Blood Relations
AND OTHER PLAYS

Blood Relations
One Tiger to a Hill
Generations
Whiskey Six Cadenza

Sharon Pollock

Edited by Anne Nothof
Prairie Play Series: 22/Series Editor, Diane Bessai

The original edition of this book published in 1981 included *Blood Relations, One Tiger
to a Hill,* and *Generations* and was #4 in the Prairie Play Series. This revised edition also
includes *Whiskey Six Cadenza* and is #22 in the Prairie Play Series.

National Library of Canada Cataloguing in Publication Data
Pollock, Sharon.
Blood relations and other plays

(Prairie play series ; 22)
ISBN 1-896300-64-2

I. Title. II. Series.
PS8581.O34B5 2002   C812'.54
C2002-910174-3   PR9199.3.P57B56 2002—

Editor for the press: Anne Nothof
Cover and interior design: Ruth Linka
Cover image: Mike Reichert Steinhauer
Interior photos: Production photos have been reproduced with the permission of the
actors appearing in them and of the photographers. Every reasonable effort has been
made to acquire permission for copyright material used in this book, and to acknowledge such indebtedness accurately. Any errors and omissions called to the publisher's
attention will be corrected in future editions.

Canadian   Patrimoine
Heritage   canadien

NeWest Press acknowledges the support of the Canada Council for the Arts and The
Alberta Foundation for the Arts for our publishing program. We also acknowledge the
financial support of the Government of Canada through the Book Publishing Industry
Development Program (BPIDP) for our publishing activities.

NeWest Press
201-8540-109 Street
Edmonton, Alberta
T6G 1E6
t: (780) 432-9427
f: (780) 433-3179
www.newestpress.com

3   4   5   13   12   11   10

PRINTED AND BOUND IN CANADA

Contents

Introduction: Painting the Background by Anne Nothof / v
Introduction to the original 1981 edition by Diane Bessai / xii

Blood Relations / 1
One Tiger to the Hill / 75
Generations / 153
Whiskey Six Cadenza / 225

Bibliography / 331
Author Biography / 337

INTRODUCTION: Painting the Background

Sharon Pollock's plays constitute kaleidoscopic worlds, constructing variable images through words, sounds, light, colour, movement. They provide alternative perspectives, realities, choices. They refuse closure, and can be endlessly replayed and interpreted. This new edition of four of Pollock's early plays reaffirms their currency and their "transcendence." Twenty-one years after the publication of "Blood Relations," "One Tiger to a Hill," and "Generations" in *Blood Relations and Other Plays* (edited by Diane Bessai, 1981), and fifteen years after the publication of "Whiskey Six Cadenza" in *NeWest Plays by Women* (edited by Diane Bessai and Don Kerr, 1987), they remain present in the landscape of Canadian drama, and have been relocated in other countries for production and study. Although Pollock has written many plays since, they remain at the core of her *oeuvre*, their images and themes refracted through different scenarios. Personal lives still inform the political scene: choices are made, usually with catastrophic consequences to individuals who reaffirm the possibility and necessity of choice. Women may be "acted on," but they also act out their own dreams and destinies. In Pollock's more recent plays, women take centre stage, and the action becomes an investigation of their inner lives. In *Doc* (1984), the family history is revisited by a daughter attempting to understand just what she has inherited from her alcoholic, suicidal mother and her work-obsessed father, a community doctor who values the lives of his patients more than the welfare of his family. In *Getting it Straight* (1989), a corrupted, decomposing world is seen through the sharp eyes of an escapee from a mental institution, hiding under the grandstand at the Calgary Stampede. In *Fair Liberty's Call* (1993), a Loyalist family relocates to New Brunswick, importing the ethical, political, and communal conundrums of the American Civil War, but also identifying the possibility of a more positive future. *Saucy Jack* (1993) replays the murders of Jack the Ripper from a woman's perspective, to show the ways in which social systems and habits are implicated in gender crimes. *Moving Pictures* (1999) uses film as a metaphor for different ways of seeing, creating, interacting. It enacts three stages of the life of silent film producer and actor, Nell Shipman, using three actors to show how the pieces of a persona clash or coalesce. It also questions the high price of creativity, and shows the personal casualties of art. *End Dream* (2000), like *Blood Relations*, uses a murder-mystery to interrogate notions of responsibility, truth, and lies. *Angel's Trumpet* (2001) questions the symbiotic and destructive relationship of muse and artist through the disastrous marriage of Zelda and Scott Fitzgerald. Pollock's focus has shifted more to the creative process, the choices necessitated by this process, and the personal consequences. Although violence against women remains endemic in Pollock's plays, they are not simply victims of systems or societies: they also make choices, knowing the likely consequences. Pollock leaves to the audience any possibility of a Last Judgement—the determination of guilt and innocence, the various degrees of responsibility in-between.

All of Pollock's plays experiment with structure and style: scenes intersect or blend, time inhabits a simultaneous present and past, characters are divided into multiple selves who interact with and observe each other. Through choreography, soundscapes, and set design, her plays suggest the illusion of reality, and the reality of dreams. For *Whiskey Six Cadenza* "the stage is filled with a gossamer depiction of Crowsnest Pass. . . . Light builds behind the image, exposing it as no more than a grey, dusty, cobwebby affair much as a spider might spin in the entrance of an abandoned mine-shaft." Even the more "naturalistic" plays, *One Tiger to a Hill* and *Generations*, have "expressionistic" elements in the settings, suggesting variant perspectives or psychological dimensions: internal prisons, internal landscapes. Lives are conditioned by spaces. Place is not only "regional," even though specific. It is multi-dimensional. Designer Richard Roberts attempted to evoke this shifting perspective in his set for the premiere of *Generations* in the Canmore Opera House:

> In initial discussions with the director it was decided that a mechanism was required to allow a flow of movement between locales—which could also be used to alter audience perspective of the locales—against a strong horizon/sky relationship. . . . the present arrangement of "wagons" . . . allows the separation of "new" and "old

places" and (when supported by light) alteration of audience perspective as the wagons move. So we have islands of related naturalistic elements ("man made"), moving within a ground of symbolic topography ("the land") against a horizontal plane ("the sky"). Into this we thrust the actors, clothed to support their roles within the play of events which carry us through time and space in performance" (Program 10).

Blood Relations remains the most popular of Pollock's plays; it has been produced around the world, from the United States to Australia to Japan, and it has provided complex material for numerous articles and theses on metatheatre, feminist theatre, and postmodern theatre. It offers good roles for women, and it appeals to different audiences: the intellectual and ideological, and "the people who are just looking for a suspenseful murder-mystery" (Pollock Interview 167). In a production directed by Martha Henry at the Grand Theatre in London Ontario, *Blood Relations* became a psychodrama played out inside the head of the Actress. Its conflation of acting with lying, of disclosures with subterfuge, of compulsion with repression, is endlessly intriguing. The compulsion to "know the truth" is sabotaged by a demonstration of the impossibility of knowing the truth: the ambiguity is fascinating. Pollock "paints the background, but leave[s] the rest to [our] imagination[s]." The complex father-daughter relationship in *Blood Relations* anticipates the love/hate symbioses in *Doc, Fair Liberty's Call, Whiskey Six Cadenza*— father as mentor, father as destroyer. Words are inherited, as well as proclivities, mannerisms, perspectives. As Lizzie tells the Actress, "I've never used a word I didn't hear from him first." Father and daughter are very much "blood relations." The daughters are not passive victims, however: they are ambitious, determined, stubborn: "If Lizzie puts her mind to a thing, she does it, and if she don't, she don't." No one is wholly innocent or completely powerless in Pollock's plays. Choice may be circumscribed, but it is still possible. Even in a prison, choices are made, and even when the outcome will almost certainly be catastrophic. "One Tiger to a Hill" is perhaps the most overtly political of the four plays in this text in its focus, raising issues of social justice and the penal system, but it also shows how one stubborn, strong-willed woman, intent on "justice," can instigate a series of disastrous events. Dede Walker believes that you should struggle for a just cause, which may be "determined by yourself," and that people are willing to die for things they're not going to win. She proves to be a case in point. But the "justice" of her cause remains in doubt—even the "cause" is somewhat compromised. Similarly, Tommy Paul, a Métis prisoner intent on escaping, is in some ways her victim as much as the victim of racism, poverty, and institutionalization, yet he asserts that he has choices, and he dies in proving this point. *One Tiger to a Hill* has had mixed reviews in Canadian productions: the premiere in Edmonton in 1980 was panned, but another production the same year at Festival Lennoxville with the same director, Richard Ouzounian, was enthusiastically received. It has been produced at the Stratford Festival and at the National Arts Centre, but it has proved more popular in the United States than in Canada. The Manhattan Theatre Club produced the play with Denzel Washington playing Tommy Paul as a young Black man who has educated himself in prison. According to Pollock, the play was "twisted in a different way" at a time in the early 1980s when Natives and Hispanics were rarely seen on stage.

Generations is popular with drama students, but is rarely produced, its complexities and ambiguities often overlooked. Again, each character makes choices that involve sacrifices—of themselves and of others. Pollock explores the viability of families and the dynamics of human sociability. She was raising six children at the time she wrote these early plays, and not surprisingly conflicting loyalties and responsibilities of family and vocation recur in her plays. The brothers David and Young Eddy Nurlin make conscious or unconscious choices about their lives in *Generations*—whether to stay on the family farm, or to leave. David's girlfriend, Bonnie also makes a choice not to marry David, fearing a loss of "self," the consequence of which may be loneliness, whereas the mother, Margaret Nurlin's decision has been to lose herself through a commitment to something bigger than herself—a dedication to the land. However, their "choices" are circumscribed—by their personal histories, by their degree of self-awareness. The issues debated in this play are not only endemic to the prairies. *Generations* has also been produced in India. According to Pollock, "someone had given a university there a batch of my plays and asked which one they wanted to do. There were a lot of farming families in the area and people who had some relationship to the land, and they chose *Generations*" (Interview 170).

With *Whiskey Six Cadenza* Pollock again unravels the fabric of Canadian history, showing how personal choices inform public performance—as in *Walsh* and *Fair Liberty's Call*. The story is partial, multivalent, as if viewed through a kaleidoscope. There is no one coherent point of view, no single perspective. It is loosely based on the tale of Emilio Piciarello (Pic) and Florence (Filumena) Losandro, a story which, according to Alberta novelist Peter Oliva, "had many angles and ironies" (*AlbertaViews* 39). Pic was the "Godfather" of the Crowsnest Pass—a bootlegger, hotel owner, and politician, who lured Filumena away from an unhappy arranged marriage to an Italian immigrant. She was living in a grungy Blairmore hotel with a husband who could not keep a job, until Pic employed him to run liquor through the Pass from British Columbia to Alberta. Filumena went along for the ride, and was ostracized by the community when she became increasingly involved with Pic. Playwright John Murrell, who has written the libretto for an opera based on the story, described Filumena as "a bit of an outsider." Like Pic she had a dream that was larger than herself: "they both wanted more than the circumstances that life offered them" (*AlbertaViews* 42). But in the original story, Filumena accompanied Pic when he shot a policeman who had wounded his son on a rum run. Filumena's public hearing was in the Coleman Opera House, and she was the first woman in twenty-four years to be hanged in Canada. She has since assumed the status of a tragic heroine. From this "history" Pollock freely creates a fiction in which the tragedy is refracted and split; it belongs to everyone in the community.

The setting in the Crowsnest Pass is described as "extend[ing] into the infinite, giving the impression of viewing eternity through a glass, a telescope, a microscope, a kaleidoscope," and the images and figures in the play are "fractured, refracted, fragmented." The play also functions like a carousel, an image Pollock has used in *Blood Relations*—reality is blurred, a fantastical, exhilarating, frightening experience which precludes an easy descent. As in her later play, *End Dream*, light and sound condition and inform the dream and the nightmare. The approaching and retreating train light is an overwhelming image of inevitability—the inescapable, exposing light that ends the dream of Mr. Big, and the love between Johnny and Leah. But there is also a strong element of individual choice in the play: Leah is Mr. Big's chosen daughter; he has in effect created her. She suffers the consequences of his choice, but she also makes her own. She chooses Johnny, and then she chooses death. Choice can be for good or ill, sometimes for both together. As Mr. Big contends, "Had Lucifer not fallen from grace there'd be no such thing as choice!"

Whiskey Six Cadenza is one of Pollock's favorite plays, but it is rarely produced, despite the best overall reviews of any play she has written. Perhaps the size of the play deters producers in a Canadian theatre scene still characterized by two-handers and a bare stage. Her other "epic" history play, *Fair Liberty's Call*, has been produced only at Stratford, and by a few university drama departments in the United States. But Sharon Pollock has made her choice to continue her active involvement in the theatre of Calgary and Canada. Her last three plays, *Moving Pictures*, *End Dream*, and *Angel's Trumpet* premiered at Theatre Junction in Calgary in 2000 and 2001, and she directed Pinter's *Betrayal* for that theatre in 2000. She has acted in her own plays—as Miss Lizzie in Theatre Calgary's production of *Blood Relations*, and in *Getting it Straight*, and she has directed her own plays, as well as those of other playwrights. She has been an artistic director—of Theatre Calgary (1984), and of Theatre New Brunswick (1988), and she has mentored playwrights and performers at the National Theatre School, the Banff School of Fine Arts, and in university theatre programs. In 1998 she was elected president of Alberta Playwrights Network, a position from which she has only recently retired. She won the Governor General's Award for *Blood Relations* in 1981, the first time it was awarded for drama, and for *Doc* in 1986. *Whiskey Six Cadenza* was nominated for the Governor General's Award in 1988. In 1999 Pollock was awarded the Harry and Martha Cohen Award for her contribution to Calgary theatre.

Sharon Pollock continues to pursue her life in art, committed to making theatre, working on "the little ball of wax" that she will form into a new play conditioned by the social traumas of September 11, 2001 in New York, and the Middle East conflict—to create a theatrical experience that penetrates audience consciousness. She believes that it is the artist's responsibility to respond to the world around her, however that manifests itself.

The publication of her plays is another part of the process of making theatre. It constitutes "a record and a documentation of what worked for a group of people in a specific time and place. . . . What you want published is a text that will stimulate the creative imagination of theatre people who are going to produce it with their own vision of the possibilities of the work. But then there's the study of the work, where students require more text than what a theatre person does. Where a designer, or actor, or director does not require editorial instructions, a student trying to envision a performance does" (Interview 173). This text, then, is a record of four Canadian plays by Sharon Pollock, incorporating her most recent revisions. "Indeed, few playwrights in Canada today have her range and technique" (Bessai xv).

WORKS CITED

Bessai, Diane. "Introduction," *Blood Relations and Other Plays*. Edmonton: NeWest Press, 2002.

Oliva, Peter. "How Do You Grow An Opera?" *Alberta Views* (Mar/Apr 2002): 38-43.

Pollock, Sharon. "Interview with Anne Nothof," *Sharon Pollock: Essays on Her Works*. Toronto: Guernica, 2000.

Roberts, Richard. Designer's Notes: "Designer as Play 'Space' Wright," Program for *Generations*, Canmore Opera House, 1980.

Anne Nothof
Athabasca University 2002

INTRODUCTION to the original 1981 edition

Sharon Pollock's importance as a playwright becomes increasingly evident each new Canadian theatre season. Her compelling
study of Lizzie Borden, *Blood Relations,* after its premiere at Theatre
Three, Edmonton in 1980, was produced at the National Arts Centre
a year later and was scheduled in the 1981-82 season at the Tarragon
in Toronto, Theatre Calgary and Centaur, Montreal. The earlier *One
Tiger to a Hill,* a hostage-taking drama, premiered at the Citadel,
Edmonton, also in 1980, was performed the following summer at
Festival Lennoxville and at the National Arts Centre's Woodshed
studio in the spring of 1981; it also had a five-week run at the
Manhattan Theatre Club, New York in November, 1980. The Alberta
Theatre Projects commission, *Generations,* for the fall of 1980 was
seen at Tarragon the following spring.

Such achievement does not come overnight, but is the fruit of
long practical experience in the theatre, both as performer and
writer. Sharon Pollock began in the mid-1960s as an actress, first in
her native New Brunswick and later in Calgary as a member of a
touring company, Prairie Players. She began to write for radio and
the stage in the early 1970s and now has to her credit seven major
stage plays, a number of children's works (mostly written for
Vancouver's Playhouse Holiday) and, in addition, a dozen radio
scripts, aired nationally and produced in the West. For *Sweet Land of
Liberty* she was awarded the Nellie, an Actra award for Best Radio
Drama, 1980. She has been head of the Playwright's Colony at
Banff, and while playwright-in-residence at ATP, Calgary, 1977-79,
conducted regular playwriting workshops. Previous to this, she
spent a year at the University of Alberta as playwriting instructor in
the drama department.

Pollock's second stage play, *Walsh,* was the first of her works to
draw national attention when it was produced in 1974 on the Stratford
Third Stage under the direction of John Wood; it had been premiered

the previous season by Harold Baldridge at Theatre Calgary. Her first play, a black comedy entitled *Compulsory Option*, won an Alberta Culture award in 1971 and was first produced by the New Play Society at the Vancouver Art Gallery in August, 1972. Later productions were mounted at Citadel Too, Festival Lennoxville, and at Theatre Passe Muraille as *No! No! No!* The Vancouver Playhouse produced her next two works, *Out Goes You*, a satiric comedy on contemporary BC politics, in 1975, and, in the season following, *The Komagata Maru Incident*, a stern indictment of Canadian racism based on a Vancouver incident in 1914 when a shipload of Sikh immigrants was refused permission to land. The latter work reinforced Pollock's growing reputation as an issue-oriented playwright, one out to re-examine the Canadian past with a disarmingly clear eye. In her opinion:

> Canadians have this view of themselves as nice civilized
> people who have never participated in historical crimes
> and atrocities. But that view is false. Our history is dull
> only because it has been dishonestly expurgated.

These remarks have a bearing on *Walsh* as well, with its examination of the ugly treatment afforded Sitting Bull and his people after their escape to Canada from their victory at Little Big Horn. Or they could apply to *One Tiger to a Hill*; this play was begun within the year of the incident that inspired it (the New Westminster penitentiary hostage-taking of 1975 in which a rehabilitation worker was shot), but it too springs from documented events that fast became history. Here the playwright attacks institutional complacency and public apathy in yet another sensitive area in Canadian public life, that of prison reform.

If one may generalize from the last three mentioned plays, one might note that Pollock's primary thematic thrust is to confront the anonymous self-protective public systems for the way they force their lieutenants into uncompromising bureaucratic decisions. Stylistically she is writing out of epic-documentary theatrical tradition, rather than naturalistic convention. This suggests that she is more interested in examining character in a social or political context than through the intimacies of psychological interiorization. These plays are direct, forceful and sometimes deliberately unsubtle in the approach to their subjects.

However, there is a notable shift of emphasis in Sharon Pollock's two most recent works, *Blood Relations*, which premiered at Theatre

Three, Edmonton, 1980[1] and *Generations*, in that both deal with private life, in particular with the politics of the family. Of course the subject of *Blood Relations* is historically speaking, very public. It is a treatment of Lizzie Borden, the New England woman who, in 1892, was charged with the axe murders of her father and step-mother. History knows that Lizzie was acquitted, but the questions of the case have been a continual source of fascination to writers since.

Not surprisingly, Pollock manages a sympathetic reconstruction of Lizzie's situation as an oppressed Victorian spinster, but, unlike the earlier plays, here the issue element is subsumed in the complexities of personality and the ambiguities of fact. The playwright is still concerned with character in its social role; in this there is a general similarity to the portrait of Walsh, as a man who is personally devastated by the public role imposed upon him from the higher authority of the system he serves. Lizzie, of course, does not literally "serve" a system, but she is the product and victim of the materialistic bourgeois social conventionality of her day that gives no breathing space either to individuality or eccentricity. Lizzie is driven to desperation by family pressures, and although the play deliberately begs the intriguing question of "did she or didn't she," in Pollock's version one sees why she might well have done so. Structurally this is the most sophisticated of the plays, taking the form of a play-within-a-play in which, ten years after her acquittal, Lizzie's actress friend (probably Nance O'Neill) acts out the crucial scenes under the stage directions of Lizzie herself.

Generations, first a radio play, is Pollock's only conventionally naturalistic work for the stage to date. A prairie farm kitchen is the focal point of the action; the subject is the tie of the land, offering a 1980s perspective on the attitudes of three generations towards their family homestead. The motivating crises of the action are recognizable contemporary problems: the Natives of a nearby reservation hold the water supply in ransom to the federal government; one of the grandsons wants to sell some land to finance his law firm, while the fiancée of the other tries to challenge his loyalty to the land with her feminist convictions. This play's power, however, lies mostly in its sympathetic evocation of family tensions and affections; at the

---

[1] An earlier version of the play was produced by Douglas College theatre department at Surrey BC in March, 1976, with the playwright in the role of Lizzie Borden. The working title was "My Name is Lisbeth." For a critical analysis of Pollock's work in Vancouver, see Malcolm Page, "Sharon Pollock: Committed Playwright," *Canadian Drama*, Fall, 1979.

same time, *Generations* is Pollock's one play conveying a strong sense of the particularities of a regional lifestyle.

Because she lives and writes in the West (her home is Calgary), Sharon Pollock is often considered a regional writer; she herself rightly chaffs at so simplistic a label, arguing that there is nothing merely local about her subjects. The regional naturalism of *Generations* is but one of several modes through which she expresses her society-oriented concerns. Indeed, few playwrights in Canada today have her range and technique.

Diane Bessai, University of Alberta, September 1981
(Revised 2002)

Blood Relations

Janet Daverne as Lizzie Borden and Judith Mabey as The Actress in the Theatre Three premiere of *Blood Relations*, Edmonton, March 1980.

"Blood Relations" [no date] 2001-16 box 5, Theatre Three fonds, University of Alberta Archives

Production History

Blood Relations was first performed at Theatre Three, Edmonton, 12 March 1980.

CAST

Miss Lizzie	*Janet Daverne*
Actress	*Judith Mabey*
Emma	*Barbara Reese*
Dr. Patrick/Defense	*Wendell Smith*
Harry	*Brian Atkins*
Mrs. Borden	*Paddy English*
Mr. Borden	*Charles Kerr*

Director	*Keith Digby*
Set and Props Designer	*J. Fraser Hiltz*
Lighting Designer	*Luciano Iogna*
Costume Designer	*Kathryn Burns*
Stage Manager	*Maureen A. Dool*

CHARACTERS

Miss Lizzie: who will play **Bridget**, the Irish maid.
The Actress: who will play **Lizzie Borden**.
Harry: Mrs. Borden's brother.
Emma: Lizzie's older sister.
Andrew: Lizzie's father.
Abigail: Lizzie's step-mother.
Dr. Patrick: the Irish doctor; sometimes **The Defense**.

SETTING

The time proper is late Sunday afternoon and evening, late fall, in Fall River, 1902; the year of the "dream thesis," if one might call it that, is 1892.

The playing areas include (a) within the Borden house: the dining room from which there is an exit to the kitchen; the parlour; a flight of stairs leading to the second floor; and (b) in the Borden yard: the walk outside the house; the area in which the birds are kept.

PRODUCTION NOTE

Action must be free-flowing. There can be no division of the script into scenes by blackout, movement of furniture, or sets. There may be freezes of some characters while other scenes are being played. There is no necessity to "get people off" and "on" again for, with the exception of The Actress and Miss Lizzie (and Emma in the final scene), all characters are imaginary, and all action in reality would be taking place between Miss Lizzie and The Actress in the dining room and parlour of her home.

The Defense may actually be seen, may be a shadow, or a figure behind a scrim.

While Miss Lizzie exits and enters with her Bridget business, she is a presence, often observing unobtrusively, when as Bridget she takes no part in the action.

ACT ONE

Lights up on the figure of a woman standing centre stage. It is a somewhat formal pose. A pause. She speaks:

> "Since what I am about to say must be but that
> Which contradicts my accusation, and
> The testimony on my part no other
> But what comes from myself, it shall scarce boot me
> To say "Not Guilty."
> But, if Powers Divine
> Behold our human action as they do,
> I doubt not than but innocence shall make
> False accusation blush and tyranny
> Tremble at . . . at . . ."

She wriggles the fingers of an outstretched hand searching for the word.

> "Aaaat" . . . Bollocks!!

She raises her script, takes a bite of chocolate.

> "Tremble at Patience," patience patience! . . .

Miss Lizzie enters from the kitchen with tea service. The Actress's attention drifts to Miss Lizzie. The Actress watches Miss Lizzie sit in the parlour and proceed to pour two cups of tea. The Actress sucks her teeth a bit to clear the chocolate as she speaks:

The Actress: Which . . . is proper, Lizzie?

Miss Lizzie: Proper?

The Actress: To pour first the cream, and add the tea—or first tea and add cream. One is proper. Is the way you do the proper way, the way it's done in circles where it counts?

Miss Lizzie: Sugar?

The Actress: Well, is it?

Miss Lizzie: I don't know. Sugar?

The Actress: Mmmn. *Miss Lizzie adds sugar.* I suppose if we had *Mrs. Beeton's Book of Etiquette*, we could look it up.

Miss Lizzie: I do have it. Shall I get it?

The Actress: No. . . . You could ask your sister, she might know.

Miss Lizzie:	Do you want this tea or not?
The Actress:	I hate tea.
Miss Lizzie:	You drink it every Sunday.
The Actress:	I drink it because you like to serve it.
Miss Lizzie:	Pppu.
The Actress:	It's true. You've no idea how I suffer from this toast and tea ritual. I really do. The tea upsets my stomach and the toast makes me fat because I eat so much of it.
Miss Lizzie:	Practise some restraint then.
The Actress:	Mmmmm. . . . Why don't we ask your sister which is proper?
Miss Lizzie:	You ask her.
The Actress:	How can I? She doesn't speak to me. I don't think she even sees me. She gives no indication of it. *She looks up the stairs.* What do you suppose she does up there every Sunday afternoon?
Miss Lizzie:	She sulks.
The Actress:	And reads the Bible I suppose, and *Mrs. Beeton's Book of Etiquette.* Oh Lizzie. . . . What a long day. The absolutely longest day. . . . When does that come anyway, the longest day?
Miss Lizzie:	June.
The Actress:	Ah yes, June. *She looks at Miss Lizzie.* June?
Miss Lizzie:	June.
The Actress:	Mmmmmm. . . .
Miss Lizzie:	I know what you're thinking.
The Actress:	Of course you do. . . . I'm thinking . . . shall I pour the sherry—or will you.
Miss Lizzie:	No.
The Actress:	I'm thinking . . . June . . . in Fall River.
Miss Lizzie:	No.

The Actress:	August in Fall River? *She smiles. Pause.*
Miss Lizzie:	We could have met in Boston.
The Actress:	I prefer it here.
Miss Lizzie:	You don't find it . . . a trifle boring?
The Actress:	Au contraire.

Miss Lizzie gives a small laugh at the affectation.

The Actress:	What?
Miss Lizzie:	I find it a trifle boring. . . . I know what you're doing. You're soaking up the ambience.
The Actress:	Nonsense, Lizzie. I come to see you.
Miss Lizzie:	Why?
The Actress:	Because . . . of us. *Pause.*
Miss Lizzie:	You were a late arrival last night. Later than usual.
The Actress:	Don't be silly.
Miss Lizzie:	I wonder why.
The Actress:	The show was late, late starting, late coming down.
Miss Lizzie:	And?
The Actress:	And—then we all went out for drinks.
Miss Lizzie:	We?
The Actress:	The other members of the cast.
Miss Lizzie:	Oh yes.
The Actress:	And then I caught a cab . . . all the way from Boston. . . . Do you know what it cost?
Miss Lizzie:	I should. I paid the bill, remember?
The Actress:	*Laughs.* Of course. What a jumble all my thoughts are. There're too many words running 'round inside my head today. It's terrible.
Miss Lizzie:	It sounds it.

Pause.

The Actress: . . . You know . . . you do this thing . . . you stare at me. . . . You look directly at my eyes. I think . . . you think . . . that if I'm lying . . . it will come up, like lemons on a slot machine. *She makes a gesture at her eyes.* Tick. Tick . . . *Pause.* In the alley, behind the theatre the other day, there were some kids. You know what they were doing?

Miss Lizzie: How could I?

The Actress: They were playing skip rope, and you know what they were singing? *She sings, and claps her hands arhythmically to:*

"Lizzie Borden took an axe,
Gave her mother forty whacks.
When the job was nicely done,
She gave her father forty-one."

Miss Lizzie: Did you stop them?

The Actress: No.

Miss Lizzie: Did you tell them I was acquitted?

The Actress: No.

Miss Lizzie: What did you do?

The Actress: I shut the window.

Miss Lizzie: A noble gesture on my behalf.

The Actress: We were doing lines—the noise they make is dreadful. Sometimes they play ball, ka-thunk, ka-thunk, ka-thunk against the wall. Once I saw them with a cat and—

Miss Lizzie: And you didn't stop them?

The Actress: That time I stopped them.

The Actress crosses to table where there is a gramophone. She prepares to play a record. She stops.

The Actress: Should I?

Miss Lizzie: Why not?

The Actress: Your sister, the noise upsets her.

Diana Leblanc as Lizzie Borden and Frances Hyland as The Actress in The Grand Theatre production of *Blood Relations*, London, Ontario, 1988.

Courtesy of The Grand Theatre

Miss Lizzie: And she upsets me. On numerous occasions.

The Actress: You're incorrigible, Lizzie.

The Actress holds out her arms to Miss Lizzie. They dance the latest "in" dance, a Scott Joplin composition. It requires some concentration, but they chat while dancing rather formally in contrast to the music.

The Actress: . . . Do you think your jawline's heavy?

Miss Lizzie: Why do you ask?

The Actress: They said you had jowls.

Miss Lizzie: Did they.

The Actress: The reports of the day said you were definitely jowly.

Miss Lizzie: That was ten years ago.

The Actress: Imagine. You were only thirty-four.

Miss Lizzie: Yes.

The Actress: It happened here, this house.

Miss Lizzie: You're leading.

The Actress: I know.

Miss Lizzie: . . . I don't think I'm jowly. Then or now. Do you?

The Actress: Lizzie? Lizzie.

Miss Lizzie: What?

The Actress: . . . Did you?

Miss Lizzie: Did I what?

Pause.

The Actress: You never tell me anything. *She turns off the music.*

Miss Lizzie: I tell you everything.

The Actress: No you don't!

Miss Lizzie: Oh yes, I tell you the most personal things about myself, my thoughts, my dreams, my—

The Actress: But never that one thing. . . . *She lights a cigarette.*

Miss Lizzie: And don't smoke those—they stink.

The Actress ignores her, inhales, exhales a volume of smoke in Miss Lizzie's direction.

Miss Lizzie: Do you suppose . . . people buy you drinks . . . or cast you even . . . because you have a "liaison" with Lizzie Borden? Do you suppose they do that?

The Actress: They cast me because I'm good at what I do.

Miss Lizzie: They never pry? They never ask? What's she really like? Is she really jowly? Did she? Didn't she?

The Actress: What could I tell them? You never tell me anything.

Miss Lizzie: I tell you everything.

The Actress: But that! *Pause.* You think everybody talks about you—they don't.

Miss Lizzie: Here they do.

The Actress: You think they talk about you.

Miss Lizzie: But never to me.

The Actress: Well . . . you give them lots to talk about.

Miss Lizzie: You know you're right, your mind is a jumble.

The Actress: I told you so.

Pause.

Miss Lizzie: You remind me of my sister.

The Actress: Oh God, in what way?

Miss Lizzie: Day in, day out, ten years now, sometimes at breakfast as she rolls little crumbs of bread in little balls, sometimes at noon, or late at night . . . "Did you, Lizzie?" "Lizzie, did you?"

The Actress: Ten years, day in, day out?

Miss Lizzie: Oh yes. She sits there where Papa used to sit and I sit there, where I have always sat. She looks at me and at her plate, then at me, and at her plate, then at me and then she says "Did you Lizzie?" "Lizzie, did you?"

The Actress: *A nasal imitation of Emma's voice.* "Did-you-Lizzie— Lizzie-did-you?" *Laughs.*

Miss Lizzie:	Did I what?
The Actress:	*Continues her imitation of Emma.* "You know."
Miss Lizzie:	Well, what do you think?
The Actress:	"Oh, I believe you didn't, in fact I know you didn't, what a thought! After all, you were acquitted."
Miss Lizzie:	Yes, I was.
The Actress:	"But sometimes when I'm on the street . . . or shopping . . . or at the church even, I catch somebody's eye, they look away . . . and I think to myself, "Did-you-Lizzie—Lizzie-did-you."
Miss Lizzie:	*Laughs.* Ah, poor Emma.
The Actress:	*Dropping her Emma imitation.* Well, did you?
Miss Lizzie:	Is it important?
The Actress:	Yes.
Miss Lizzie:	Why?
The Actress:	I have . . . a compulsion to know the truth.
Miss Lizzie:	The truth?
The Actress:	Yes.
Miss Lizzie:	. . . Sometimes I think you look like me, and you're not jowly.
The Actress:	No.
Miss Lizzie:	You look like me, or how I think I look, or how I ought to look . . . sometimes you think like me . . . do you feel that?
The Actress:	Sometimes.
Miss Lizzie:	*Triumphant.* You shouldn't have to ask then. You should know. "Did I, didn't I?" You tell me.
The Actress:	I'll tell you what I think . . . I think . . . that you're aware there is a certain fascination in the ambiguity. . . . You always paint the background but leave the rest to my imagination. Did Lizzie Borden take an axe? . . . If you didn't I should be disappointed . . . and

	if you did I should be horrified.
Miss Lizzie:	And which is worse?
The Actress:	To have murdered one's parents, or to be a pretentious small-town spinster? I don't know.
Miss Lizzie:	Why're you so cruel to me?
The Actress:	I'm teasing, Lizzie, I'm only teasing. Come on, paint the background again.
Miss Lizzie:	Why?
The Actress:	Perhaps you'll give something away.
Miss Lizzie:	Which you'll dine out on.
The Actress:	Of course. *Laughs.* Come on, Lizzie. Come on.
Miss Lizzie:	A game.
The Actress:	What?
Miss Lizzie:	A game? . . . And you'll play me.
The Actress:	Oh—
Miss Lizzie:	It's your stock in trade, my love.
The Actress:	Alright. . . . A game!
Miss Lizzie:	Let me think . . . Bridget . . . Brrridget. We had a maid then. And her name was Bridget. Oh, she was a great one for stories, stood like this, very straight back, and her hair . . . and there she was in the courtroom in her new dress on the stand. "Do you swear to tell the truth, the whole truth, and nothing but the truth, so help you God?" *Imitates Irish accent.*

"I do sir," she said.

"Would you give the court your name."

"Bridget O'Sullivan, sir."

Very faint echo of the voice of the Defense under Miss Lizzie's next line.

"And occupation."

"I'm like what you'd call a maid, sir. I do a bit of everything, cleanin' and cookin'."

The actual voice of The Defense is heard alone; he may also be seen.

The Defense: You've been in Fall River how long?

Miss Lizzie: *Who continues as Bridget, while The Actress (who will play Lizzie) observes.* Well now, about five years sir, ever since I came over. I worked up on the hill for a while but it didn't—well, you could say, suit me, too lah-de-dah—so I—

The Defense: Your employer in June of 1892 was?

Bridget: Yes sir. Mr. Borden, sir. Well, more rightly, Mrs. Borden for she was the one who—

The Defense: Your impression of the household?

Bridget: Well . . . the man of the house, Mr. Borden, was a bit of a . . . tightwad, and Mrs. B. could nag you into the grave, still she helped with the dishes and things which not everyone does when they hire a maid. *Harry appears on the stairs; approaches Bridget stealthily. She is unaware of him.* Then there was the daughters, Miss Emma and Lizzie, and that day, Mr. Wingate, Mrs. B.'s brother who'd stayed for the night and was—*Harry grabs her ass with both hands. She screams.*

Bridget: Get off with you!

Harry: Come on, Bridget, give me a kiss!

Bridget: I'll give you a good poke in the nose if you don't keep your hands to yourself.

Harry: Ohhh-hh-hh Bridget!

Bridget: Get away you old sod!

Harry: Haven't you missed me?

Bridget: I have not! I was pinched black and blue last time . . . and I'll be sufferin' the same before I see the end of you this time.

Harry: *Tilts his ass at her.* You want to see my end?

Bridget: You're a dirty old man.

Harry:	If Mr. Borden hears that, you'll be out on the street. *Grabs her.* Where's my kiss!
Bridget:	*Dumps glass of water on his head.* There! *Harry splutters.* Would you like another? You silly thing you— and leave me towels alone!
Harry:	You've soaked my shirt.
Bridget:	Shut up and pour yourself a cup of coffee.
Harry:	You got no sense of fun, Bridget.
Bridget:	Well now, if you tried actin' like the gentleman farmer you're supposed to be, Mr. Wingate—
Harry:	I'm tellin' you you can't take a joke.
Bridget:	If Mr. Borden sees you jokin', it's not his maid he'll be throwin' out on the street, but his brother-in-law, and that's the truth.
Harry:	What's between you and me's between you and me, eh?
Bridget:	There ain't nothin' between you and me.
Harry:	. . . Finest cup of coffee in Fall River.
Bridget:	There's no gettin' on the good side of me now, it's too late for that.
Harry:	. . . Bridget? . . . You know what tickles my fancy?
Bridget:	No and I don't want to hear.
Harry:	It's your Irish temper.
Bridget:	It is, is it? . . . Can I ask you something?
Harry:	Ooohhh—anything.
Bridget:	*Innocently.* Does Miss Lizzie know you're here? . . . I say does Miss Lizzie—
Harry:	Why do you bring her up?
Bridget:	She don't then, eh? *Teasing.* It's a surprise visit?
Harry:	No surprise to her father.
Bridget:	Oh?

Harry:	We got business.
Bridget:	I'd of thought the last bit of business was enough.
Harry:	It's not for— [*you to say*]
Bridget:	You don't learn a thing, from me or Lizzie, do you?
Harry:	Listen here—
Bridget:	You mean you've forgotten how mad she was when you got her father to sign the rent from the mill house over to your sister? Oh my.
Harry:	She's his wife, isn't she?
Bridget:	*Lightly.* Second wife.
Harry:	She's still got her rights.
Bridget:	Who am I to say who's got a right? But I can tell you this—Miss Lizzie don't see it that way.
Harry:	It don't matter how Miss Lizzie sees it.
Bridget:	Oh it matters enough—she had you thrown out last time, didn't she? By jasus that was a laugh!
Harry:	You mind your tongue.
Bridget:	And after you left, you know what happened?
Harry:	Get away.
Bridget:	She and sister Emma got her father's rent money from the other mill house to make it all even-ste-ven—and now, here you are back again? What kind of business you up to this time? *Whispers in his ear.* Mind Lizzie doesn't catch you.
Harry:	Get away!
Bridget:	*Laughs.* Ohhhh—would you like some more coffee, sir? It's the finest coffee in all Fall River! *She pours it.* Thank you sir. You're welcome, sir. *She exits to the kitchen.*
Harry:	There'll be no trouble this time!! Do you hear me!
Bridget:	*Off.* Yes sir.

Harry:	There'll be no trouble. *Sees a basket of crusts.* What the hell's this? I said is this for breakfast!
Bridget:	*Entering.* Is what for—oh no—Mr. Borden's not economizin' to that degree yet, it's the crusts for Miss Lizzie's birds.
Harry:	What birds?
Bridget:	Some kind of pet pigeons she's raisin' out in the shed. Miss Lizzie loves her pigeons.
Harry:	Miss Lizzie loves kittens and cats and horses and dogs. What Miss Lizzie doesn't love is people.
Bridget:	*Some* people. *She looks past Harry to The Actress/ Lizzie. Harry turns to follow Bridget's gaze. Bridget speaks, encouraging, an invitation for The Actress to join her.* Good mornin' Lizzie.
The Actress:	*She is a trifle tentative in the role of Lizzie.* Is the coffee on?
Bridget:	Yes ma'am.
Lizzie:	I'll have some then.
Bridget:	Yes ma'am. *She makes no move to get it, but watches as Lizzie stares at Harry.*
Harry:	Well . . . I think . . . maybe I'll . . . just split a bit of that kindling out back. *He exits.*
Lizzie:	Silly ass.
Bridget:	Oh Lizzie. *She laughs. She enjoys the Actress/Lizzie's comments as she guides her into her role by "painting the background."*
Lizzie:	Well, he is. He's a silly ass.
Bridget:	Can you remember him last time with your Papa? Oh, I can still hear him: "Now Andrew, I've spent my life raisin' horses and I'm gonna tell you somethin'— a *woman* is just like a *horse*! You keep her on a tight rein, or she'll take the bit in her teeth and next thing you know, road, destination, and purpose is all behind you, and you'll be damn lucky if she don't

	pitch you right in a sewer ditch!"
Lizzie:	Stupid bugger.
Bridget:	Oh Lizzie, what language! What would your father say if he heard you?
Lizzie:	Well . . . I've never used a word I didn't hear from him first.
Bridget:	Do you think he'd be congratulatin' you?
Lizzie:	Possibly. *Bridget gives a subtle shake of her head.* Not.
Bridget:	Possibly not is right. . . . And what if *Mrs.* B. should hear you?
Lizzie:	I hope and pray that she does. . . . Do you know what I think, Bridget? I think there's nothing wrong with Mrs. B. . . . that losing eighty pounds and tripling her intellect wouldn't cure.
Bridget:	*Loving it.* You ought to be ashamed.
Lizzie:	It's the truth, isn't it?
Bridget:	Still, what a way to talk of your mother.
Lizzie:	Step-mother.
Bridget:	Still, you don't mean it, do you?
Lizzie:	Don't I? *Louder.* She's a *silly ass* too!
Bridget:	Shhhh.
Lizzie:	It's alright, she's deaf as a picket fence when she wants to be. . . . What's he here for?
Bridget:	Never said.
Lizzie:	He's come to worm more money out of Papa I bet.
Bridget:	Lizzie.
Lizzie:	What.
Bridget:	Your sister, Lizzie. *Bridget indicates Emma. Lizzie turns to see her on the stairs.*
Emma:	You want to be quiet, Lizzie, a body can't sleep for the racket upstairs.

Lizzie:	Oh?
Emma:	You've been makin' too much noise.
Lizzie:	It must have been Bridget. She dropped a pot, didn't you, Bridget.
Emma:	A number of pots from the sound of it.
Bridget:	I'm all thumbs this mornin', ma'am.
Emma:	You know it didn't sound like pots.
Lizzie:	Oh.
Emma:	Sounded more like voices.
Lizzie:	Oh?
Emma:	Sounded like your voice, Lizzie.
Lizzie:	Maybe you dreamt it.
Emma:	I wish I had, for someone was using words no lady would use.
Lizzie:	When Bridget dropped the pot, she did say "pshaw!" didn't you, Bridget.
Bridget:	Pshaw! That's what I said.
Emma:	That's not what I heard.

Bridget will withdraw.

Lizzie:	Pshaw?
Emma:	If mother heard you, you know what she'd say.
Lizzie:	She's not my mother or yours.
Emma:	Well she married our father twenty-seven years ago, if that doesn't make her our mother—
Lizzie:	It doesn't.
Emma:	Don't talk like that.
Lizzie:	I'll talk as I like.
Emma:	We're not going to fight, Lizzie. We're going to be quiet and have our breakfast!

Lizzie:	Is that what we're going to do?
Emma:	Yes.
Lizzie:	Oh.
Emma:	At least—that's what I'm going to do.
Lizzie:	Bridget, Emma wants her breakfast!
Emma:	I could have yelled myself.
Lizzie:	You could, but you never do.

Bridget serves Emma, Emma is reluctant to argue in front of Bridget.

Emma:	Thank you, Bridget.
Lizzie:	Did you know Harry Wingate's back for a visit? . . . He must have snuck in late last night so I wouldn't hear him. Did you? *Emma shakes her head. Lizzie studies her.*
Lizzie:	Did you know he was coming?
Emma:	No.
Lizzie:	No?
Emma:	But I do know he wouldn't be here unless Papa asked him.
Lizzie:	That's not the point. You know what happened last time he was here. Papa was signing property over to her.
Emma:	Oh Lizzie.
Lizzie:	Oh Lizzie nothing. It's bad enough Papa's worth thousands of dollars, and here we are, stuck in this tiny bit of a house on Second Street, when we should be up on the hill and that's her doing. Or her's and Harry's.
Emma:	Shush.
Lizzie:	I won't shush. They cater to Papa's worst instincts.
Emma:	They'll hear you.
Lizzie:	I don't care if they do. It's true, isn't it? Papa tends to

	be miserly, he probably has the first penny he ever earned—or more likely she has it.
Emma:	You talk rubbish.
Lizzie:	Papa can be very warm-hearted and generous but he needs encouragement.
Emma:	If Papa didn't save his money, Papa wouldn't have any money.
Lizzie:	And neither will we if he keeps signing things over to her.
Emma:	I'm not going to listen.
Lizzie:	Well try thinking.
Emma:	Stop it.
Lizzie:	*Not a threat, a simple statement of fact.* Someday Papa will die—
Emma:	Don't say that.
Lizzie:	Some day Papa will die. And I don't intend to spend the rest of my life licking Harry Wingate's boots, or toadying to his sister.
Mrs. Borden:	*From the stairs.* What's that?
Lizzie:	Nothing.
Mrs. Borden:	*Making her way downstairs.* Eh?
Lizzie:	I said, nothing!
Bridget:	*Holds out basket of crusts. Lizzie looks at it.* For your birds, Miss Lizzie.
Lizzie:	*She takes the basket.* You want to know what I think? I think she's a fat cow and I hate her. *She exits to watch scene.*
Emma:	. . . Morning, Mother.
Mrs. Borden:	Morning Emma.
Emma:	. . . Did you have a good sleep?

Bridget will serve breakfast.

Mrs. Borden: So so. . . . It's the heat you know. It never cools off proper at night. It's too hot for a good sleep.

Emma: . . . Is Papa up?

Mrs. Borden: He'll be down in a minute. . . . Sooo . . . what's wrong with Lizzie this morning?

Emma: Nothing.

Mrs. Borden: . . . Has Harry come down?

Emma: I'm not sure.

Mrs. Borden: Bridget. Has Harry come down?

Bridget: Yes ma'am.

Mrs. Borden: And?

Bridget: And he's gone out back for a bit.

Mrs. Borden: Lizzie see him?

Bridget: Yes ma'am. *Beats it back to the kitchen. Emma concentrates on her plate.*

Mrs. Borden: . . . You should have said so. . . . She have words with him?

Emma: Lizzie has more manners than that.

Mrs. Borden: She's incapable of disciplining herself like a lady and we all know it.

Emma: Well she doesn't make a habit of picking fights with people.

Mrs. Borden: That's just it. She does.

Emma: Well . . . she may—

Mrs. Borden: And you can't deny that.

Emma: *Louder.* Well this morning she may have been a bit upset because no one told her he was coming and when she came down he was here. But that's all there was to it.

Mrs. Borden: If your father wants my brother in for a stay, he's to ask Lizzie's permission I suppose.

Emma: No.

Mrs. Borden: You know, Emma—

Emma: She didn't argue with him or anything like that.

Mrs. Borden: You spoiled her. You may have had the best of intentions, but you spoiled her.

Miss Lizzie/Bridget is speaking to Actress/Lizzie.

Miss Lizzie/Bridget: I was thirty-four years old, and I still daydreamed . . . I did . . . I daydreamed . . . I dreamt that my name was Lisbeth . . . and I lived up on the hill in a corner house . . . and my hair wasn't red. I hate red hair. When I was little, everyone teased me. . . . When I was little, we never stayed in this house for the summer, we'd go to the farm. . . . I remember . . . my knees were always covered with scabs, god knows how I got them, but you know what I'd do? I'd sit in the field, and haul up my skirts, and my petticoat and my bloomers and roll down my stockings and I'd *pick* the scabs on my knees! And Emma would catch me! You know what she'd say? "Nice little girls don't have scabs on their knees!"

They laugh.

Lizzie: Poor Emma.

Miss Lizzie/Bridget: I dreamt . . . someday I'm going to live . . . in a corner house on the hill. . . . I'll have parties, grand parties. I'll be . . . witty, not biting, but witty. Everyone will be witty. Everyone who is *anyone* will want to come to my parties . . . and if . . . I can't . . . live in a corner house on the hill . . . I'll live on the farm, all by myself on the farm! There was a barn there, with barn cats and barn kittens and two horses and barn swallows that lived in the eaves. . . . The birds I kept here were pigeons, not swallows. They were grey, a dull grey . . . but . . . when the sun struck their feathers, I'd see blue, a steel blue with a sheen, and when they'd move in the sun they were bright blue and maroon and over it all, an odd sparkle as if you'd . . . grated a new silver dollar and the gratings caught in their feathers. . . . Most of the time they were dull . . . and stupid perhaps . . . but they weren't really. They were . . . hiding I think. . . . They knew me. . . . They liked me. The truth . . . is—

The Actress/Lizzie: The truth is . . . thirty-four is too old to day-dream.

Mrs. Borden: The truth is she's spoilt rotten. *Mr. Borden will come downstairs and take his place at the table. Mrs. Borden continues for his benefit. Mr. Borden ignores her. He has learned the fine art of tuning her out. He is not intimidated or hen-pecked.* And we're paying the piper for that. In most of the places I've been the people who pay the piper call the tune. Of course I haven't had the advantage of a trip to Europe with a bunch of lady friends like our Lizzie had three years ago, all expenses paid by her father.

Emma: Morning Papa.

Mr. Borden: Mornin'.

Mrs. Borden: I haven't had the benefit of that experience. . . . Did you know Lizzie's seen Harry?

Mr. Borden: Has she.

Mrs. Borden: You should have met him downtown. You should never have asked him to stay over.

Mr. Borden: Why not?

Mrs. Borden: You know as well as I do why not. I don't want a repeat of last time. She didn't speak civil for months.

Mr. Borden: There's no reason for Harry to pay for a room when we've got a spare one. . . . Where's Lizzie?

Emma: Out back feeding the birds.

Mr. Borden: She's always out at those birds.

Emma: Yes Papa.

Mr. Borden: And tell her to get a new lock for the shed. There's been someone in it again.

Emma:	Alright.
Mr. Borden:	It's those little hellions from next door. We had no trouble with them playin' in that shed before, they always played in their own yard before.
Emma:	. . . Papa?
Mr. Borden:	It's those damn birds, that's what brings them into the yard.
Emma:	. . . About Harry . . .
Mr. Borden:	What about Harry?
Emma:	Well . . . I was just wondering why . . . [he's here]
Mr. Borden:	You never mind Harry—did you speak to Lizzie about Johnny MacLeod?
Emma:	I ah—
Mr. Borden:	Eh?
Emma:	I said I tried to—
Mr. Borden:	What do you mean, you tried to.
Emma:	Well, I was working my way 'round to it but—
Mr. Borden:	What's so difficult about telling Lizzie Johnny MacLeod wants to call?
Emma:	Then why don't you tell her? I'm always the one that has to go running to Lizzie telling her this and telling her that, and taking the abuse for it!
Mrs. Borden:	We all know why that is, she can wrap her father 'round her little finger, always has, always could. If everything else fails, she throws a tantrum and her father buys her off, trip to Europe, rent to the mill house, it's all the same.
Emma:	Papa, what's Harry here for?
Mr. Borden:	None of your business.
Mrs. Borden:	And don't you go runnin' to Lizzie stirring things up.
Emma:	You know I've never done that!

Mr. Borden: What she means—

Emma: *With anger but little fatigue.* I'm tired, do you hear? Tired! *She gets up from the table and leaves for upstairs.*

Mr. Borden: Emma!

Emma: You ask Harry here, you know there'll be trouble, and when I try to find out what's going on, so once again good old Emma can stand between you and Lizzie, all you've got to say is "none of your business!" Well then, it's *your* business, you look after it, because I'm not! *She exits.*

Mrs. Borden: . . . She's right.

Mr. Borden: That's enough. I've had enough. I don't want to hear from you too.

Mrs. Borden: I'm only saying she's right. You have to talk straight and plain to Lizzie and tell her things she don't want to hear.

Mr. Borden: About the farm?

Mrs. Borden: About Johnny MacLeod! Keep your mouth shut about the farm and she won't know the difference.

Mr. Borden: Alright.

Mrs. Borden: Speak to her about Johnny MacLeod.

Mr. Borden: Alright!

Mrs. Borden: You know what they're sayin' in town. About her and that doctor.

Miss Lizzie/Bridget is speaking to the Actress/Lizzie.

Miss Lizzie/Bridget: They're saying if you live on Second Street and you need a housecall, and you don't mind the Irish, call Dr. Patrick. Dr. Patrick is very prompt with his Second Street house calls.

The Actress/Lizzie: Do they really say that?

Miss Lizzie/Bridget: No they don't. I'm telling a lie. But he is very prompt with a Second Street call. Do you know why that is?

The Actress/Lizzie: Why?

Miss Lizzie/Bridget: Well—he's hoping to see someone who lives on Second Street—someone who's yanking up her skirt and showing her ankle—so she can take a decent-sized step—and forgetting everything she was ever taught in Miss Cornelia's School for Girls, and talking to the Irish as if she never heard of the Pope! Oh yes, he's very prompt getting to Second Street. . . . Getting away is something else . . .

Dr. Patrick: Good morning, Miss Borden!

Lizzie: I haven't decided . . . if it is . . . or it isn't. . . .

Dr. Patrick: No, you've got it all wrong. The proper phrase is, "Good morning, Dr. Patrick," and then you smile, discreetly of course, and lower the eyes just a titch, twirl the parasol—

Lizzie: The parasol?

Dr. Patrick: The parasol, but not too fast; and then you murmur in a voice that was ever sweet and low, "And how are you doin' this morning, Dr. Patrick?" Your education's been sadly neglected, Miss Borden.

Lizzie: You're forgetting something. You're married—and Irish besides—I'm supposed to ignore you.

Dr. Patrick: No.

Lizzie: Yes. Don't you realize Papa and Emma have fits every time we engage in "illicit conversation." They're having fits right now.

Dr. Patrick: Well, does Mrs. Borden approve?

Lizzie: Ahhh. She's the real reason I keep stopping and talking. Mrs. Borden is easily shocked. I'm hoping she dies from the shock.

Dr. Patrick: *Laughs.* Why don't you . . . run away from home, Lizzie?

Lizzie: Why don't you "run away" with me?

Dr. Patrick: Where'll we go?

Lizzie:	Boston.
Dr. Patrick:	Boston?
Lizzie:	For a start.
Dr. Patrick:	And when will we go?
Lizzie:	Tonight.
Dr. Patrick:	But you don't really mean it, you're havin' me on.
Lizzie:	I do mean it.
Dr. Patrick:	How can you joke—and look so serious?
Lizzie:	It's a gift.
Dr. Patrick:	*Laughs.* Oh Lizzie—
Lizzie:	Look!
Dr. Patrick:	What is it?
Lizzie:	It's those little beggars next door. Hey! Hey get away! Get away there! . . . They break into the shed to get at my birds and Papa gets angry.
Dr. Patrick:	It's a natural thing.
Lizzie:	Well Papa doesn't like it.
Dr. Patrick:	They just want to look at them.
Lizzie:	Papa says what's his is his own—you need a formal invitation to get into our yard. . . . *Pause.* How's your wife?
Dr. Patrick:	My wife.
Lizzie:	Shouldn't I ask that? I thought nice polite ladies always inquired after the wives of their friends or acquaintances or . . . whatever.

Harry observes them.

Dr. Patrick:	You've met my wife, my wife is always the same.
Lizzie:	How boring for you.
Dr. Patrick:	Uh-huh.

Lizzie:	And for her—
Dr. Patrick:	Yes indeed.
Lizzie:	And for me.
Dr. Patrick:	Do you know what they say, Lizzie? They say if you live on Second Street, and you need a house call, and you don't mind the Irish, call Dr. Patrick. Dr. Patrick is very prompt with his Second Street house calls.
Lizzie:	I'll tell you what I've heard them say—Second Street is a nice place to visit, but you wouldn't want to live there. I certainly don't.
Harry:	Lizzie.
Lizzie:	Well, look who's here. Have you had the pleasure of meeting my uncle, Mr. Wingate.
Dr. Patrick:	No Miss Borden, that pleasure has never been mine.
Lizzie:	That's exactly how I feel.
Dr. Patrick:	Mr. Wingate, sir.
Harry:	Dr. . . . Patrick is it?
Dr. Patrick:	Yes it is, sir.
Harry:	Who's sick? [*In other words, "What the hell are you doing here?"*]
Lizzie:	No one. He just dropped by for a visit; you see Dr. Patrick and I are very old, very dear friends, isn't that so?

Harry stares at Dr. Patrick.

Dr. Patrick:	Well . . . *Lizzie jabs him in the ribs.* Ouch! It's her sense of humour, sir . . . a rare trait in a woman. . . .
Harry:	You best get in, Lizzie, it's gettin' on for lunch.
Lizzie:	Don't be silly, we just had breakfast.
Harry:	You best get in!
Lizzie:	. . . Would you give me your arm, Dr. Patrick? *She moves away with Dr. Patrick, ignoring Harry.*

Dr. Patrick:	Now see what you've done?
Lizzie:	What?
Dr. Patrick:	You've broken two of my ribs and ruined my reputation all in one blow.
Lizzie:	It's impossible to ruin an Irishman's reputation.
Dr. Patrick:	*Smiles.* . . . I'll be seeing you, Lizzie . . .
Miss Lizzie/Bridget:	They're sayin' it's time you were married.
Lizzie:	What time is that?
Miss Lizzie/Bridget:	You need a place of your own.
Lizzie:	How would getting married get me that?
Miss Lizzie/Bridget:	Though I don't know what man would put up with your moods!
Lizzie:	What about me putting up with his!
Miss Lizzie/Bridget:	Oh Lizzie!
Lizzie:	What's the matter, don't men have moods?
Harry:	I'm tellin' you, as God is my witness, she's out in the walk talkin' to that Irish doctor, and he's fallin' all over her.
Mrs. Borden:	What's the matter with you. For her own sake you should speak to her.
Mr. Borden:	I will.
Harry:	The talk around town can't be doin' you any good.
Mrs. Borden:	Harry's right.
Harry:	Yes sir.
Mrs. Borden:	He's tellin' you what you should know.
Harry:	If a man can't manage his own daughter, how the hell can he manage a business—that's what people say, and it don't matter a damn whether there's any sense in it or not.
Mr. Borden:	I know that.

Mrs. Borden: Knowin' is one thing, doin' something about it is another. What're you goin' to do about it?

Mr. Borden: God damn it! I said I was goin' to speak to her and I am!

Mrs. Borden: Well speak good and plain this time!

Mr. Borden: Jesus christ woman!

Mrs. Borden: Your "speakin' to Lizzie" is a ritual around here.

Mr. Borden: Abbie—

Mrs. Borden: She talks, you listen, and nothin' changes!

Mr. Borden: That's enough!

Mrs. Borden: Emma isn't the only one that's fed to the teeth!

Mr. Borden: Shut up!

Mrs. Borden: You're gettin' old, Andrew! You're gettin' old! *She exits.*

An air of embarrassment from Mr. Borden at having words in front of Harry. Mr. Borden fumbles with his pipe.

Harry: *Offers his pouch of tobacco.* Here . . . have some of mine.

Mr. Borden: Don't mind if I do. . . . Nice mix.

Harry: It is.

Mr. Borden: . . . I used to think . . . by my seventies . . . I'd be bouncin' a grandson on my knee. . . .

Harry: Not too late for that.

Mr. Borden: Nope . . . never had any boys . . . and girls . . . don't seem to have the same sense of family. . . . You know it's all well and good to talk about speakin' plain to Lizzie, but the truth of the matter is, if Lizzie puts her mind to a thing, she does it, and if she don't, she don't.

Harry: It's up to you to see she does.

Mr. Borden: It's like Abigail says, knowin' is one thing, doin' is another. . . . You're lucky you never brought any children into the world, Harry, you don't have to deal with them.

Harry: Now that's no way to be talkin'.

Mr. Borden: There's Emma . . . Emma's a good girl . . . when Abbie and I get on, there'll always be Emma. . . . Well! You're not sittin' here to listen to me and my girls, are you, you didn't come here for that. Business, eh Harry?

Harry whips out a sheet of figures.

Miss Lizzie/Bridget: I can remember distinctly . . . that moment I was undressing for bed, and I looked at my knees—and there were no scabs! At last! I thought I'm the nice little girl Emma wants me to be! . . . But it wasn't that at all. I was just growing up. I didn't fall down so often. . . . *She smiles.* Do you suppose . . . do you suppose there's a formula, a magic formula for being "a woman?" Do you suppose every girl baby receives it at birth, it's the last thing that happens just before birth, the magic formula is stamped indelibly on the brain Ka Thud!! *Her mood of amusement changes.* . . . and through some terrible oversight . . . perhaps the death of my mother . . . I didn't get that Ka Thud!! I was born . . . defective. . . . *She looks at the Actress.*

Lizzie: *Low.* No.

Miss Lizzie/Bridget: Not defective?

Lizzie: Just . . . born.

The Defense: Gentlemen of the Jury!! I ask you to look at the defendent, Miss Lizzie Borden. I ask you to recall the nature of the crime of which she is accused. I ask you—do you believe Miss Lizzie Borden, the youngest daughter of a scion of our community, a recipient of the fullest amenities our society can bestow upon its most fortunate members, do you believe Miss Lizzie Borden capable of wielding the murder weapon—thirty-two blows, gentlemen, thirty-two blows—fracturing Abigail Borden's skull, leaving her bloody and broken body in an upstairs bedroom, then, Miss Borden, with no hint of frenzy, hysteria, or trace of blood upon her person, engages in casual conversation with the maid, Bridget O'Sullivan, while awaiting her father's return home, upon which, after sending Bridget to her attic room, Miss Borden deals thirteen blows to the head of her father, and minutes later—in a state utterly compatible with that of a loving daughter upon discovery of murder most foul—Miss Borden calls for aid! Is this the aid we give her? Accusation of the most heinous and infamous of crimes? Do you believe Miss Lizzie Borden capable of these acts? I can tell you I do not!! I can tell you these acts of violence are acts of madness!! Gentlemen! If this gentlewoman is capable of such an act—I say to you—look to your daughters—if this gentlewoman is capable of such an act, which of us can lie abed at night, hear a step upon the stairs, a rustle in the hall, a creak outside the door? . . . Which of you can plump your pillow, nudge your wife, close your eyes, and sleep? Gentlemen, Lizzie Borden is not mad. Gentlemen, Lizzie Borden is not guilty.

Mr. Borden:	Lizzie?
Lizzie:	Papa . . . have you and Harry got business?
Harry:	'Lo Lizzie. I'll ah . . . finish up later. *He exits with the figures. Lizzie watches him go.*
Mr. Borden:	Lizzie?
Lizzie:	What?
Mr. Borden:	Could you sit down a minute?
Lizzie:	If it's about Dr. Patrick again, I—
Mr. Borden:	It isn't.
Lizzie:	Good.
Mr. Borden:	But we could start there.
Lizzie:	Oh Papa.
Mr. Borden:	Sit down Lizzie.

Lizzie: But I've heard it all before, another chat for a wayward girl.

Mr. Borden: *Gently.* Bite your tongue, Lizzie.

She smiles at him, there is affection between them. She has the qualities he would like in a son but deplores in a daughter.

Mr. Borden: Now . . . first off. . . I want you to know that I . . . understand about you and the doctor.

Lizzie: What do you understand?

Mr. Borden: I understand . . . that it's a natural thing.

Lizzie: What is?

Mr. Borden: I'm saying there's nothing unnatural about an attraction between a man and a woman. That's a natural thing.

Lizzie: I find Dr. Patrick . . . amusing and entertaining . . . if that's what you mean . . . is that what you mean?

Mr. Borden: This attraction . . . points something up—you're a woman of thirty-four years—

Lizzie: I know that.

Mr. Borden: Just listen to me, Lizzie. . . . I'm choosing my words, and I want you to listen. Now . . . in most circumstances . . . a woman of your age would be married, eh? Have children, be running her own house, that's the natural thing, eh? *Pause.* Eh, Lizzie?

Lizzie: I don't know.

Mr. Borden: Of course you know.

Lizzie: You're saying I'm unnatural . . . am I supposed to agree, is that what you want?

Mr. Borden: No, I'm not saying that! I'm saying the opposite to that! . . . I'm saying the feelings you have towards Dr. Patrick—

Lizzie: What feelings?

Mr. Borden: What's . . . what's happening there, I can understand, but what you have to understand is that he's a mar-

	ried man, and there's nothing for you there.
Lizzie:	If he weren't married, Papa, I wouldn't be bothered talking to him! . . . It's just a game, Papa, it's a game.
Mr. Borden:	A game.
Lizzie:	You have no idea how boring it is looking eligible, interested, and alluring, when I feel none of the three. So I play games. And it's a blessed relief to talk to a married man.
Mr. Borden:	What're his feelings for you?
Lizzie:	I don't know, I don't care. Can I go now?
Mr. Borden:	I'm not finished yet! . . . You know Mr. MacLeod, Johnny MacLeod?
Lizzie:	I know his three little monsters.
Mr. Borden:	He's trying to raise three boys with no mother!
Lizzie:	That's not my problem! I'm going.
Mr. Borden:	Lizzie!
Lizzie:	What!
Mr. Borden:	Mr. MacLeod's asked to come over next Tuesday.
Lizzie:	I'll be out that night.
Mr. Borden:	No you won't!
Lizzie:	Yes I will! . . . Whose idea was this?
Mr. Borden:	No one's.
Lizzie:	That's a lie. She wants to get rid of me.
Mr. Borden:	I want what's best for you!
Lizzie:	No you don't! 'Cause you don't care what I want!
Mr. Borden:	You don't know what you want!
Lizzie:	But I know what you want! You want me living my life by the *Farmers' Almanac*; having everyone over for Christmas dinner; waiting up for my husband; and *serving at socials*!

Mr. Borden:	It's good enough for your mother!
Lizzie:	She is *not* my *mother*!
Mr. Borden:	. . . John MacLeod is looking for a wife.
Lizzie:	No, god damn it, he isn't!
Mr. Borden:	Lizzie!
Lizzie:	He's looking for a housekeeper and it isn't going to be me!
Mr. Borden:	You've a filthy mouth!
Lizzie:	Is that why you hate me?
Mr. Borden:	You don't make sense.
Lizzie:	Why is it when I pretend things I don't feel, that's when you like me?
Mr. Borden:	You talk foolish.
Lizzie:	I'm supposed to be a mirror. I'm supposed to reflect what you want to see, but everyone wants something different. If no one looks in the mirror, I'm not even there, I don't exist!
Mr. Borden:	Lizzie, you talk foolish!
Lizzie:	No, I don't, that isn't true.
Mr. Borden:	About Mr. MacLeod—
Lizzie:	You can't make me get married!
Mr. Borden:	Lizzie, do you want to spend the rest of your life in this house?
Lizzie:	No . . . No . . . I want out of it, but I won't get married to do it.
Mrs. Borden:	*On her way through to the kitchen.* You've never been asked.
Lizzie:	Oh listen to her! I must be some sort of failure, then, eh? You had no son and a daughter that failed! What does that make you, Papa!
Mr. Borden:	I want you to think about Johnny MacLeod!

Lizzie: To hell with him!!!

Mr. Borden appears defeated. After a moment, Lizzie goes to him, she holds his hand, strokes his hair.

Lizzie: Papa? . . . Papa, I love you, I try to be what you want, really I do try, I try . . . but . . . I don't want to get married. I wouldn't be a good mother, I—

Mr. Borden: How do you know—

Lizzie: I know it! . . . I want out of all this . . . I hate this house, I hate . . . I want out. Try to understand how I feel. . . . Why can't I do something? . . . Eh? I mean . . . I could . . . I could go into your office. . . . I could . . . learn how to keep books?

Mr. Borden: Lizzie.

Lizzie: Why can't I do something like that?

Mr. Borden: For god's sake, talk sensible.

Lizzie: Alright then! Why can't we move up on the hill to a house where we aren't in each other's laps!

Mrs. Borden: *Returning from kitchen.* Why don't you move out!

Lizzie: Give me the money and I'll go!

Mrs. Borden: Money.

Lizzie: And give me enough that I won't ever have to come back!

Mrs. Borden: She always gets 'round to money!

Lizzie: You drive me to it!

Mrs. Borden: She's crazy!

Lizzie: You drive me to it!

Mrs. Borden: She should be locked up!

Lizzie: *Begins to smash the plates in the dining room.* There!! There!!

Mr. Borden: Lizzie!

Mrs. Borden: Stop her!

Lizzie: There!

Mr. Borden attempts to restrain her.

Mrs. Borden: For god's sake, Andrew!

Lizzie: Lock me up! Lock me up!

Mr. Borden: Stop it! Lizzie!

She collapses against him, crying.

Lizzie: Oh, Papa, I can't stand it.

Mr. Borden: There, there, come on now, it's alright, listen to me, Lizzie, it's alright.

Mrs. Borden: You may as well get down on your knees.

Lizzie: Look at her. She's jealous of me. She can't stand it whenever you're nice to me.

Mr. Borden: There now.

Mrs. Borden: Ask her about Dr. Patrick.

Mr. Borden: I'll handle this my way.

Lizzie: He's an entertaining person, there're very few around!

Mrs. Borden: Fall River ain't Paris and ain't that a shame for our Lizzie!

Lizzie: One trip three years ago and you're still harping on it; it's true, Papa, an elephant never forgets!

Mr. Borden: Show some respect!

Lizzie: She's a fat cow and I hate her!

Mr. Borden slaps Lizzie. There is a pause as he regains control of himself.

Mr. Borden: Now . . . now . . . you'll see Mr. MacLeod Tuesday night.

Lizzie: No.

Mr. Borden: God damn it!! I said you'll see Johnny MacLeod Tuesday night!!

Joan Orenstein as Abigail Borden, Patricia Collins as The Actress/Lizzie and Derek Ralston as Andrew Borden in the National Arts Centre production of *Blood Relations*, Ottawa, Ontario, 1981.

Courtesy of Photo Features Ltd

Lizzie:	No.
Mr. Borden:	Get the hell upstairs to your room!
Lizzie:	No.
Mr. Borden:	I'm telling you to go upstairs to your room!!
Lizzie:	I'll go when I'm ready.
Mr. Borden:	I said, Go!

He grabs her arm to move her forcibly, she hits his arm away.

Lizzie:	No! . . . There's something you don't understand, Papa. You can't make me do one thing that I don't want to do. I'm going to keep on doing just what I want just when I want—like always!
Mr. Borden:	*Shoves her to the floor to gain a clear exit from the room. He stops on the stairs, looks back to her on the floor. . . .* I'm . . . *He continues off.*
Mrs. Borden:	*Without animosity.* You know, Lizzie, your father keeps you. You know you got nothing but what he gives you. And that's a fact of life. You got to come to deal with facts. I did.
Lizzie:	And married Papa.
Mrs. Borden:	And married your father. You never made it easy for me. I took on a man with two little ones, and Emma was your mother.
Lizzie:	You got stuck so I should too, is that it?
Mrs. Borden:	What?
Lizzie:	The reason I should marry Johnny MacLeod.
Mrs. Borden:	I just know, this time, in the end, you'll do what your Papa says, you'll see.
Lizzie:	No, I won't. I have a right. A right that frees me from all that.
Mrs. Borden:	No, Lizzie, you got no rights.
Lizzie:	I've a legal right to one-third because I am his flesh and blood.

Mrs. Borden:	What you don't understand is your father's not dead yet, your father's got many good years ahead of him, and when his time comes, well, we'll see what his will says then. . . . Your father's no fool, Lizzie. . . . Only a fool would leave money to you. *She exits.*

After a moment, Bridget enters from the kitchen.

Bridget:	Ah Lizzie . . . you outdid yourself that time. *She is comforting Lizzie.* . . . Yes you did . . . an elephant never forgets!
Lizzie:	Oh Bridget.
Bridget:	Come on now.
Lizzie:	I can't help it.
Bridget:	Sure you can . . . sure you can . . . stop your cryin' and come and sit down . . . you want me to tell you a story?
Lizzie:	No.
Bridget:	Sure, a story. I'll tell you a story. Come on now . . . now . . . before I worked here I worked up on the hill and the lady of the house . . . are you listenin'? Well, she swore by her cook, finest cook in creation, yes, always bowin' and scrapin' and smilin' and givin' up her day off if company arrived. Oh the lady of the house she loved that cook—and I'll tell you her name! It was Mary! Now listen! Do you know what Mary was doin'? *Lizzie shakes her head.* Before eatin' the master'd serve drinks in the parlour—and out in the kitchen, Mary'd be spittin' in the soup!
Lizzie:	What?
Bridget:	She'd spit in the soup! And she'd smile when they served it!
Lizzie:	No.
Bridget:	Yes. I've seen her cut up hair for an omelette.
Lizzie:	You're lying.
Bridget:	Cross me heart. . . . They thought it was pepper!

Lizzie:	Oh, Bridget!
Bridget:	These two eyes have seen her season up mutton stew when it's off and gone bad.
Lizzie:	Gone bad?
Bridget:	Oh and they et it, every bit, and the next day they was hit with . . . *stomach flu!* So cook called it. By jasus Lizzie, I daren't tell you what she served up in their food, for fear you'd be sick!
Lizzie:	That's funny. . . . *A fact—Lizzie does not appear amused.*
Bridget:	*Starts to clear up the dishes.* Yes, well, I'm tellin' you I kept on the good side of cook.

Lizzie watches her for a moment.

Lizzie:	. . . Do you . . . like me?
Bridget:	Sure I do. . . . You should try bein' more like cook, Lizzie. Smile and get 'round them. You can do it.
Lizzie:	It's not . . . *fair* that I have to.
Bridget:	There ain't nothin' fair in this world.
Lizzie:	Well then . . . well then, I don't want to!
Bridget:	You dream, Lizzie . . . you dream dreams . . . Work. Be sensible. What could you do?
Lizzie:	I could
Miss Lizzie/Bridget:	No.
Lizzie:	I could
Miss Lizzie/Bridget:	No.
Lizzie:	I could
Miss Lizzie/Bridget:	No!
Lizzie:	I . . . dream.
Miss Lizzie/Bridget:	You dream . . . of a carousel . . . you see a carousel . . . you see lights that go on and go off . . . you see yourself on a carousel horse, a red-painted horse

with its head in the air, and green staring eyes, and a white flowing mane, it looks wild! . . . It goes up and comes down, and the carousel whirls round with the music and lights, on and off . . . and you watch . . . watch yourself on the horse. You're wearing a mask, a white mask like the mane of the horse, it looks like your face except that it's rigid and white . . . and it changes! With each flick of the lights, the expression, it changes, but always so rigid and hard, like the flesh of the horse that is red that you ride. You ride with no hands! No hands on this petrified horse, its head flung in the air, its wide staring eyes like those of a doe run down by the dogs! . . . And each time you go 'round, your hands rise a fraction nearer the mask . . . and the music and the carousel and the horse . . . they all three slow down, and they stop. . . . You can reach out and touch . . . you . . . you on the horse . . . with your hands so at the eyes. . . . You look into the eyes! *A sound from Lizzie, she is horrified and frightened. She covers her eyes.* There are none! None! Just black holes in a white mask. . . . *Pause.* The eyes of your birds . . . are round . . . and bright . . . a light shines from inside . . . they . . . can see into your heart . . . they're pretty . . . they love you.

Mr. Borden: I want this settled, Harry, I want it settled while Lizzie's out back.

Miss Lizzie/Bridget draws Lizzie's attention to the Mr. Borden/Harry scene. Lizzie listens, will move closer.

Harry: You know I'm for that.

Mr. Borden: I want it all done but the signin' of the papers tomorrow, that's if I decide to—

Harry: You can't lose, Andrew. That farm's just lyin' fallow.

Mr. Borden: Well, let's see what you got.

Harry: *Gets out his papers.* Look at this . . . I'll run horse auctions and a buggy rental—now I'll pay no rent for the house or pasturage but you get twenty per cent, eh? That figure there—

Mr. Borden:	Mmmn.
Harry:	From my horse auctions last year, it'll go up on the farm and you'll get twenty per cent off the top. . . . My buggy rental won't do so well . . . that's that figure there, approximate . . . but it all adds up, eh? Adds up for you.
Mr. Borden:	It's a good deal, Harry, but . . .
Harry:	Now I know why you're worried—but the farm will still be in the family, 'cause aren't I family? And whenever you or the girls want to come over for a visit, why I'll send a buggy from the rental, no need for you to have the expense of a horse, eh?
Mr. Borden:	It looks good on paper.
Harry:	There's . . . ah something else, it's a bit awkward but I got to mention it; I'll be severin' a lot of my present connections, and what I figure I've a right to, is some kind of guarantee. . . .
Mr. Borden:	You mean a renewable lease for the farm?
Harry:	Well—what I'm wondering is . . . No offense, but you're an older man, Andrew . . . now if something should happen to you, where would the farm stand in regards to your will? That's what I'm wondering.
Mr. Borden:	I've not made a will.
Harry:	You know best—but I wouldn't want to be in a position where Lizzie would be havin' anything to do with that farm. The less she knows now the better, but she's bound to find out—I don't feel I'm steppin' out of line by bringin' this up.

Lizzie is within earshot. She is staring at Harry and Mr. Borden. They do not see her.

Mr. Borden:	No.
Harry:	If you mind you come right out and say so.
Mr. Borden:	That's alright.
Harry:	Now . . . if you . . . put the farm—in Abbie's name,

	what do you think?
Mr. Borden:	I don't know, Harry.
Harry:	I don't want to push.
Mr. Borden:	. . . I should make a will . . . I want the girls looked after, it don't seem like they'll marry . . . and Abbie, she's younger than me, I know Emma will see to her, still . . . money-wise I got to consider these things. . . . It makes a difference no men in the family.
Harry:	You know you can count on me for whatever.
Mr. Borden:	If . . . *If* I changed title to the farm, Abbie'd have to come down to the bank, I wouldn't want Lizzie to know.
Harry:	You can send a note for Abbie when you get to the bank; she can say it's a note from a friend, and come down and meet you. Simple as that.
Mr. Borden:	I'll give it some thought.
Harry:	You see, Abbie owns the farm, it's no difference to you, but it gives me protection.
Mr. Borden:	Who's there?
Harry:	It's Lizzie.
Mr. Borden:	What do you want? . . . Did you lock the shed? . . . Is the shed locked! *Lizzie makes a slow motion which Mr. Borden takes for assent.* Well you make sure it stays locked! I don't want any more of those god damned . . . I . . . ah . . . I think we about covered everything, Harry, we'll . . . ah . . . we'll let it go till tomorrow.
Harry:	Good enough . . . well . . . I'll just finish choppin' that kindlin', give a shout when it's lunchtime. *He exits.*

Lizzie and Mr. Borden stare at each other for a moment.

Lizzie:	*Very low.* What are you doing with the farm?

Mr. Borden slowly picks up the papers, places them in his pocket.

Lizzie:	Papa! . . . Papa. I want you to show me what you put in your pocket.

Mr. Borden:	It's none of your business.
Lizzie:	The farm is my business.
Mr. Borden:	It's nothing.
Lizzie:	Show me!
Mr. Borden:	I said it's nothing!

Lizzie makes a quick move towards her father to seize the paper from his pocket. Even more quickly and smartly he slaps her face. It is all very quick and clean. A pause as they stand frozen.

Harry:	*Off.* Andrew, there's a bunch of kids broken into the shed!
Mr. Borden:	Jesus christ.
Lizzie:	*Whispers.* What about the farm?
Mr. Borden:	You! You and those god damn birds! I've told you! I've told you time and again!
Lizzie:	What about the farm!
Mr. Borden:	Jesus christ . . . You never listen! Never!
Harry:	*Enters carrying the hand hatchet.* Andrew!!
Mr. Borden:	*Grabs the hand hatchet from Harry, turns to Lizzie.* There'll be no more of your god damn birds in this yard!!
Lizzie:	No!

Mr. Borden raises the hatchet and smashes it into the table as Lizzie screams.

Lizzie:	No Papa!! Nooo!!

The hatchet is embedded in the table. Mr. Borden and Harry assume a soft freeze as Actress/Lizzie whirls to see Miss Lizzie/Bridget observing the scene.

Lizzie:	Nooo!
Miss Lizzie:	I loved them.

BLACKOUT

ACT TWO

Lights come up on The Actress/Lizzie sitting at the dining room table. She is very still, her hands clasped in her lap. Miss Lizzie/Bridget is near her. She too is very still. A pause.

Actress/Lizzie: *Very low.* Talk to me.

Miss Lizzie/Bridget: I remember . . .

Actress/Lizzie: *Very low.* No.

Miss Lizzie/Bridget: On the farm, Papa's farm, Harry's farm, when I was little and thought it was my farm and I loved it, we had some puppies, the farm dog had puppies, brown soft little puppies with brown ey . . . . [*She does not complete the word "eyes"*] And one of the puppies got sick. I didn't know it was sick, it seemed like the others, but the mother, she knew. It would lie at the back of the box, she would lie in front of it while she nursed all the others. They ignored it, that puppy didn't exist for the others. . . . I think inside it was different, and the mother thought the difference she sensed was a sickness . . . and after a while . . . anyone could tell it was sick. It had nothing to eat! And Papa took it and drowned it. That's what you do on a farm with things that are different.

Actress/Lizzie: Am I different?

Miss Lizzie/Bridget: You kill them.

Actress/Lizzie looks at Miss Lizzie/Bridget. Miss Lizzie/Bridget looks towards the top of the stairs. Bridget gets up and exits to the kitchen. Emma appears at the top of the stairs. She is dressed for travel and carries a small suitcase and her gloves. She stares down at Lizzie still sitting at the table. After several moments Lizzie becomes aware of that gaze and turns to look at Emma. Emma then descends the stairs. She puts down her suitcase. She is not overjoyed at seeing Lizzie, having hoped to get away before Lizzie arose; nevertheless she begins with an excess of enthusiasm to cover the implications of her departure.

Emma: Well! You're up early. . . . Bridget down? . . . Did you put the coffee on? *She puts her gloves on the table.* My goodness, Lizzie, cat got your tongue? *She exits to the*

kitchen. Lizzie picks up the gloves. Emma returns.
Bridget's down, she's in the kitchen. . . . Well, looks
like a real scorcher today, doesn't it?

Lizzie:	What's the bag for?
Emma:	I . . . decided I might go for a little trip, a day or two, get away from the heat. . . . The girls've rented a place out beach way and I thought . . . with the weather and all . . .
Lizzie:	How can you do that?
Emma:	Do what? . . . Anyway I thought I might stay with them a few days. . . . Why don't you come with me?
Lizzie:	No.
Emma:	Just for a few days, come with me.
Lizzie:	No.
Emma:	You know you like the water.
Lizzie:	I said no!
Emma:	Oh, Lizzie.

Pause.

Lizzie:	I don't see how you can leave me like this.
Emma:	I asked you to come with me.
Lizzie:	You know I can't do that.
Emma:	Why not?
Lizzie:	Someone has to *do* something, you just run away from things.

Pause.

Emma:	. . . Lizzie . . . I'm sorry about the— [*birds*]
Lizzie:	No!
Emma:	Papa was angry.
Lizzie:	I don't want to talk about it.
Emma:	He's sorry now.

Lizzie:	Nobody *listens* to me, can't you hear me? I said *don't* talk about it. I don't want to talk about it. Stop talking about it!!

Bridget enters with the coffee.

Emma:	Thank you, Bridget.

Miss Lizzie/Bridget sits in the parlour.

Emma:	Well! . . . I certainly can use this this morning. . . . Your coffee's there.
Lizzie:	I don't want it.
Emma:	You're going to ruin those gloves.
Lizzie:	I don't care.
Emma:	Since they're not yours.

Lizzie bangs the gloves down on the table. A pause. Then Emma picks them up and smooths them out.

Lizzie:	Why are you leaving me?
Emma:	I feel like a visit with the girls. Is there something wrong with that?
Lizzie:	How can you go now?
Emma:	I don't know what you're getting at.
Lizzie:	I heard them. I heard them talking yesterday. Do you know what they're saying?
Emma:	How could I?
Lizzie:	"How could I?" What do you mean "How could I?" Did you know?
Emma:	No, Lizzie, I did not.
Lizzie:	*Did-not-what.*
Emma:	Know.
Lizzie:	But you know now. How do you know now?
Emma:	I've put two and two together and I'm going over to the girls' for a visit!

Lizzie:	Please Emma!
Emma:	It's too hot.
Lizzie:	I need you, don't go.
Emma:	I've been talking about this trip.
Lizzie:	That's a lie.
Emma:	They're expecting me.
Lizzie:	You're lying to me!
Emma:	I'm going to the girls' place. You can come if you want, you can stay if you want. I planned this trip and I'm taking it!
Lizzie:	Stop lying!
Emma:	If I want to tell a little white lie to avoid an altercation in this house, I'll do so. Other people have been doing it for years!
Lizzie:	You don't understand, you don't understand anything.
Emma:	Oh, I understand enough.
Lizzie:	You don't! Let me explain it to you. You listen carefully, you listen. . . . Harry's getting the farm, can you understand that? Harry is here and he's moving on the farm and he's going to be there, on the farm, living on the farm. *Our farm.* Do you understand that? . . . Do you understand that!
Emma:	Yes.
Lizzie:	Harry's going to be on the farm. That's the first thing. No . . . no it isn't. . . . The first thing . . . was the mill house, that was the first thing! And *now* the farm. You see there's a pattern, Emma, you can see that, can't you?
Emma:	I don't—
Lizzie:	You can see it! The mill house, then the farm, and the next thing is the papers for the farm—do you know what he's doing, Papa's doing? He's signing the farm over to her. It will never be ours, we will never have

	it, not ever. It's ours by rights, don't you feel that?
Emma:	The farm—has always meant a great deal to me, yes.
Lizzie:	Then what are you doing about it! You can't leave me now . . . but that's not all. Papa's going to make a will, and you can see the pattern, can't you, and if the pattern keeps on, what do you suppose his will will say. What do you suppose, answer me!
Emma:	I don't know.
Lizzie:	Say it!
Emma:	He'll see we're looked after.
Lizzie:	I don't want to be looked after! What's the matter with you? Do you really want to spend the rest of your life with that cow, listening to her drone on and on for years! That's just what they think you'll do. Papa'll leave you a monthly allowance, just like he'll leave me, just enough to keep us all living together. We'll be worth millions on paper, and be stuck in this house and by and by Papa will die and Harry will move in and you will wait on that cow while she gets fatter and fatter and I—will—sit in my room.
Emma:	Lizzie.
Lizzie:	We have to do something, you can see that. We have to do something!
Emma:	There's nothing we can do.
Lizzie:	Don't say that!
Emma:	Alright, then, what can we do?
Lizzie:	I . . . I . . . don't know. But we have to do something, you have to help me, you can't go away and leave me alone, you can't do that.
Emma:	Then—
Lizzie:	You know what I thought? I thought you could talk to him, really talk to him, make him understand that we're people. *Individual people,* and we have to live separate lives, and his will should make it possible for

	us to do that. And the farm can't go to Harry.
Emma:	You know it's no use.
Lizzie:	I can't talk to him anymore. Every time I talk to him I make everything worse. I hate him, no. No I don't. I hate her.

Emma looks at her brooch watch.

Lizzie:	Don't look at the time.
Emma:	I'll miss my connections.
Lizzie:	No!
Emma:	*Puts on her gloves.* Lizzie. There's certain things we have to face. One of them is, we can't change a thing.
Lizzie:	I won't let you go!
Emma:	I'll be back on the weekend.
Lizzie:	He killed my birds! He took the axe and he killed them! Emma, I ran out and held them in my hands, I felt their hearts throbbing and pumping and the blood gushed out of their necks, it was all over my hands, don't you care about that?
Emma:	I . . . I . . . have a train to catch.
Lizzie:	He didn't care how much he hurt me and you don't care either. Nobody cares.
Emma:	I . . . have to go now.
Lizzie:	That's right. Go away. I don't even like you, Emma. Go away! *Emma leaves, Lizzie runs after her calling.* I'm sorry for all the things I told you! Things I really felt! You pretended to me, and I don't like you!! Go away!!

Lizzie looks after Emma's departing figure. After a moment she slowly turns back into the room. Miss Lizzie/Bridget is there.

Lizzie:	I want to die . . . I want to die, but something inside won't let me . . . inside something says *no. She shuts her eyes.* I can do anything.
Defense:	Miss Borden.

Both Lizzies turn.

Defense: Could you describe the sequence of events upon your father's arrival home?

Lizzie: *With no animation.* Papa came in . . . we exchanged a few words . . . Bridget and I spoke of the yard goods sale downtown, whether she would buy some. She went up to her room . . .

Defense: And then?

Lizzie: I went out back . . . through the yard . . . I picked up several pears from the ground beneath the trees . . . I went into the shed . . . I stood looking out the window and ate the pears . . .

Defense: How many?

Lizzie: Four.

Defense: It wasn't warm, stifling in the shed?

Lizzie: No, it was cool.

Defense: What were you doing, apart from eating the pears?

Lizzie: I suppose I was thinking. I just stood there, looking out the window, thinking, and eating the pears I'd picked up.

Defense: You're fond of pears?

Lizzie: Otherwise, I wouldn't eat them.

Defense: Go on.

Lizzie: I returned to the house. I found—Papa. I called for Bridget.

Mrs. Borden descends the stairs. Lizzie and Miss Lizzie/Bridget turn to look at her. Mrs. Borden is only aware of Lizzie's stare. Pause.

Mrs. Borden: . . . What're you staring at? . . . I said what're you staring at?

Lizzie: *Continuing to stare at Mrs. Borden.* Bridget.

Bridget: Yes ma'am.

Pause.

Mrs. Borden: Just coffee and a biscuit this morning, Bridget, it's too hot for a decent breakfast.

Bridget: Yes ma'am.

She exits for the biscuit and coffee. Lizzie continues to stare at Mrs. Borden.

Mrs. Borden: . . . Tell Bridget I'll have it in the parlour.

Is making an effort to be pleasant, to be "good." Mrs. Borden is more aware of this as unusual behaviour from Lizzie than were she to be rude, biting, or threatening. Lizzie, at the same time, feels caught in a dimension other than the one in which the people around her are operating. For Lizzie, a bell-jar effect. Simple acts seem filled with significance. Lizzie is trying to fulfill other people's expectations of "normal."

Lizzie: It's not me, is it?

Mrs. Borden: What?

Lizzie: You're not moving into the parlour because of me, are you?

Mrs. Borden: What?

Lizzie: I'd hate to think I'd driven you out of your own dining room.

Mrs. Borden: No.

Lizzie: Oh good, because I'd hate to think that was so.

Mrs. Borden: It's cooler in the parlour.

Lizzie: You know, you're right.

Mrs. Borden: Eh?

Lizzie: It is cooler. . . .

Bridget enters with the coffee and biscuit.

Lizzie: I will, Bridget.

She takes the coffee and biscuit, gives it to Mrs. Borden. Lizzie watches her eat and drink. Mrs. Borden eats the biscuit delicately. Lizzie's attention is caught by it. Miss Lizzie/Bridget sits in the dining room.

Lizzie: Do you like that biscuit?

Mrs. Borden: It could be lighter.

Lizzie: You're right.

Mr. Borden enters, makes his way into the kitchen, Lizzie watches him pass.

Lizzie: You know, Papa doesn't look well, Papa doesn't look well at all. Papa looks sick.

Mrs. Borden: He had a bad night.

Lizzie: Oh?

Mrs. Borden: Too hot.

Lizzie: But it's cooler in here, isn't it? . . . *Not trusting her own evaluation of the degree of heat.* Isn't it?

Mrs. Borden: Yes, yes, it's cooler in here.

Mr. Borden enters with his coffee. Lizzie goes to him.

Lizzie: Papa? You should go in the parlour. It's much cooler in there, really it is.

He goes into the parlour. Lizzie remains in the dining room. She sits at the table, folds her hands in her lap, a mirror image of Miss Lizzie/ Bridget. Mr. Borden begins to read the paper.

Mrs. Borden: . . . I think I'll have Bridget do the windows today . . . they need doing . . . get them out of the way first thing. . . . Anything in the paper, Andrew? *Pause.*

Mr. Borden: *As he continues to read.* Nope.

Mrs. Borden: There never is . . . I don't know why we buy it. *Pause.*

Mr. Borden: *Reading.* Yup.

Mrs. Borden: You going out this morning? *Pause.*

Mr. Borden: Business.

Mrs. Borden: . . . Harry must be having a bit of a sleep-in. *Pause.*

Mr. Borden: Yup.

Mrs. Borden: He's always up by—*Harry starts down the stairs.* Well, speak of the devil—coffee and biscuits?

| Harry: | Sounds good to me. |

Mrs. Borden starts off to get it. Lizzie looks at her, catching her eye. Mrs. Borden stops abruptly.

| Lizzie: | *Her voice seems too loud.* Emma's gone over to visit at the girls' place. *Mr. Borden lowers his paper to look at her. Harry looks at her. Suddenly aware of the loudness of her voice, she continues softly, too softly. . . .* Till the weekend. |

| Mr. Borden: | She didn't say she was going, when'd she decide that? |

Lizzie looks down at her hands, doesn't answer. A pause. Then Mrs. Borden continues out to the kitchen.

| Harry: | Will you be ah . . . going downtown today? |

| Mr. Borden: | This mornin'. I got . . . business at the bank. |

A look between them. They are very aware of Lizzie's presence in the dining room.

| Harry: | This mornin' eh? Well now . . . that works out just fine for me. I can . . . I got a bill to settle in town myself. |

Lizzie turns her head to look at them.

| Harry: | I'll be on my way after that. |

| Mr. Borden: | Abbie'll be disappointed you're not stayin' for lunch. |

| Harry: | 'Nother time. |

| Mr. Borden: | *Aware of Lizzie's gaze.* I . . . I don't know where she is with that coffee. I'll— |

| Harry: | Never you mind, you sit right there, I'll get it. *He exits.* |

Lizzie and Mr. Borden look at each other. The bell-jar effect is lessened.

| Lizzie: | *Softly.* Good mornin' Papa. |

| Mr. Borden: | Mornin' Lizzie. |

| Lizzie: | Did you have a good sleep? |

| Mr. Borden: | Not bad. |

Lizzie:	Papa?
Mr. Borden:	Yes Lizzie.
Lizzie:	You're a very strong-minded person, Papa, do you think I'm like you?
Mr. Borden:	In some ways . . . perhaps.
Lizzie:	I must be like someone.
Mr. Borden:	You resemble your mother.
Lizzie:	I look like my mother?
Mr. Borden:	A bit like your mother.
Lizzie:	But my mother's dead.
Mr. Borden:	Lizzie—
Lizzie:	I remember you told me she died because she was sick . . . I was born and she died . . . Did you love her?
Mr. Borden:	I married her.
Lizzie:	Can't you say if you loved her.
Mr. Borden:	Of course I did, Lizzie.
Lizzie:	Did you hate me for killing her?
Mr. Borden:	You don't think of it that way, it was just something that happened.
Lizzie:	Perhaps she just got tired and died. She didn't want to go on, and the chance came up and she took it. I could understand that. . . . Perhaps she was like a bird, she could see all the blue sky and she wanted to fly away but she couldn't. She was caught, Papa, she was caught in a horrible snare, and she saw a way out and she took it. . . . Perhaps it was a very brave thing to do, Papa, perhaps it was the only way, and she hated to leave us because she loved us so much, but she couldn't breathe all caught in the snare. . . . *Long pause.* Some people have very small wrists, have you noticed. Mine aren't. . . .

There is a murmur from the kitchen, then muted laughter. Mr. Borden looks towards it.

Lizzie:	Papa! . . . I'm a very strong person.
Mrs. Borden:	*Off, laughing.* You're tellin' tales out of school, Harry!
Harry:	*Off.* God's truth. You should have seen the buggy when they brought it back.
Mrs. Borden:	*Off.* You've got to tell Andrew. *Pokes her head in.* Andrew, come on out here, Harry's got a story. *Off.* Now you'll have to start at the beginning again, oh my goodness.

Mr. Borden starts for the kitchen. He stops, and looks back at Lizzie.

Lizzie:	Is there anything you want to tell me, Papa?
Mrs. Borden:	*Off.* Andrew!
Lizzie:	*Softly, an echo.* Andrew.
Mr. Borden:	What is it, Lizzie?
Lizzie:	If I promised to be a good girl forever and ever, would anything change?
Mr. Borden:	I don't know what you're talkin' about.
Lizzie:	I would be lying . . . Papa! . . . Don't do any business today. Don't go out. Stay home.
Mr. Borden:	What for?
Lizzie:	Everyone's leaving. Going away. Everyone's left.
Mrs. Borden:	*Off.* Andrew!
Lizzie:	*Softly, an echo.* Andrew.
Mr. Borden:	What is it?
Lizzie:	I'm calling you.

Mr. Borden looks at her for a moment, then leaves for the kitchen.

Dr. Patrick is heard whistling very softly. Lizzie listens.

Lizzie:	Listen . . . can you hear it . . . can you?
Miss Lizzie/Bridget:	I can hear it. . . . It's stopped.

Dr. Patrick can't be seen. Only his voice is heard.

Dr. Patrick:	*Very low.* Lizzie?

Lizzie:	*Realization.* I could hear it before [*you*]. *Pause.* It sounded so sad I wanted to cry.
Miss Lizzie/Bridget:	You mustn't cry. *She exits.*
Lizzie:	I mustn't cry.
Dr. Patrick:	I bet you know this one. *He whistles an Irish jig.*
Lizzie:	I know that! *She begins to dance.*

Dr. Patrick enters. He claps in time to the dance. Lizzie finishes the jig. Dr. Patrick applauds.

Dr. Patrick:	Bravo! Bravo!!
Lizzie:	You didn't know I could do that, did you?
Dr. Patrick:	You're a woman of many talents, Miss Borden.
Lizzie:	You're not making fun of me?
Dr. Patrick:	I would never do that.
Lizzie:	I can do anything I want.
Dr. Patrick:	I'm sure you can.
Lizzie:	If I wanted to die—I could even do that, couldn't I.
Dr. Patrick:	Well now, I don't think so.
Lizzie:	Yes, I could!
Dr. Patrick:	Lizzie—
Lizzie:	You wouldn't know—you can't see into my heart.
Dr. Patrick:	I think I can.
Lizzie:	Well you can't!
Dr. Patrick:	. . . It's only a game.
Lizzie:	I never play games.
Dr. Patrick:	Sure you do.
Lizzie:	I hate games.
Dr. Patrick:	You're playin' one now.
Lizzie:	You don't even know me!

Dr. Patrick:	Come on Lizzie, we don't want to fight. I know what we'll do . . . we'll start all over. . . . Shut your eyes, Lizzie. *She does so.* Good mornin' Miss Borden. . . . Good mornin' Miss Borden. . . .
Lizzie:	. . . I haven't decided. . . . *She slowly opens her eyes . . .* if it is or it isn't.
Dr. Patrick:	Much better . . . and now . . . would you take my arm, Miss Borden? How about a wee promenade?
Lizzie:	There's nowhere to go.
Dr. Patrick:	That isn't so. . . . What about Boston? . . . Do you think it's too far for a stroll? . . . I know what we'll do, we'll walk 'round to the side and you'll show me your birds. *They walk.* . . . I waited last night but you never showed up . . . there I was, travellin' bag and all, and you never appeared. . . . I know what went wrong! We forgot to agree on an hour! Next time, Lizzie, you must set the hour. . . . Is this where they're kept?

Lizzie nods, she opens the cage and looks in it.

Dr. Patrick:	It's empty. *He laughs.* And you say you never play games?
Lizzie:	They're gone.
Dr. Patrick:	You've been havin' me on again, yes you have.
Lizzie:	They've run away.
Dr. Patrick:	Did they really exist?
Lizzie:	I had blood on my hands.
Dr. Patrick:	What do you say?
Lizzie:	You can't see it now, I washed it off, see?
Dr. Patrick:	*Takes her hands.* Ah Lizzie . . .
Lizzie:	Would you . . . help someone die?
Dr. Patrick:	Why do you ask that?
Lizzie:	Some people are better off dead. I might be better off dead.

Kaori Ogura as Dr. Patrick and Izumi Imazeki as Lizzie Borden in the
Bunka-Za Theatre production of *Blood Relations*, Tokyo, Japan.
Translated into Japanese by Toyoshi (Yoshi) Yoshihara.
Directed by Takehisa (Tak) Kaiyama.

Courtesy of Tadao Shase

Dr. Patrick:	You're a precious and unique person, Lizzie, and you shouldn't think things like that.
Lizzie:	Precious and unique?
Dr. Patrick:	All life is precious and unique.
Lizzie:	I am precious and unique? . . . I *am* precious and unique. You said that.
Dr. Patrick:	Oh, I believe it.
Lizzie:	And I am. I know it. People mix things up on you, you have to be careful. I am a person of worth.
Dr. Patrick:	Sure you are.
Lizzie:	Not like that fat cow in there.
Dr. Patrick:	Her life too is—
Lizzie:	No!
Dr. Patrick:	Liz—
Lizzie:	Do you know her!
Dr. Patrick:	That doesn't matter.
Lizzie:	Yes it does, it does matter.
Dr. Patrick:	You can't be—
Lizzie:	You're a doctor, isn't that right?
Dr. Patrick:	Right enough there.
Lizzie:	So, tell me, tell me, if a dreadful accident occurred . . . and two people were dying . . . but you could only save one. . . . Which would you save?
Dr. Patrick:	You can't ask questions like that.
Lizzie:	Yes I can, come on, it's a game. How does a doctor determine? If one were old and the other were young—would you save the younger one first?
Dr. Patrick:	Lizzie.
Lizzie:	You said you liked games! If one were a bad person and the other was good, was trying to be good, would you save the one who was good and let the bad person

	die?
Dr. Patrick:	I don't know.
Lizzie:	Listen! If you could go back in time . . . what would you do if you met a person who was evil and wicked?
Dr. Patrick:	Who?
Lizzie:	I don't know, Attila the Hun!
Dr. Patrick:	*Laughs.* Oh my.
Lizzie:	Listen, if you met Attila the Hun, and you were in a position to kill him, would you do it?
Dr. Patrick:	I don't know.
Lizzie:	Think of the suffering he caused, the unhappiness.
Dr. Patrick:	Yes, but I'm a doctor, not an assassin.
Lizzie:	I think you're a coward.
Pause.	
Dr. Patrick:	What I do is try to save lives.
Lizzie:	But you put poison out for the slugs in your garden.
Dr. Patrick:	You got something mixed up.
Lizzie:	I've never been clearer. Everything's clear. I've lived all of my life for this one moment of absolute clarity! If war were declared, would you serve?
Dr. Patrick:	I would fight in a war.
Lizzie:	You wouldn't fight, you would kill—you'd take a gun and shoot people, people who'd done nothing to you, people who were trying to be good, you'd kill them! And you say you wouldn't kill Attila the Hun, or that that stupid cow's life is precious—*My life is precious!!*
Dr. Patrick:	To you.
Lizzie:	Yes to me, are you stupid!?
Dr. Patrick:	And hers is to her.
Lizzie:	I don't care about her! *Pause.* I'm glad you're not my doctor, you can't make decisions, can you? You are a

coward.

Dr. Patrick starts off.

Lizzie: You're afraid of your wife . . . you can only play games. . . . If I really wanted to go to Boston, you wouldn't come with me because you're a coward! *I'm not a coward!!*

Lizzie turns to watch Mrs. Borden enter the parlour and sit with needle work. After a moment Mrs. Borden looks at Lizzie, aware of her scrutiny.

Lizzie: . . . Where's Papa?

Mrs. Borden: Out.

Lizzie: And Mr. Wingate?

Mrs. Borden: He's out too.

Lizzie: So what are you going to do . . . Mrs. Borden?

Mrs. Borden: I'm going to finish this up.

Lizzie: You do that. . . . *Pause.* Where's Bridget?

Mrs. Borden: Out back washing windows. . . . You got clean clothes to go upstairs, they're in the kitchen.

Pause.

Lizzie: Did you know Papa killed my birds with the axe? He chopped off their heads. *Mrs. Borden is uneasy.* . . . It's alright. At first I felt bad, but I feel better now. I feel much better now. . . . I am a woman of decision, Mrs. Borden. When I decide to do things, I do them, yes, I do. *Smiles.* How many times has Papa said—when Lizzie puts her mind to a thing, she does it—and I do. . . . It's always me who puts the slug poison out because they eat all the flowers and you don't like that, do you? They're bad things, they must die. You see, not all life is precious, is it?

Mrs. Borden: *After a moment makes an attempt casually to gather together her things, to go upstairs. She does not want to be in the room with Lizzie.*

Lizzie: Where're you going?

Mrs. Borden: Upstairs. . . . *An excuse.* The spare room needs changing.

A knock at the back door . . . A second knock.

Lizzie: Someone's at the door. . . . *A third knock.* I'll get it.

She exits to the kitchen. Mrs. Borden waits. Lizzie returns. She's a bit out of breath. She carries a pile of clean clothes which she puts on the table. She looks at Mrs. Borden.

Lizzie: Did you want something?

Mrs. Borden: Who was it?—the door?

Lizzie: Oh yes. I forgot. I had to step out back for a moment and—it's a note. A message for you.

Mrs. Borden: Oh.

Lizzie: Shall I open it?

Mrs. Borden: That's alright. *She holds out her hand.*

Lizzie: Looks like Papa's handwriting. . . . *She passes over the note.* Aren't you going to open it?

Mrs. Borden: I'll read it upstairs.

Lizzie: Mrs. Borden! . . . Would you mind . . . putting my clothes in my room? *She gets some clothes from the table, Mrs. Borden takes them, something she would never normally do. Before she can move away, Lizzie grabs her arm.* Just a minute . . . I would like you to look into my eyes. What's the matter? Nothing's wrong. It's an experiment. . . . Look right into them. Tell me . . . what do you see . . . can you see anything?

Mrs. Borden: . . . Myself.

Lizzie: Yes. When a person dies, retained on her eye is the image of the last thing she saw. Isn't that interesting? *Pause.*

Mrs. Borden slowly starts upstairs. Lizzie picks up remaining clothes on table. The hand hatchet is concealed beneath them. She follows Mrs. Borden up the stairs.

Lizzie:	Do you know something? If I were to kill someone, I would come up behind them very slowly and quietly. They would never even hear me, they would never turn around. *Mrs. Borden stops on the stairs. She turns around to look at Lizzie who is behind her.* They would be too frightened to turn around even if they heard me. They would be so afraid they'd see what they feared. *Mrs. Borden makes a move which might be an effort to go past Lizzie back down the stairs. Lizzie stops her.* Careful. Don't fall. *Mrs. Borden turns and slowly continues up the stairs with Lizzie behind her.* And then, I would strike them down. With them not turning around, they would retain no image of me on their eye. It would be better that way.

Lizzie and Mrs. Borden disappear at the top of the stairs. The stage is empty for a moment. Bridget enters. She carries the pail for washing the windows. She sets the pail down, wipes her forehead. She stands for a moment looking towards the stairs as if she might have heard a sound. She picks up the pail and exits to the kitchen. Lizzie appears on the stairs. She is carrying the pile of clothes she carried upstairs. The hand hatchet is concealed between the clothes. Lizzie descends the stairs, she seems calm, self-possessed. She places the clothes on the table. She pauses, then she slowly turns to look at Mrs. Borden's chair at the table. After a moment she moves to it, pauses a moment, then sits down in it. She sits there at ease, relaxed, thinking. Bridget enters from the kitchen, she sees Lizzie. Bridget tidies. She picks up the pile of clothes. Its weight is unusual. She puts the pile down, lifts a portion of the pile. She sees the hatchet. She replaces clothes on top of hatchet. She takes in Lizzie sitting in Mrs. Borden's chair. Bridget glances towards the stairs, back to Lizzie. Lizzie looks, for the first time, at Bridget.

Lizzie:	We must hurry before Papa gets home.
Bridget:	Lizzie?
Lizzie:	I have it all figured out, but you have to help me, Bridget, you have to help me.
Bridget:	What have you done?
Lizzie:	He would never leave me the farm, not with her on his back, but now *(She gets up from the chair)* I will have the farm, and I will have the money, yes, to do what I please! And you too Bridget, I'll give you some

of my money but you've got to help me. *She moves towards Bridget who backs away a step.* Don't be afraid, it's me, it's Lizzie, you like me!

Bridget: What have you done! *Pause. Bridget moves towards the stairs.*

Lizzie: Don't go up there!

Bridget: You killed her!

Lizzie: Someone broke in and they killed her.

Bridget: They'll know!

Lizzie: Not if you help me.

Bridget: I can't, Miss Lizzie, I can't!

Lizzie: *Grabs Bridget's arm.* Do you want them to hang me! Is that what you want! Oh Bridget, look! Look! *She falls to her knees.* I'm begging for my life, I'm begging. Deny me, and they will kill me. Help me, Bridget, please help me.

Bridget: But . . . what . . . could we do?

Lizzie: *Up off her knees.* Oh I have it all figured out. I'll go downtown as quick as I can and you leave the doors open and go back outside and work on the windows.

Bridget: I've finished them, Lizzie.

Lizzie: Then do them again! Remember last year when the burglar broke in? Today someone broke in and she caught them.

Bridget: They'll never believe us.

Lizzie: Have coffee with Lucy next door, stay with her till Papa gets home and he'll find her, and then each of us swears she was fine when we left, she was alright when we left!—it's going to work, Bridget, I know it!

Bridget: Your papa will guess.

Lizzie: *Getting ready to leave for downtown.* If he found me here he might guess, but he won't.

Bridget: Your papa will know!

Lizzie:	Papa loves me, if he has another story to believe, he'll believe it. He'd want to believe it, he'd have to believe it.
Bridget:	Your papa will know.
Lizzie:	Why aren't you happy? I'm happy. We both should be happy! *Lizzie embraces Bridget. Lizzie steps back a pace.* Now—how do I look?

Mr. Borden enters. Bridget sees him. Lizzie slowly turns to see what Bridget is looking at.

Lizzie:	Papa?
Mr. Borden:	What is it? Where's Mrs. Borden?
Bridget:	I . . . don't know . . . sir . . . I . . . just came in, sir.
Mr. Borden:	Did she leave the house?
Bridget:	Well, sir . . .
Lizzie:	She went out. Someone delivered a message and she left. *Lizzie takes off her hat and looks at her father.*
Lizzie:	. . . You're home early, Papa.
Mr. Borden:	I wanted to see Abbie. She's gone out, has she? Which way did she go? *Lizzie shrugs, he continues, more thinking aloud.* Well . . . I . . . I . . . best wait for her here. I don't want to miss her again.
Lizzie:	Help Papa off with his coat, Bridget. . . . I hear there's a sale of dress goods on downtown. Why don't you go buy yourself a yard?
Bridget:	Oh . . . I don't know, ma'am.
Lizzie:	You don't want any?
Bridget:	I don't know.
Lizzie:	Then . . . why don't you go upstairs and lie down. Have a rest before lunch.
Bridget:	I don't think I should.
Lizzie:	Nonsense.
Bridget:	Lizzie, I—
Lizzie:	You go up and lie down. I'll look after things here.

Lizzie smiles at Bridget. Bridget starts up the stairs, suddenly stops. She looks back at Lizzie.

Lizzie: It's alright . . . go on . . . it's alright. *Bridget continues up the stairs. She stops on the stairs and watches as Miss Lizzie. For the last bit of interchange, Mr. Borden has lowered the paper he's reading. Lizzie looks at him.* Hello Papa. You look so tired. . . . I make you unhappy. . . . I don't like to make you unhappy. I love you.

Mr. Borden: *Smiles and takes her hand.* I'm just getting old, Lizzie.

Lizzie: You've got on my ring. . . . Do you remember when I gave you that? . . . When I left Miss Cornelia's—it was in a little blue velvet box, you hid it behind your back, and you said, "Guess which hand, Lizzie!" And I guessed. And you gave it to me and you said, "It's real gold, Lizzie, it's for you because you are very precious to me." Do you remember, Papa? *Mr. Borden nods.* And I took it out of the little blue velvet box, and I took your hand, and I put my ring on your finger and I said "Thank you, Papa, I love you." . . . You've never taken it off . . . see how it bites into the flesh of your finger. *She presses his hand to her face.* I forgive you, Papa, I forgive you for killing my birds. . . . You look so tired, why don't you lie down and rest, put your feet up, I'll undo your shoes for you. *She kneels and undoes his shoes.*

Mr. Borden: You're a good girl.

Lizzie: I could never stand to have you hate me, Papa. Never. I would do anything rather than have you hate me.

Mr. Borden: I don't hate you, Lizzie.

Lizzie: I would not want you to find out anything that would make you hate me. Because I love you.

Mr. Borden: And I love you, Lizzie, you'll always be precious to me.

Lizzie: *Looks at him, and then smiles.* Was I—when I had scabs on my knees?

Mr. Borden: *Laughs.* Oh yes. Even then.

Lizzie: *Laughs.* Oh Papa! . . . Kiss me! *He kisses her on the forehead.* Thank you, Papa.

Mr. Borden: Why're you crying?

Lizzie: Because I'm so happy. Now . . . put you feet up and
get to sleep . . . that's right . . . shut your eyes . . . go
to sleep . . . go to sleep.

*She starts to hum, continues humming as Mr. Borden falls asleep. Lizzie
still humming, moves to the table, slips her hand under the clothes, with-
draws the hatchet. She approaches her father with the hatchet behind her
back. She stops humming. A pause, then she slowly raises the hatchet very
high to strike him. Just as the hatchet is about to start its descent, there is
a blackout. Children's voices are heard singing:*

> "Lizzie Borden took an axe,
> Gave her mother forty whacks.
> When the job was nicely done,
> She gave her father forty-one!
> Forty-one!
> Forty-one!"

*The singing increases in volume and in distortion as it nears the end of the
verse till the last words are very loud but discernible, just. Silence. Then the
sound of slow measured heavy breathing which is growing into a wordless
sound of hysteria. Light returns to the stage, dim light from late in the day.
The Actress stands with the hatchet raised in the same position in which we
saw her before the blackout, but the couch is empty. Her eyes are shut. The
sound comes from her. Miss Lizzie is at the foot of the stairs. She moves to
The Actress, reaches up to take the hatchet from her. When Miss Lizzie's
hand touches The Actress's, The Actress releases the hatchet and whirls
around to face Miss Lizzie who is left holding the hatchet. The Actress backs
away from Miss Lizzie. There is a flickering of light at the top of the stairs.*

Emma: *From upstairs.* Lizzie! Lizzie! You're making too much
noise!

*Emma descends the stairs carrying an oil lamp. The Actress backs away
from Lizzie and moves into the shadows. Miss Lizzie turns to see Emma.
The hand hatchet is behind Miss Lizzie's back concealed from Emma.
Emma pauses for a moment.*

Emma: Where is she?

Miss Lizzie: Who?

Emma: *A pause then Emma moves to the window and glances
out.* It's raining.

Michele Vance Hehir as The Actress/Miss Lizzie and John Hutchison as Andrew Borden in the Walterdale Theatre Associates production of *Blood Relations*, Edmonton, Alberta, 1998.

Courtesy of the Walterdale Theatre Associates

Miss Lizzie:	I know.
Emma:	*Puts the lamp down, sits, lowers her voice.* Lizzie.
Miss Lizzie:	Yes?
Emma:	I want to speak to you, Lizzie.
Miss Lizzie:	Yes Emma.
Emma:	That . . . actress who's come up from Boston.
Miss Lizzie:	What about her?
Emma:	People talk.
Miss Lizzie:	You needn't listen.
Emma:	In your position you should do nothing to inspire talk.
Miss Lizzie:	People need so little in the way of inspiration. And Miss Cornelia's classes didn't cover "Etiquette for Acquitted Persons."
Emma:	Common sense should tell you what you ought or ought not do.
Miss Lizzie:	Common sense is repugnant to me. I prefer uncommon sense.
Emma:	I forbid her in this house, Lizzie!
Pause.	
Miss Lizzie:	Do you?
Emma:	*Backing down, softly.* It's . . . disgraceful.
Miss Lizzie:	I see.
Emma:	I simply cannot—
Miss Lizzie:	You could always leave.
Emma:	Leave?
Miss Lizzie:	Move. Away. Why don't you?
Emma:	I—
Miss Lizzie:	You could never, could you?
Emma:	If I only—

Miss Lizzie:	Knew.
Emma:	Lizzie, did you?
Miss Lizzie:	Oh Emma, do you intend asking me that question from now till death us do part?
Emma:	It's just—
Miss Lizzie:	For if you do, I may well take something sharp to you.
Emma:	Why do you joke like that!
Miss Lizzie:	*Emma sees the hatchet for the first time. Emma's reaction is not any verbal or untoward movement. She freezes as Miss Lizzie advances on her.* Did you never stop and think that if I did, then you were guilty too?
Emma:	What?
Miss Lizzie:	It was you who brought me up, like a mother to me. Almost like a mother. Did you ever stop and think that I was like a puppet, your puppet. My head your hand, yes, your hand working my mouth, me saying all the things you felt like saying, me doing all the things you felt like doing, me spewing forth, me hitting out, and you, you—!
The Actress:	*Quietly.* Lizzie.

Miss Lizzie is immediately in control of herself.

Emma:	*Whispers.* I wasn't even here that day.
Miss Lizzie:	I can swear to that.
Emma:	Do you want to drive me mad?
Miss Lizzie:	Oh yes.
Emma:	You didn't . . . did you?
Miss Lizzie:	Poor . . . Emma.
The Actress:	Lizzie. *She takes the hatchet from Miss Lizzie.* Lizzie, you did.
Miss Lizzie:	I didn't. You did. *The Actress looks to the hatchet then to the audience.*

BLACKOUT

One Tiger to a Hill

Shaun Austin-Olsen as Everett Chalmers, Joe-Norman Shaw as Tommy Paul, and Roger Honeywell as Gillie Dermott in the Stratford Festival production of *One Tiger to a Hill*, Stratford, Ontario, 1990.

Courtesy of the Stratford Festival Archives

Production History

One Tiger to a Hill was first performed at the Citadel Theatre, Edmonton, 20 February 1980.

CAST

Everett Chalmers	*Raymond Clarke*
Tommy Paul	*Michael Ball*
Carl Hanzuk	*Jean-Pierre Fournier*
Richard Wallace	*Brendan Barry*
George McGowan	*Paul Craig*
Frank Soholuk	*William Forrest MacDonald*
Dede Walker	*Michelle Fisk*
Gillie Dermott	*Raymond Skipp*
Cecil Stocker	*William Fisher*
Lena Benz	*Doris Chillcott*
Director	*Richard Ouzounian*
Set Designer	*Lawrence Schafer*
Costume Designer	*Garry Dahms*
Lighting Designer	*Bill Williams*
Stage Manager	*Sherrel Clelland*

ACKNOWLEDGEMENT

With thanks to Richard Ouzounian for the Festival Lennoxville production under his direction.

Everett Chalmers: a corporation lawyer, early thirties.
Lena Benz: a social activist, old leftist, about sixty.
Richard Wallace: warden of the prison, late fifties.
George McGowen: Head of Security, late fifties.
Carl Hanzuk: a guard, mid-thirties.
Gillie MacDermott: a prisoner, in his twenties.
Tommy Paul: a Métis prisoner, late twenties.
Dede (Deed) Walker: a rehabilitation officer, late twenties.
Frank Soholuk: a rehabilitation officer, late twenties.
Cecil Stocker: a schoolteacher, pronounced English accent, early forties.

SETTING

The events of the play cover forty-eight hours, and take place within a maximum security prison built in the 19th century.

The set conveys the impression of bars, and of confinement. There are at least two levels. On an upper level is the warden's office. A corridor, referred to as the tier corridor, runs from a SR exit from the warden's office to the extreme SR of the playing area. It makes a right-angle turn, and runs directly DS ending at the extreme DSR of the playing area. An exit offstage is located at the extreme USR right-angle turn. Near the DSR end of the tier corridor is a flight of stairs which descends to what is referred to as the landing area. There is a built-in cupboard in this area which contains two speakers, and which is large enough to contain the cleaning caddy which, at the opening, sits in the landing area. The cleaning caddy is on wheels and on it is cleaning apparatus which includes two large bottles of Javex. A pail of water sits on the caddy. There is a squeezing device mounted on the pail. A commercial cleaning-sized mop is in the pail.

A corridor runs from the landing area SR to the extreme DSL of the playing area. Here it makes a right-angle turn to run directly US to a dead end. Just around this corner is the entrance to Walker's office referred to as the outer office. One must cross through Walker's office to enter Soholuk's office which is situated SR of Walker's office and is referred to as the inner office. These are make-shift offices used as a result of overcrowding in the prison. There is a rug covering the floor of the warden's office, but other areas are defined by tile, the corridor and landing differing from the outer and inner office. Any walls or doorways in the outer and inner offices are skeletal.

The flow from scene to scene is most important. There is always some light on, for example, the warden's office, when a scene is being played in the outer or inner office. The lighting transition from scene to scene is not that of a cross fade, for before light in the active scene is fading, light for the next scene is building, anticipating the scene. There is often activity in both scenes as they begin or end, with one beginning to seize focus, the other to release it. During the body of a scene, characters not in the prime scene will assume a soft freeze. The electronic and theme music referred to in the script are excerpts chosen from The BC Pen Symphony, composed by J. Douglas Dodd.

ACT ONE

Blackout. A definite light on the prison, but one that enhances shadows, starkness, harshness. There is a faint electronic hum which contains within it the clanking of closing doors, footsteps, and rattling keys. It builds in volume. As it does so, the following characters enter on the tier corridor. They do not rush. Their progress to their positions is slow and measured.

Tommy Paul and Hanzuk walk along the tier corridor, and descend the stairs to the landing. Wallace enters his office, he looks down at a report on his desk. Dede Walker enters and stands as if caught in mid-stride at DSR *end of the tier corridor. McGowen too assumes a position near Wallace's office in the tier corridor. As Hanzuk watches him, Paul grasps mop handle with one hand, squeeze device with other hand. Electronic sound ceases as soon as he does this. All characters assume a soft freeze.*

The picture seen: Tommy Paul in the landing area, one hand on mop, one on squeezer; Hanzuk a short distance from Paul and watching him; Wallace in his office gazing down at the report; McGowen in the tier corridor on his way to Wallace's office; Walker a distance from McGowen but apparently following him. The characters hold the soft freeze.

Theme music.

Chalmers enters the tier corridor. He will not acknowledge the presence of the characters, and their position is such that it is never necessary for him to brush past them. There is always space between him and them as he walks to the top of the stairs. He stops at the top of the stairs. There is a slight increase of light on him. The theme ends with a drawn out electronic sound that echoes, reverberates, fades away. A pause. Chalmers speaks to the audience.

Chalmers: My name is Ev Chalmers, Everett Chalmers. *He descends the stairs, stops at the bottom.* Everett. . . . No one calls their kids that any more. It's all Robyn and Jason today. My kids—Robyn and Jason—and Anne with an e, that's my wife. *He will walk along the lower level corridor speaking to the audience.* I'm a lawyer, corporate law, my own firm. Well, our firm. I've a partner, Joe Wetmore, good guy, lot of fun. Bit of a kook. In my experience all criminal lawyers are kooks, and Joe's into criminal law real heavy. It's like in medicine, they say all psychiatrists are nuts, you know what I mean? . . . Anyway, that's Joe. . . . I live on a street that borders a park. . . .

On the other side of the park there's a street and a hill. At the foot of the hill, there's the pen.

Tommy Paul pushes the handle squeezing the water from the mop, he lifts the mop from the pail onto the floor. Hanzuk takes a few steps away from him, then turns to watch him.

Wallace sits at the desk, picks up the report to study it.

Chalmers does not acknowkdge their movement. He is silent with his own thoughts.

All freeze as he speaks.

Chalmers: For nine years, twice a day, almost every day, I drove past the pen. Grey stone walls, turrets at the corners, bleak, oppressive, looked like a medieval fortress. Whenever I noticed the place, it always seemed to be raining. Sometimes I wondered what it was like being inside, locked up. I suppose there was always this question at the back of my mind and the question went like this—what if? What if the things you hear, the things you don't want to hear, the things they won't let you hear, what if those things really happen inside? Would I be any different in essence from all those good Germans who passed Dachau and Buchenwald, and never asked questions? In those nine years there were riots inside, prisoners died inside, there were charges, counter charges, all those news items you and I read. . . . I did nothing, but when the weather was bad, the traffic slow, I occasionally wondered. . . . And then, by accident, because Joe was away, couldn't be reached, I got involved, and two people died to confirm a resolve, a resolve that was slowly, reluctantly, growing in me—a resolve to find out what happens to them—and to us—when we condemn men to that wastebasket we call the pen. This place is the pen. These are the people. It happened like this.

Paul begins washing the floor, Hanzuk shifts his stance watching him, Wallace puts down the report and begins to work at his desk. This happens simultaneously as Chalmers steps out of the playing area of the stage and exits.

Hanzuk: *With no particular malice, more passing time.* Hey.

Paul looks at Hanzuk.

Hanzuk: *Indicating the floor already washed.* Again . . . Again.

Paul resumes washing the floor, redoing the area already washed.

McGowen starts walking towards the warden's office.

Walker: Mr. McGowen!

McGowen continues. Walker runs after him.

Walker: I wanna talk to you, George!

McGowen: Later.

Walker: Now! *She follows McGowen.*

McGowen enters Wallace's office with Walker after him.

Wallace: Good morning, George.

McGowen: Yeah.

Walker: I just heard about Desjardins.

McGowen: You want coffee?

Walker: Shove the coffee, George. I wanna know if you're gonna take some action against the guard.

McGowen: There's no negligence involved, read the report.

Walker: Desjardin's dead and I wanna know what you're gonna do about it.

McGowen: *Stirs his coffee.* You ah . . . want my recommendation as Head of Security?

Walker: That's right, George.

McGowen: Bury him. Forget him.

Walker looks from McGowen to Wallace. He says nothing, but returns her stare.

Walker: Jeezuz. *She whirls out the door and along the tier corridor. Wallace looks at McGowen, smiles, shakes his head.*

Wallace: Christ, George, if it weren't for the union I'd fire you.

McGowen: If I weren't so old, I'd quit.

Walker descends the stairs and sees Paul washing the floor.

Walker: What's he doing, he's got a meeting at ten.

Hanzuk: Your watch say ten?

Walker gives him a vicious finger, and sails past Paul along the corridor to her office.

Walker: I'll see you at ten.

Paul looks after her.

Hanzuk: Hey. . . . Again.

Paul redoes the area already washed. Walker enters her office and sits at her desk.

Walker: Shit. *She begins work.*

Wallace: Come on, George, be reasonable. We got a death in solitary, and we got a citizens' committee coming in on Thursday. Lena Benz is on it, and if there's a leak somewhere and—

McGowen: You mean Walker.

Wallace: Whoever. If there's a leak and Benz gets hold of this, then—

McGowen: So keep her out.

Wallace: And how do I do that.

McGowen: You've done it before. Get a court order, an injunction.

Wallace: What reason this time?

McGowen: Provoking, inciting, defacing government property. Hell, run your finger down a list, you'll come up with something.

Wallace: Alright. Suppose we can take care of Benz, there's still Tommy Paul. He was close to Desjardins and the next thing we know he's gonna be hollering for his lawyer, and once Joe Wetmore's in here, he'll give Wetmore an earful.

McGowen: Yeah, well, Paul won't be talkin' to anyone if he's top tier.

Wallace: But he's not top tier. Is he?

McGowen: He will be.

Wallace: What do you mean, are there internal charges pending against Tommy Paul?

McGowen: No charges, not at the moment.

Wallace: God damn it, George, we can't use punitive isolation to gag Paul.

McGowen: Who's doin' that?

Wallace: When I asked you to handle sentencing for isolation it was because I knew you wouldn't abuse it.

McGowen: In the last four years Tommy Paul's spent eight hundred and four days in solitary. As of now he's general population eighty-two days. Now he's never gone more than a month before without charges of some sort, and I don't have to run a kangaroo court to say—he's overdue.

Wallace: We can defuse the whole thing by taking some disciplinary action against the guard.

McGowen: The guard does a good job.

Wallace: That's not the point.

McGowen: I back the guard, the union backs the guard, that's the point.

Wallace: If Benz finds out, do you think she'll back the guard?

McGowen: So you tell the committee she's *persona non grata*. If you have to, you get a court order.

Wallace: I don't want to do that!

McGowen: Look, we're not runnin' Open House with Multiple Listing, we're runnin' a maximum security pen.

Wallace: With a parliamentary paper on penal reform coming out.

McGowen: Your coffee stinks.

Wallace: You should know, you're drinking it.

McGowen: And I'm sayin' it stinks.

Wallace: Alright. The coffee stinks.

Wallace looks through the papers on his desk. McGowen drinks his coffee. Tommy Paul pushes the cleaning caddy down the corridor, and around SL corner, Hanzuk follows him. Paul begins washing the corridor floor near the entrance to Walker's office.

Wallace: You read this rehab report on Paul?

McGowen: I read all the crap that passes my desk.

Wallace: So what do you think?

McGowen: Ms. Walker doesn't know what she's talkin' about.

Wallace: Come on, George, tell me how you account for her positive assessment.

McGowen: You really want to know?

Wallace: Yeah.

McGowen: He screws her.

Wallace: George, it's only Monday, would you gimme a break?

McGowen: Rehab's a pain in the ass.

Wallace: Security shouldn't say things like that.

McGowen: Especially on Thursday, eh?

Wallace: Especially this Thursday. Soholuk's report on the community orientation program's here.

McGowen: He's fronting for Walker.

Wallace: Maybe, but he makes a few points, new points.

McGowen: You know how I feel.

Wallace: Put it on paper.

McGowen: It's already on paper.

Wallace: Well, it's on the agenda for—

McGowen: Alright. *He takes the report.* But ah—Soholuk's not walkin' a tier.

McGowen exits from Wallace's office, down the tier corridor and offstage.

Wallace sits at his desk with his paper work.

Hanzuk: You know somethin', Paul? You're doin' a shitty job there, real shitty. I mean, we can't have Ms. Walker walkin' down dirty hallways, now can we? This time why don't you do it for her?

Paul pushes the caddy along the corridor back towards the landing area. He is almost there when Hanzuk speaks, and Paul stops.

Hanzuk: I . . . ah . . . hear there's a vacancy top tier. I hear they got a hold on it. It's like . . . reserved for someone.

Tommy Paul looks directly at Hanzuk.

Hanzuk: You got any thoughts on that? . . . No?

Soholuk enters the tier corridor, descends the stairs. Paul pushes the caddy into the landing area and begins washing the floor. Soholuk is on his way to his office.

Soholuk: Hanzuk. *He passes Hanzuk in the corridor, then stops.* Oh. Almost forgot. *Turns back to Hanzuk, he searches through his pockets.* Got a visitor to the area here. . . . Not workin' up top? You miss the view?

Hanzuk: Very funny.

Soholuk: You're not laughin'. Hey, you got all this stress, Hanzuk, you gotta relax. *He gives Hanzuk a coloured slip.* You don't, you'll get arteriosclerosis, no kiddin'.

Hanzuk: You wanna know somethin', Soholuk?

Soholuk: Rehab's a pain in the ass, right? . . . I'm a pain in the ass!

Hanzuk: *Smiles.* Right.

Soholuk: See how much better you feel? Blood pumpin' to the brain! They move Walker yet?

Hanzuk: Where to? There ain't no room.

Soholuk: Well, shit, man, we ain't got no room in there either.

Soholuk continues down the corridor into the outer (Walker's) office. Hanzuk moves to the landing area where Paul is washing the floor. Walker is bent over the filing cabinet, her back to Soholuk. He sneaks up behind her, grabs her, nuzzles her neck. Without turning around, she hits him on the head with a file folder.

Walker:	You're a pig, Frank.
Soholuk:	A lovable pig?
Walker:	A plain pig.
Soholuk:	You didn't always say that. You mean what I thought was love was just—
Walker:	Too much Donini.
Soholuk:	Well, that covers the first time.
Walker:	You're a pig.
Soholuk:	Aah, I dunno what I see in you, Dede—unless it's your tits.
Walker:	What tits.
Soholuk:	I'm into small tits.
Walker:	God, you're disgusting.
Soholuk:	Latent homosexual, what do you think?
Walker:	Blatant heterosexual–that's what I think.
Soholuk:	You betcha. *He moves into the inner office, his office, preparing to start work.*
Walker:	Did you hear about Desjardins?
Soholuk:	Yeah.
Walker:	Well?
Soholuk:	Well what?
Walker:	Well what're we gonna do about it?
Soholuk:	We're gonna wait. We're gonna take it as it comes.
Walker:	Uh-uh.
Soholuk:	Hell, I know it's hard, but we gotta kiss ass, we gotta fill out forms, and beat 'em at their own game.
Walker:	I can't operate like that.
Soholuk:	You don't try.
Walker:	I do try! Jesus, I don't believe this. Desjardins' dead.

Desjardins' dead, and you're tellin' me how to "work the system." What the hell's wrong with you?

Soholuk: Drop it.

Walker: Fuck it. Now get out of here, I got work to do.

She returns to work. Soholuk watches her for a moment, from the inner office doorway.

Soholuk: Deed? . . . Deed, I wanna talk to you.

Walker: You can't tell me anything I don't know.

Soholuk: Sometimes when someone else says it, it makes more sense, eh?

Walker: Save the counselling trip for the inmates, OK?

Soholuk: OK. *He gets a chair; sits, watches her work for a bit. She looks up at him. A pause.*

Walker: What're you doin' here anyway, I thought you weren't in today.

Soholuk: Yeah, well I got an appointment, a teacher.

Walker: For inside?

Soholuk: Nah, nothin' like that. He wants me to talk to his class.

Walker: Oh.

Soholuk: "Rehabilitation and the Penal System"—How does that sound for a topic?

Walker: Be a very short talk.

Soholuk: Bit-ter.

Walker: You got it.

Soholuk: Know somethin'? I bet you were the kinda kid that was always luggin' home birds with a broken wing.

Walker: What've you been doin', talkin' to my mother?

Soholuk: Bet you put 'em in a box by the bed and in the mornin', you discovered your cat ate 'em, nothin' left but feathers on the floor.

Walker: Alright, Frank. What're you gettin' at.

Soholuk:	You got this job, Deed, and there's certain things you gotta accept.
Walker:	Like what.
Soholuk:	Like in a maximum pen, rehab can only do so much.
Walker:	Like nothin'.
Soholuk:	Would you listen?
Walker:	I heard it before.
Soholuk:	Look, you gotta—
Walker:	I don't *gotta do anything!*
Soholuk:	One thing! One thing, Deed. You gotta accept the fact that if you keep on, for anyone on your caseload you're a liability, not an asset.
Walker:	Would you get the hell out of my office!
Soholuk:	You think you're helpin' Tommy Paul?
Walker:	Yes!
Soholuk:	Get real.
Walker:	He's outa solitary two and a half months!
Soholuk:	Yeah! And when he goes back, they're throwin' away the key.
Walker:	Who says back!
Soholuk:	I do.
Walker:	Why?
Soholuk:	'Cause they're out to get him.
Walker:	Why!
Soholuk:	'Cause they don't like him comin' in for a session, and gettin' laid!

Walker slaps his face. Soholuk grabs her hand. Pause.

Soholuk:	We've been friends a long time, Deed. That's why I feel I can tell you this. What you're doin' is stupid. Get outa here.

Walker:	You don't know what I'm doin'.
Soholuk:	Get a transfer.
Walker:	I don't want to.
Soholuk:	Check the board.
Walker:	No.
Soholuk:	Come on, listen to your good friend Frankie Soholuk. He knows what he's talkin' about. You're bangin' your head on a steel door here. Go where you can do some real good, and I don't mean fuckin' an inmate. Get a transfer to minimum.
Walker:	I hear you.
Soholuk:	You're a sweetie, did I ever tell you that?
Walker:	Yeah, Frank, many times.
Soholuk:	I mean it . . . soooo . . . *He gets up to return to his office, stops, looks back at Walker. She is unaware of his scrutiny.* . . . Hey . . . ah . . . I got a copy of that commu-nity orientation paper. You got a minute we could go over it.
Walker:	Yeah.

Soholuk enters his office. After a moment Walker follows him. Paul pushes the caddy to the stage left end of the corridor and washes the floor.

Walker:	Frank.
Soholuk:	Mmn.
Walker:	If I told you, no matter what people think, it's not what they think, between Tommy and me, would you believe me?
Soholuk:	I dunno, hum a few bars.
Walker:	Come on, Frank.
Soholuk:	Me? Sure, I'd believe you. Some reason I shouldn't?
Walker:	No.
Soholuk:	There you go. Now. *Passes her the orientation report.* I want you to read the recommendations, and the resolu-

tion at the end.

Walker reads the report. Hanzuk, his back to the stairs, does not see Gillie who enters the tier corridor, and stops at the top of the stairs looking down at Paul and Hanzuk.

Hanzuk: Hey, Paul, you know that room top tier they got reserved? Last tenant's under the apple tree. Rumour has it next tenant's leavin' the same way. You got any thoughts on that? No?

Paul's glance shifts from Hanzuk to Gillie. Hanzuk, suddenly aware of this, quickly turns to see Gillie. Gillie descends the stairs.

Gillie: There's a coupla speakers I'm supposed to take into the office there.

Hanzuk: Yeah.

Gillie: *Is fumbling for a slip he will pass to Hanzuk.* It's for a meetin'.

Hanzuk: Yeah.

Gillie: They're in the cupboard. You want me to bring 'em up? It's on the slip I should bring 'em up.

Hanzuk: Yeah.

Gillie moves to the landing area where the cupboard is located. Hanzuk moves down the corridor to Paul.

Hanzuk: It's ten o'clock, Paul.

Hanzuk remains in the corridor and watches Paul push the caddy down the corridor. When Paul moves into the landing area he cannot be seen by Hanzuk. Before stepping out of sight, he stares back at Hanzuk for a moment, his face is neutral.

Stocker enters the tier corridor. He is a bit confused about directions. He sees Hanzuk in the lower corridor and descends the stairs, down the corridor to speak to him. He neither sees, nor is seen by, Paul and Gillie.

While Stocker is speaking to Hanzuk, Gillie and Paul are busy in the landing area. Gillie removes the two speakers from the cupboard. Paul quickly shoves the cleaning caddy into the cupboard, first removing the two bottles of Javex from it. Gillie and Paul crouch around the corner of the landing; they remove knives from their pant legs. Using the knives they remove the backs of the speakers, place the Javex inside the speakers, replace the backs of the speakers, return their knives to their pant legs.

Stocker: I, ah, I've been directed to this area for a Mr. Frank Soholuk? *Hanzuk holds out his hand.* Ah. Yes. Quite. Here it is. *He passes Hanzuk a slip of paper.* All in order I think. Ten I believe. Ten o'clock.

Hanzuk: First door on the left, second office.

Stocker: Right.

He moves down the corridor past Hanzuk who waits till he's past him before barking:

Hanzuk: Hey! *Stocker stops, turns back to Hanzuk who smiles holding out the slip.* You'll need this to get out.

Stocker: Ah. Right. Thank you. Good. *He takes the slip.* First door, second office.

Hanzuk waits a moment, then follows Stocker down the corridor. He listens outside Walker's office. Soholuk and Walker are in the inner office. Stocker stops in the outer office.

Stocker: Mr. Soholuk?

Soholuk: Yeah?

Soholuk and Walker join Stocker.

Stocker: Stocker. Cecil Stocker.

Soholuk: Pleasure. . . . My fellow worker, Deed Walker.

Stocker: Miss Walker.

Soholuk: We're just finishing up here—if you wouldn't mind waiting inside?

Stocker: No hurry, no hurry at all. I'll just . . . wait inside.

He enters the inner office. Hanzuk moves away from the door, back down the corridor to the landing area where he stops Gillie and Paul who are about to start down the corridor, each carrying a speaker.

After a brief scrutiny he nods Gillie on. Gillie waits down the corridor for Paul. Paul is expressionless as he waits for Hanzuk to give him the nod. Eventually Hanzuk does. As Paul moves to join Gillie he winks at Gillie. Hanzuk relaxes for a smoke. During this Soholuk and Walker continue their dialogue in the outer office. Walker smiles as she watches Stocker enter the inner office.

Soholuk: Shaddup.

Walker: Did I say something?

Soholuk: You were thinkin' something. OK now. *He refers to the community orientation report he has carried from the inner office.* This paper, it's on the agenda for the next team meeting, Thursday I think. Wallace has already got a copy.

Walker: So I pretend it's a great new proposal.

Soholuk: That's right, but I don't want you to second my motion.

Walker: Sure. I won't second your motion, if you *will* second mine.

Soholuk: What do you mean?

Walker: I want Desjardins' death in the minutes.

Gillie and Paul are at the office door.

Soholuk: You never listen, do you!

Gillie: We're here with them speakers.

Walker: Great, stick 'em in the corner.

As Soholuk draws Walker away a bit for a private chat, Paul and Gillie draw their knives, and remove the Javex from the speakers, their backs to Soholuk and Walker. Hanzuk is having his smoke at the foot of the stairs, Stocker is in the inner office unknown to Gillie and Paul.

Soholuk: We are not bringin' up you-know-what-about-you-know-who at the meeting. It's not the time, it's not the place.

Walker: That's bullshit.

Soholuk: You'll endanger programs and not gain a thing.

Walker: We've got to do something!

Soholuk: They'll stonewall it, believe me.

Walker: So what can we do?

Soholuk: I dunno. Write a . . . what's that smell?

Walker: Eh?

Soholuk: Is that gas? . . . Is that gasoline?

He and Walker turn towards the corner. The open Javex bottles are full of gasoline. As Walker and Soholuk move towards them, Gillie and Paul launch themselves with knives drawn. Paul is going for Walker. Gillie for Soholuk.

Paul: *A scream.* Gooooooo!

Soholuk: Hanzuk! Hanzuk!

Gillie swipes at Soholuk with the knife. Soholuk leaps back. Gillie starts out into the corridor, Soholuk makes a grab for him. Gillie gives him a hard elbow in the gut. Soholuk falls.

Hanzuk runs down the corridor in reaction to Soholuk's yell. He is met by Gillie with the knife who makes several swipes at him. Walker is taken by Paul fairly easily.

Walker: No, Tommy, no, it's me, it's me, Tommy!

Gillie: *To Hanzuk in the corridor.* Come on, I'm gonna getcha, getcha good!

Paul is yelling for Gillie to get back into the office.

Paul: Gillie! Gillie!

Hanzuk runs back to the landing where he punches an alarm, and grabs the phone.

Soholuk has run into the corridor just as Gillie turns from Hanzuk.

Gillie: Come on!

Soholuk: I'm on your side, man!

Wallace picks up the phone. McGowen rushes into his office.

Gillie: Kill you, you fucker, gonna kill you!

Walker: Don't!

Paul: It's OK.

Soholuk: It's me, Soholuk, you don't wanna kill me!

Gillie: Getcha good!

Gillie ends up driving Soholuk back into the office. Soholuk is on the floor with Gillie on top of him, the knife under Soholuk's chin. The alarm stops.

Hanzuk will put down the phone but remain at his post at the top of the stairs or in the landing area till near the end of Act One.

Paul: Gillie.

Gillie: *Whose focus is on the knife and Soholuk's chin.* Yeah.

Paul: Give a holler to Hanzuk.

Gillie: Yeah.

Paul: Hanzuk.

Gillie: Yeah. Hanzuk! Hanzuk!

Hanzuk puts down the phone. Turns to listen.

Gillie: There's someone wants to talk to you, Hanzuk! You out there, Hanzuk?

Paul pulls Walker into the corridor. Hanzuk stage right, Paul and Walker stage left end of the corridor.

Paul: Hanzuk!

Hanzuk: What do you want.

Paul: Somethin' wrong with your hearin'?

Hanzuk: No.

Paul: What?

Hanzuk: No.

Paul: I said what?

Hanzuk: There's nothin' wrong with my hearin'!

Paul: Good.

Hanzuk: So what do you want.

Paul: It's like this, Hanzuk. I got my knife under Walker's ear here, and Gillie's keepin' very close to Soholuk, and Soholuk's not lookin' too good.

Hanzuk: You OK, Soholuk!

Soholuk:	*Gillie indicates for him to answer.* Yeah, Carl, I'm OK.
Paul:	The thing is, the situation could change. We got one hundred and eight ounces of gasoline and we got weapons—You got any thoughts on that? . . . No? . . . We're thinkin' of soakin' the inner office, I'm thinkin' of stickin' Soholuk in there, and lettin' Gillie play with his lighter. . . . You got any thoughts on that?
Hanzuk:	Keep goin'.
Paul:	I want Joe Wetmore down here, and I want him here fast. You got that?
Hanzuk:	I got it.
Paul:	Then move it!!

He drags Walker back into the office. Gillie indicates for Soholuk to get up and sit in one of the chairs. Gillie and Paul can use the speakers to sit on. They smile and prepare to wait it out. Paul gets paper and pencil and writes. Hanzuk speaks on the phone briefly, then prepares to remain at his post near the top of the stairs or near the foot of the landing.

Wallace puts the phone down.

McGowen:	So what're we gonna tell Paul?
Wallace:	The truth, he'll have to believe it. Wetmore's off fishing, some goddamn bush camp according to his secretary, so that's it, end of story, kaput. We'll have to find someone else.
McGowen:	I don't want the Mounties inside.
Wallace:	They won't be.
McGowen:	It's an institutional problem, and the institution will handle it.
Wallace:	We're together on that.
McGowen:	No interference, provincial or federal.
Wallace:	George, I spoke to the Minister—he agrees—it's our problem.
McGowen:	I know those Ottawa bastards, they sign the chit, and we shovel the shit.

Wallace: First thing we need is an alternative to Wetmore, one Paul will accept.

McGowen: We should have kept him top tier, solitary.

Wallace: Forget that.

McGowen: Now he's got three people in there, and one of them's Walker.

Wallace: We need a med—

McGowen: That doesn't strike you as funny? It sure as hell strikes me as funny.

Wallace: For god's sake, George! . . . Look, we don't know what Walker's involvement is, but we do know that when the chips are down, Tommy Paul will cut her throat just as quick as he'd cut yours or mine. Right now what we need is someone from outside to replace Wetmore, someone he'll go for.

McGowen: I say we keep it internal.

Wallace: I'm thinking of Wetmore's partner, Ev Chalmers.

McGowen: No.

Wallace: I know Ev, he's solid.

McGowen: No!

Wallace: We tell Paul we tried to get Wetmore, and we can't, but we're continuing to act in good faith, eh? Then we put forward Chalmers. If Paul takes him at least we know we're dealing with someone we trust.

McGowen: I don't know that. What the hell's Chalmers to me? I don't golf, I don't curl. You say he's solid, so what?

Wallace: If we don't take the initiative here, we could end up with anyone.

McGowen: You do what you like with the goddamn mediator. What I want is a list of the guards that are classified marksmen.

Wallace: We've got two of our people in there, plus this fellow Stocker. I want to see them walk out in one piece. That's the priority.

Gillie: *Shaking paper from the three hole punch, softly.* Oooooooo-eeeeeee.

Wallace: Do we understand that?

McGowen: You want to come out clean. I want to come out clean. I know the priority.

He exits from the office, and offstage along the tier corridor. Wallace sits at his desk.

Stocker is motionless hiding in the inner office. Gillie shakes more bits of paper out of the three hole punch. Paul sits close to Walker. Soholuk is sitting, holding his arm against his chest, as if in a sling.

Gillie: Who . . . whoo . . . whooooeeeee . . . hey look, Tommy, it's snowin' . . . big flakes, eh, big flakes is comin' downnnn . . . *The punch is empty, Gillie shakes it.* Shhit. *Discards the punch, sees the wastebasket and empties it on the floor.* Hey make a good fire, eh? We can toast weinies, eh? Weinies and mushmellows!

Paul: What the hell's a mushmellow?

Gillie: A mushmellow.

Paul: Marshmellow.

Gillie: Yeah, you toast 'em en they get all black on the outside en catch fire you know en you hoo hoo hoo blow 'em out en they're all black on the outside en inside they're all runny. You ever been to one of them camps you toast weinies and mushmellows?

Paul: You?

Gillie: Nah, fuckin' camps all work camps, but I toasted mushmellows before. *He throws a file folder up in the air. It falls with a thud to the floor.* Wish paper was heavier.

Paul: Lighter.

Gillie: Yeah, wish it would go like them little glass jars, you know, you shake 'em up . . . only upside down, that's what you gotta do first, upside down, turn 'em over, hold 'em, and all this here snow comes down on a little house or somethin'. . . . I had one once, got it from Woolwords. Snuck the old hand under the glass, shit I was only little, I was only 'bout five, but smooth, man. I got my little hand under that big glass counter, lifted that little jar thing, smooooth, man, right in the jacket. This old dyke on the door . . . I just coasted through, man, easy—she'd of come on to me, I'd a . . . *He leaps about in exaggerated karate poses. It's all fun, a joke. Paul is amused by him.* Eyyuh! Uu! Eyyhh! Owohhh! And Yuh! Last little kid she'll piss on, eh?

Paul: You bet. Eh Deed?

McGowen and Chalmers enter the tier corridor, and move to the top of the stairs.

Gillie: *Sees a first aid kit. He's talking to himself.* Here's one of them kits.

Paul: What's the matter?

Walker: You should have told me, Tommy.

Paul: I wanted to.

Walker: But you didn't.

Gillie: *Examining the kit, he will put streaks of iodine on his face, still talking to himself.* Get on the war paint, scare the shit outa Hanzuk.

Paul: I tried, but I didn't have the words, are you mad at me?

Walker: I just wish you'd have told me.

Paul: Are you scared? I'm scared, scared shitless, but being scared can help, can give you a high, an edge, make you think, keep on thinkin'.

Walker: But you were doin' so well. You had a chance.

Paul: Inside I got no chance.

Walker: You can change.

Paul: That's what I'm doin'.

Walker: I don't mean like this.

Paul: So what do you want? Mandatory parole? Hell, that's

	only 'bout fifty years, why not, eh?
Walker:	What'll this get you?
Paul:	You.
Gillie:	*Leaps about making war whoops.* Hah hahahahahaha! Ah Hahahahahahah! *When he gets close to Soholuk he whirls on him without any malice, but the knife is right at Soholuk's throat.* Don't piss on little kids, man!

McGowen signals to Hanzuk.

Hanzuk:	Paul! Paul! Someone comin' in, Paul!

A look of triumph between Paul and Gillie, each pulls his hostage closer. Chalmers steps into the office. Paul is expecting Wetmore.

Paul:	Back off! Get the hell out!
Chalmers:	Wallace—
Paul:	Joe! Joe!!
Chalmers:	He's not out there.
Paul:	Jooeeeee!
Chalmers:	He's up north, he's fishin'.

Paul shoves Walker aside and shoves his knife at Chalmers's throat.

Paul:	Liar.
Chalmers:	You know how he takes off. They tried to reach him, and they can't.

Paul feels for and finds Chalmers's wallet as well as giving him a quick frisk.

Paul:	You get him.
Walker:	Tommy—
Paul:	Shaddup.
Chalmers:	I work with him, my name's Chalmers, Ev Chalmers.
Paul:	*Stepping away to check the wallet.* You're stupid.
Chalmers:	Yeah . . . well . . . Joe says . . . I'm stupid, but honest.

Paul is slightly amused by this, the slightest ease of tension.

Paul: And you work with Joe.

Chalmers: Yeah.

Paul: So what does Joe say about me?

Hanzuk and McGowen in the landing area light cigarettes as they wait for Chalmers.

Chalmers: He says . . . you may be nuts—but you're not unreasonable.

Paul smiles at this.

Soholuk: Hey Tommy—a compromise—he's honest and you're reasonable?

Paul: *Tosses the wallet back to Chalmers.* Shaddup.

Gillie: Hey you—you see . . . this is the gas . . . and this is the lighter, just have to kick it over and . . . whooosh!

Chalmers: Ah-huh.

Gillie: And this is the war paint. *Indicating his face.*

Chalmers: Ah-huh.

Gillie: Fuckin' A.

Soholuk: As you can see, I'm not in the barbecue. . . . *Indicating the inner office, his signal that Stocker is undiscovered.*

Gillie: Shaddup.

Soholuk: Just makin' convers—

Gillie: *Pulls his head back, knife at the throat.* Shaddup!

Paul: *A hand on Gillie's shoulder which restrains him.* OK! It's OK. . . . Now you listen, here's what I want, we want, Gillie and me, when I talk I'm talkin' for both of us, see? First off, I want someone else besides you, I want—

Walker: *Quietly, to Paul.* What about Lena Benz, she'd be good.

Chalmers is aware of Walker's interjection.

Paul: Yeah, Lena Benz, get her in on this thing.

Chalmers: I can't promise. I can just negotiate.

Paul:	Just tell them, OK! Lena Benz! The rest is like in two parts—for Gillie and me, we want a flight out, Cuba, Russia, someone will take us, and we want fifty thousand bucks. You tell them that's what it costs to keep Gillie and me inside for a year, just a year. So they're gettin' a bargain.
Chalmers:	OK.
Walker:	Second part?
Paul:	Part Two. *A look to Walker, back to Chalmers.* I got a list. Shower time, recreation, job trainin', all the things they say they're doin' and they don't! And I want solitary top tier to go by the court rulin' we got last year. It was Wetmore's case and you remember he won it. Cruel and Unusual punishment! That's what the judge said, and nothin's changed! Fuck-all! You hear me?
Chalmers:	Yeah.
Paul:	Last—very important—not "negotiable"—we want an inquiry into what happened to Guy Desjardins in solitary. That's it.
Chalmers:	Well . . . I'll be back. *He exits down the corridor.*
Paul:	With Lena Benz! Bring Lena Benz!

Chalmers meets McGowen on the landing. He and McGowen make their way up the stairs, along the tier corridor to Wallace's office. Wallace shakes his head, takes the list, sits at his desk, indicating a chair for Chalmers. They remain thus.

The scene in the outer office is meanwhile continuing.

Paul:	*Turning from Chalmers' exit to Gillie.* What'd I tell you?
Gillie:	Yeah.
Walker:	You're bringin' some good focus, Tommy, on the right things.
Paul:	I got it all figured out. You'll see.
Soholuk:	Tommy?
Paul:	What do you want?

Soholuk:	My arm, man, do you think I could get an elastic bandage from the kit?
Paul:	. . . Yeah, sure, go ahead. *Indicates for Gillie to toss Soholuk a bandage. He does so.*
Soholuk:	Could ah . . . could Deed gimme a hand here. It's gonna be bloody awkward.

Walker moves to help him, then stops, looks to Paul for permission.

Paul:	Yeah . . . Dede. *Indicates for her to help Soholuk. Soholuk and Walker are a bit apart from Gillie and Paul.*
Gillie:	Now all we gotta do is wait, eh, just gotta wait.
Walker:	Does it hurt?
Soholuk:	Not as much as you think.
Walker:	What do you mean?
Soholuk:	Take your time with the bandage and listen—you know what's gonna happen, don't you?
Walker:	I'm just takin' it as it comes, Frank.
Soholuk:	We make a move, Deed, and security'll be through that door like gangbusters backin' us up. . . . We don't make a move, security can still do its gangbusters' bit, only we're gonna get caught in the middle.
Walker:	No.
Soholuk:	You gotta help me. If I try to take Gillie, can you handle Tommy, I mean just for a minute till—
Walker:	I wanna wait, Frank.
Soholuk:	Things are not gonna get better, things are gonna get worse.
Walker:	I wanna wait.
Soholuk:	Help me!
Gillie:	*Suddenly aware of them talking, comes towards them with the knife.* What're you doin' over here, what're you doin'!
Walker:	*Backs up quickly away from Soholuk into Paul.* I was just fixin' his arm.

Gillie: Yeah . . . OK . . . OK . . .

He sits on a speaker beside Soholuk. Paul guides Walker to the chair at the desk. He sits on the arm of the chair as:

Chalmers: It's someone he trusts.

Wallace: Do you know Lena Benz, have you heard of her?

Chalmers: You say priority's the release of the hostages. If Benz is for that, do her politics matter?

Wallace: We talked about it this morning. No entry. And that was before any of this happened. We'd be crazy to ask her in now.

Chalmers: Well, I don't think he'll take me alone.

McGowen: Benz is out.

Wallace: The money, the plane—we've got nothing to do with that. You tell him.

Chalmers: If I don't get back in, I can't tell him anything.

Wallace: His request's been forwarded to Ottawa. You tell him when we hear from them, he'll be the first to know.

Chalmers: I said he won't take me alone! You should consider Lena Benz as a second.

Wallace: No.

Pause.

Chalmers: OK . . . what about this list of things?

Wallace: The institution is run according to the federal Penitentiary Act.

Chalmers: He says it isn't.

Wallace: Well, whose word do you take there?

Chalmers: He makes some—ah—pretty specific charges.

McGowen: Look, we got five hundred and sixty hardcore offenders in a pen built for four forty, so what do you want? Early to bed and no cookies?

Chalmers: I don't want anything! I'm tryin' to figure out what I say to the guy, if and when. Now what about solitary—the judge made a number of recommendations, didn't he?

Wallace: Which are being implemented.

Chalmers: It's over a year now.

McGowen: That's right.

Pause.

Chalmers: Desjardins. What's that?

Wallace: A discipline problem with one of the guards. Paul's tryin' to blow it up into something else.

McGowen: That's a non-negotiable item.

Chalmers: What the hell did you call me in for?

Wallace: George—

McGowen: You know how I feel.

Wallace: The prio—

McGowen: Look, Stocker's safe for the moment, and Walker is safe.

Chalmers: Walker, why's Walker safe?

McGowen: There's only Soholuk to worry about.

Chalmers: Why's Walker safe?

Pause.

Wallace: George here reads the situation a bit different than I do.

Chalmers: What do you mean?

Wallace: He feels there may be evidence linking Walker as an accessory.

Chalmers: What evidence?

Wallace: Dede Walker is Tommy Paul's rehabilitation officer, his counsellor.

Chalmers: And?

Wallace: And the grapevine has it he gets more than counselling. George is a bit blunter than that. He says she screws him.

McGowen: She's what you call a liberated woman.

Chalmers: Have you got any real evidence linking her to Paul's actions?

McGowen: What the hell do you want? How many times have we sat in on those damn team meetings and listened to Walker mouth off 'bout shower time, job trainin', recreation? Those are Walker's demands, not Paul's. Before he met her he didn't know his ass from his elbow—he thought the Penitentiary Act was a sexual offense for christ's sake. And now what? He's down there makin' demands with that crazy MacDermott, and guess who? Walker! So what kinda evidence do you want? A polaroid print!

Wallace: We need time. Time works for us.

Chalmers: Well—No Benz. No plane. No money. Changes to solitary are pending, and Desjardins is internal! You know what that's gonna buy you? Not time. *Pause.* Christ, there's three people in there! *Pause.* So what do you want me to do?

Wallace: Alright.

McGowen: We don't want Lena Benz.

Wallace: We've got no choice.

McGowen: We got choices. You don't want to make them.

Wallace: Look George, we give them Lena Benz and they talk. So long as they're talking, they're not doing anything else. So for the moment—we just keep them talking.

Wallace, McGowen, and Chalmers will assume a soft freeze. Gillie tosses his knife from hand to hand. He cautiously looks down the corridor, he sees Hanzuk at the end of it. Returns to outer office, paces.

Gillie: Why ain't nobody here yet?

Paul: Takes time.

Gillie: You think they take us serious?

Paul: Sure they do.

Gillie:	Then what's takin' so long!
Walker:	It takes time, Gillie.
Gillie:	Maybe they don't take us serious, what about that?
Paul:	It's alright.
Gillie:	Then why ain't we heard nothin' yet!
Paul:	It's OK!

He grasps Gillie's shoulder to comfort him.

Gillie:	You said—*Paul nods reassuringly at Gillie who is silent for a moment, then walks away from Paul to sit on a speaker. He continues to talk to himself.*
Gillie:	We was gonna put 'em in the office . . .
Paul:	You tired?
Walker:	No.
Gillie:	You gotta do what you say you're gonna do . . .
Walker:	You could change things, Tommy, you can get real changes made.
Gillie:	I know that.
Paul:	The main line's to get the hell outa here.
Walker:	The other's important.
Paul:	You're funny.
Walker:	I'm serious, Tommy.
Paul:	Yeah, but you go home at night.

He looks over at Gillie, moves to him, puts his arm around him. He whispers encouragement in his ear. Gillie nods. He moves over towards the exit to the corridor. Paul looks at Soholuk, then Paul picks up some of the paper Gillie has strewn about. He stuffs it back in the wastebasket. Soholuk watches him for a moment, then switches his focus to Gillie.

Soholuk:	Gillie?
Gillie:	Shaddup.
Soholuk:	Hey, it's Frank you're talkin' to.

Soholuk slowly makes his way over to Gillie who is paying no particular attention to him. Only Gillie stands between Soholuk and the exit to the corridor.

Gillie: I don't wanna talk.

Soholuk: I'm not one of your screws.

Gillie: No difference.

Soholuk: Come on.

Gillie: *Taps his head.* They beat on the outside, you fuck around with the inside, what's the difference.

Soholuk: You got me there.

Gillie: No difference.

Soholuk: No difference, eh Deed?

He suddenly makes a move to yank Gillie's arm up behind him, hoping to disable him for a moment, swing him out of the doorway. Gillie, at the same moment, as much in frustration as in any real knowledge of what Soholuk is attempting, just as suddenly smashes Soholuk, knocking him down, then driving him into the inner office. Walker screams, Paul grabs her restraining her as Gillie threatens Soholuk.

Gillie: Hey! Open your ears, man, get in that office eh! Get in! *He grabs a bottle of Javex as he drives Soholuk into the inner office.* Get in there! You're gonna be nothin' but a big slab a charcoal meat, man, you're— *He catches sight of Stocker.* Hey! Another one!

Paul: What?

Gillie: 'Nother one hidin', dumb bastard hidin' in here! Go on! Get! *He drives Stocker into the outer office. Stocker makes a run for the door to the corridor. Paul steps in front of him.* Say hello to Tommy.

Stocker: Hello.

Gillie: *Laughs.* What?

Stocker: Hello.

Paul: Who is he?

Walker: A teacher, come in to see Frank.

Gillie:	You hear that? "A-low" . . . A-low, what the hell's that, a-low—cup a teh, whatta we got here, eh? *He drives Stocker with the knife towards the swivel chair on wheels behind the desk.*
Gillie:	'Ave a go, good show. *He shoves him into the chair.* Your name Harry?
Paul:	The man asked you a question.
Gillie:	What's your name! Your name Harry!
Walker:	Tommy—
Paul:	It's OK.
Gillie:	'Arry!
Stocker:	No. No, that's not my name.
Gillie:	Talk some more.
Stocker:	Well I—
Paul:	What's your name!
Stocker:	Cecil—
Gillie:	Cecil!
Stocker:	Cecil Stocker.
Gillie:	Cecil a-low a-low Cecil.
Stocker:	Hello.

Gillie gives the odd feint and jab at Cecil with the knife, he runs it around his ear as he questions him.

Gillie:	You don't know a Harry?
Stocker:	I may do.
Gillie:	*Gives a guffaw.* "May do?"
Walker:	Make him stop.
Stocker:	It's a common name.
Paul:	It keeps him loose.
Gillie:	Mister Harry Sir! *He lunges at him with the knife.*

Stocker:	Ahh!
Gillie:	Oh you like that, eh? Sir! *He lunges again. To Paul.* You 'member that camp I told you?
Paul:	Yeah?
Gillie:	It's him, talks just like him.
Paul:	You were waitin' in there, were you?
Stocker:	That's right, I was just sitting and . . . waiting.
Paul:	What else you do?
Gillie:	Mr. Harry Sir!

Paul notices that Soholuk has come to the doorway of the inner office.

Stocker:	I looked 'round for a door of course but—
Paul:	But. *He gestures with Soholuk to get back in the inner office.*
Gillie:	But.
Stocker:	There was none.
Gillie:	Hey! *Makes a sweep with the knife at Stocker who jumps up from the chair to make a dash around the desk to the door. Gillie steps in front of him. Paul is on the other side of him.*
Paul:	Disappointed?
Stocker:	What?
Gillie:	Wot wot wot!
Paul:	No door.
Stocker:	Yes.
Paul:	What!
Gillie:	Duck! *Gillie throws a punch which Stocker ducks. Gillie begins to dance and weave throwing punches.* Hey come on, come on there boy, put 'em up, come on, weave boy weave, bob boy bob, hey watch the left—and a left—and a right!

He lands several punches, the last one knocks Stocker down. Paul has stepped back and holds Walker. Soholuk unobserved has once again come to the doorway of the inner office. Gillie is laughing having a wonderful time. He bends down beside Stocker.

Paul: *To Walker.* It's OK. Relax.

Gillie: You be a good teacher, you gotta learn.

Walker: I don't like it.

Gillie: Teachin', learnin', one's just the other turned round.

Walker: That's enough, Tommy.

Paul: OK.

Gillie: Turnin' the other cheek, you know that one?

Paul: Hey Gillie.

Gillie: An eye for an eye—

Paul: Gillie.

Gillie: for an eye?

Paul: Put him in with Soholuk.

Gillie: I wanna hear him talk—say Gilbert MacDermott is the best boy we ever had at this camp, go on, say it!

Paul: I want him inside.

Stocker: Gilbert MacDermott is the best boy we ever had at this camp.

Soholuk is making his way towards the exit to the corridor unseen by Walker, Gillie, or Paul.

Gillie: *Laughs, gets up.* You hear that? Evah had at this camp!

Paul: Now put him inside.

Gillie: No, I wanna— [hear him talk]

Paul: And I want him inside!

Gillie: And I don't!

Paul: You! Inside!

Stocker sits up. Gillie turns to him with the knife. Stocker stops, freezes. Gillie laughs. Soholuk is edging his way along towards the door.

Gillie: Hey, he knows who's solid, who's the Big Man!

Paul: Who? *Gillie looks at him. Pause.*

Gillie: You are.

Soholuk makes a dash for the door. Paul sees him.

Walker: Frank!!

Paul grabs Soholuk, throws him into the filing cabinet. Gillie grabs Stocker, shoves him into the inner office. He then runs to cautiously check the corridor.

Soholuk: *To Walker.* What're you doin'!

Walker: I said wait, Frank, I wanna wait!

Paul grabs him from the floor.

Soholuk: Sure wait, there's always time to die, isn't there!

Paul: *Throwing him in the inner office.* Next time I'll cut your fuckin' throat!

At this point, Lena Benz is entering the tier corridor, making her way to Wallace's office.

Benz: Last time I was here, I was "forcibly removed from the premises."

Wallace: *Smiles.* It's called "illegal entry"—and into my office at that.

Benz: If I waited for an invitation I'd never get in.

Wallace: Well it looks like you're wrong there.

Benz: Did you ever read that petition I left?

Wallace: Oh yes.

Benz: And?

Wallace: "No comment." *To Chalmers.* Lena Benz is the only person I know who breaks into a prison.

Benz: Hell, I came in with a visitor's permit and just . . . made my way . . . up to the office. . . . How's the family, George, boys still in school?

Wallace: She's got all our case histories.

Benz: I operate just like the government. I make it my business to know what's none of my business. *She winks at Chalmers.*

Wallace: Well—you've been briefed on the situation of the hostages; you know the background of the prisoners; you know our position; now—*Benz tosses a bound document on the desk.* What's that?

Benz: It's ah . . . what you might call a private copy of the paper on penal reform, hot from the office of the Solicitor General. Hasn't been released yet—will probably be buried.

McGowen: One of your stoolies send it to you?

Benz: That's right. And it makes interesting reading. Says things like—autocratic administrative structure—well-established resistance to significant change—bureaucratic norms that promote men with no professional qualifications in penology—

Wallace: What does it say about operating in a 19th century fortress with no financial support for progressive programming—with forty per cent more inmates than we're equipped to handle, and all of them clamouring for "privileges"—what does it say about trying to recruit and maintain staff in a hostile environment with low pay and no status!

Benz: *Picks up the document, passes it to Chalmers.* Page thirty-four—the documentation on punitive isolation . . . without cause . . . restriction of privileges . . . without cause . . . excessive force to subdue . . .

McGowen: You're so goddamn smart you tell me what's excessive when a 250 pound inmate comes at you with a shiv, a honed piece a steel, you tell me, is that in your bloody paper?

Benz: The point is Paul is asking for changes, minor changes inside, that this government paper endorses.

McGowen: The point is unless the people who wrote that paper start working inside, those changes aren't gonna happen!

Benz:	*To Wallace.* In the light of this document, what can we negotiate in the way of internal conditions?
Wallace:	Nothing.
Chalmers:	*Has been studying the document.* Why not?
Wallace:	The institution is run accord—
Benz:	I challenge that.
McGowen:	Jesus.
Chalmers:	But the recommendations in here seem to be what Paul's asking for in the way of recreation, job training—
McGowen:	No!
Chalmers:	But it's the difference between Paul making reasonable demands and unreasonable demands. I mean this government paper backs his demands. *He tosses the document back on the desk.*
Benz:	What about solitary, top tier?
Wallace:	Is under renovation, he knows that!
Benz:	And Desjardins?
McGowen:	I'm standin' here listenin' to what about this, what about that! Let's talk reality, eh? What's real? What's real is no money. What's real is nobody wants those bastards, not Cuba, not Russia, not us. What's real is your parliamentary paper is just that, nothin' but paper! Bleedin' hearts and MPs don't run a maximum security pen, we do, and we're all servin' time, the guards, the prisoners, everyone! . . . Now you tell them to send the hostages out, one at a time, then they come out—Or else we go in!
Wallace:	Wait a minute.
McGowen:	You "negotiate" and you're gonna have inmates grabbin' hostages like kids grabbin' candy—and we're the ones who work inside. Not you, not them [*the document*]—Us.
Chalmers:	Is the priority the release of the hostages?

Benz: Or the retention of power by the prison!

Wallace: It is not an either-or question!

McGowen: Look—Stocker is safe. Walker is in on it.

Chalmers: We don't know that!

McGowen: If we rush 'em we can free 'em, but we gotta move before they find Stocker.

Wallace: No! For the moment . . . we talk.

McGowen: So you talk to MacDermott, who shot some poor Chinese grocer in front of his kids. He shot him four times 'cause he wasn't fast enough with the till. And Tommy Paul, who got a contract and knocked on a door and when the door opened, he blew half a girl's head away, and he shut the door, ditched the gun, and went out for a beer. That's who you're talkin' to. You don't make deals with people like that!

Benz: Your government does every day. South Africa, Chile, Brazil, Arg—

Chalmers: Lena.

Benz: What!

Chalmers: Why don't we . . . take a break and cool off, eh? Then we'll go in and see Paul, alright?

Benz: Alright . . . *She starts to leave, stops, indicates the document.* Read it why don't you? Read it!

She and Chalmers make their way along the tier corridor, down the stairs to the landing area.

McGowen: There's a decision to be made. Soon you're gonna have to make it.

Wallace: But not yet. Not now.

McGowen exits from the office and offstage. Wallace sits at his desk. Benz gives a hard stare to Hanzuk who is near the top of the stairs as they descend. Hanzuk moves a short distance up the tier corridor leaving Benz and Chalmers alone on the landing. Benz shoves her shoulder bag at Chalmers for him to hold while she has a smoke. There's a large bag in the shoulder bag.

Chalmers: What's in the bag?

Benz: Kentucky fried. First time I ever been in one of these numbers they didn't demand 'tucky fried.

Chalmers smiles. A pause.

Chalmers: They had no trouble finding you?

Benz: Hell no. I was in the Eddy havin' a beer.

Chalmers: Oh.

Benz: Yeah. I was in a women's march this mornin' and I met an old friend, Charlie Wilson.

Chalmers: In a women's march?

Benz: Not Charlie, *me.* I was striding forth, and I heard this here voice yellin' "Lena Benz, you old bitch, what'll you be onto next?" I craned my neck round, and I seen Charlie Wilson takin' a pull on the biggest damn bottle of vanilla. Last time I seen Charlie he'd just got the shit beat outa him in an IWA strike in Prince George— Anyways, there he was lyin' in the gutter and drinkin' vanilla, and there I was with my Charlotte Whitton T-shirt "whatever my sex, I'm no lady," and Charlie says, "Truer words was never written," and I says "Dump the vanilla and I'll buy you a beer in the Eddy!" . . . So . . . that's where they found me.

Chalmers: I see.

Benz: What about you . . . what's a nice boy like you doin' in a place like this?

Chalmers: Tryin' to help.

Benz: Put a torch to the place. That's the best help we can give. Not reform. Abolish. *Chalmers smiles.* No, listen, here's the dilemma, it's like this. A man comes up to you and he says, listen—I'm thinkin' of killin' all the Jews in the world, do you think I should do that? What do you say? Hell no! And he says, well, I'm gonna do it anyway. Should I transport them by freight train, or by truck? What do you say? Same thing.

Chalmers: As reforming the penal system? I don't think so.

Benz: Listen. You're sittin' by a little kid on the bus. You say, "Hello there, what do you want to be when you grow up?" The kid says, "A prison guard!" Would you not think there's some cause for concern with that kid?

Chalmers: You're a great one for stories.

Benz: Yes I am. I certainly am . . . here's a story. A true story. In Ohio a bunch of guards rounded up these pet cats the prisoners befriended, including six four-day-old kittens. And in front of the prison population, they dashed their brains out against a wall. The incident was leaked, and letters poured in by the hundreds—all from Irate Cat Lovers. Not one expressed concern for the poor buggers locked up in an institution where those guards wield power without restraint, and virtually no review.

Chalmers: That's not a nice story.

Benz: It's better than some . . . hell, prime ministers, politicians, and presidents kill more men than the inmates of this place ever did.

Chalmers: There's a difference you know.

Benz: To me, it seems more a matter of quantity . . . so, we go in, and we talk. And we pray to God George doesn't rush the place while we're there.

Chalmers: You don't think he'd do that.

Benz: Look, you and I can be straight with each other. We know we got nothing to say.

Chalmers: So why are you here?

Benz: Same question for you.

Chalmers: I told you. I thought I could help.

Benz: Some reason I can't feel the same?

She signals to Hanzuk, takes the shoulder bag, with chicken.

Hanzuk: Paul! Paul!

Benz and Chalmers go down the corridor to the outer office.

Paul: What'd I tell you?

Gillie nods.

Benz: Well sir—good to see you, Tommy.

Paul: Same here.

Benz: And you too, Gillie boy.

Gillie: Yeah.

Benz: *Passes him the chicken bag.* Kentucky fried in the bag, it's cold, but greasy.

Gillie: *Takes the bag.* Fuckin' A.

Benz: Really done it this time, eh?

Paul: Do or die.

Chalmers: Where's Soholuk?

Paul: In the office.

Gillie: *Into the chicken.* With the other one.

Benz moves into the inner office to check Stocker and Soholuk.

Paul: Seems there was a bonus in the bottom of the box.

Chalmers: You alright?

Walker: Yeah.

Paul: You got Lena for me.

Chalmers: Yup.

Paul: So I'm sayin' thanks.

Chalmers: You could do me a favour, and let her relax a bit.

Paul: I like her close, she's a good friend.

Chalmers: She looks tired.

Paul: You tired?

Walker: I'm alright.

Paul: See?

A pause. Chalmers looks over towards Gillie. He catches Gillie's eye. Gillie tenses, puts down the chicken, takes out his knife. Chalmers and Gillie eye each other.

Paul: Let's get goin', OK? Lena?

Benz joins them in the outer office.

Benz: Well boys—we're gonna be straight with you, Ev and me, 'cause we think you can handle it, no horseshit.

Stocker and Soholuk drift to the doorway to listen.

Paul: Yeah.

Benz: No fifty thousand bucks.

Paul: Who says?

Chalmers: Ottawa.

Paul: Jesus.

Benz: Look, they won't deal for money, but for the flight out, they're still lookin'.

Paul: What're the chances?

Benz: I dunno.

Paul: Who're they askin'?

Benz: Cuba, Algeria, it's gonna take time.

Paul: Fuck!

Walker: Tommy, category two, changes inside.

Paul: Yeah. *Pause.* Nobody's sayin' nothin'.

Benz: We discussed them.

Walker: You discussed them?

Chalmers: McGowen and Wallace're studying them.

Paul: No.

Chalmers: In principle we agree with the changes, eh Lena?

Paul: Not good enough.

Chalmers: They say top tier is under renovation.

Walker: They're liars.

Gillie: All they done is painted the walls!

Paul:	Don't your fuckin' courts mean anything! We got a rulin' last year, cruel and unusual punishment, and nothin's changed except the fuckin' paint on the fuckin' walls!
Gillie:	You gotta do what you say you're gonna do else no one believes you!
Paul:	Lemme handle this!
Benz:	Hold on.
Paul:	No, what the hell's goin' on, you come in here with nothin'!
Benz:	Will you listen!
Paul:	Why? You got nothin' to say!
Benz:	I come in with a paper, it's gonna mean changes!
Paul:	Nothin' changes!
Benz:	It's gonna have to this time.
Chalmers:	The recommendations mirror your demands.
Walker:	Why won't Wallace deal then?
Benz:	He's workin' in a system, the system takes time to turn 'round.
Chalmers:	Concentrate on the flight out.
Gillie:	Are there gonna be changes or not!
Paul:	Take it easy!
Gillie:	I wanna know!
Benz:	There's gonna be changes!
Chalmers:	They're not gonna happen tomorrow!
Paul:	It's alright!
Gillie:	You gotta do what you say!
Paul:	It's OK.
Gillie:	Gotta burn one, do what you say!

He grabs the gasoline, sloshes it into the inner office hitting Stocker in the doorway, Soholuk leaps back to avoid getting hit.

Paul: Gillie!

Gillie: Stupid bastard, gonna kill you!

Walker backs away screaming, Gillie kicks at Stocker on the floor.

Paul: *To Chalmers.* Grab him! *To Benz.* Get outa here! Tell 'em they come in the whole works goes up!

Chalmers attempts to grab Gillie from behind. Gillie jabs him in the gut. Chalmers falls into the inner office. Benz runs down the corridor to Hanzuk. Hanzuk grabs the phone. Benz exits offstage along the tier corridor. Gillie has the lighter out, is on his knees trying to light it.

Walker: Tommy! Stop him! Tommy!

Paul grabs Gillie, throws him across the room, is down on top of him, his knife in his hand.

Paul: Gillie! Gillie, you bugger! You listen to me! You wanna burn us all up, man? Is that what you want! You do what I say when I say how I say! I'm your friend, eh? Don't I listen, eh? Look after each other?

Gillie: Yeah.

Paul: What do you do with your aces, man?

Gillie: Save 'em.

Paul: That's right, and that's what we're doin'. We're savin' all those aces till the end, man. We don't blow nothin' now. . . . *He takes the lighter from Gillie's hand. He helps him up.* Come on, eh?

Chalmers and Soholuk have Stocker sitting on the desk in the inner office. He has his hand over his eyes.

Chalmers: Get his jacket off, and anything else that's got gas on it, I'll take it out when I leave.

Soholuk: Jesus.

Chalmers: Did it hit your eyes? Is that what's the matter?

Stocker: . . . I'm alright . . . just need a minute.

Soholuk: Is security puttin' together a squad?

Chalmers: I dunno.

Soholuk: There's nothin' we can do here. You tell 'em that. We can't initiate nothin' from here.

Chalmers: I'll tell 'em.

Soholuk: You know I wasn't even supposed to come in today? Shit, half these guys I went to school with. Them or people just like them. I could have turned up a con, but I got smart. I got smart, and now somebody's sittin' up there sayin' "OK. Soholuk, you smart ass, Gotcha anyway!" . . . What a piss-off! . . . You tell em, whatever they do, think it through, eh? Like . . . it's just us in here . . . think it through. . . .

Chalmers exits from the inner office. He stands just inside the outer office watching Paul and Gillie.

Gillie: We gettin' a plane?

Paul: Sure we will.

Gillie: I never been on a plane before. . . . What about Desjardins, we wouldn't just forget about him, would we?

Paul: No, we wouldn't do that.

Gillie: Sometimes I just want to hit somethin'.

Walker: *To Chalmers.* Is he OK?

Chalmers: Someone should look at him, a doctor.

Paul: No one comes in except you and Benz.

Gillie: Sometimes it's just like a dream. . . . Hey, man, I get you one there with the elbow?

Chalmers: Right in the gut.

Gillie: Yeah? I didn't mean to hurt you or nothin', eh Deed? . . . What's the matter with her?

Paul: She don't like it when you're loud.

Gillie: I'm sorry, Deed, I don't mean nothin' by it. Deed?

Walker: What?

Gillie: It's the same way, Deed, just the same. I mean, the Chinaman, the Chink, the guy in the store. I didn't mean to hurt him or nothin'. I said, "hurry up! hurry up!" And these three little kids, they kept cryin' and Jesus, he kept fumblin' away there and he wouldn't be quick and he wouldn't shut up, just kept up this jabber, Chink jabber and Jesus! I dunno it all. . . . I can hardly remember. All's I wanted him to do was shut up and give me the money, that's all I wanted. Why couldn't he do that! Why couldn't he do that!

Walker: I dunno.

Gillie: He was on the floor and I run out the door and I run right in the side of a cop car! *He laughs.* What a piece a bad luck, eh? . . . Jesus, my whole life's a piece a bad luck.

Walker: . . . We're gonna die, Tommy.

Paul: Everyone's gonna die, Deed.

Walker: I never thought I was gonna die like this.

Paul: You aren't. We're gonna go someplace where it never snows, and you're gonna get old and wrinkly, and I'm gonna shrink like my grampa.

Pause. Then Chalmers starts out. As he's about to exit into the corridor.

Paul: Tell 'em we'll settle for a flight out, and Desjardins.

Chalmers continues out the outer office, down the corridor, up the stairs, and exits offstage from the tier corridor.

Gillie moves to pick up the fried chicken bag. He stops, looks at Walker, after a moment he makes an attempt at apology.

Gillie: You . . . got nice hair, Deed.

Walker: You like it?

Gillie: My mum had nice hair . . . long hair.

Pause. He gets the chicken, sits down to eat it. Takes only one bite, then merely holds it, clutching the bag.

Walker: God, Tommy, how does everything happen?

Paul: I was doin' time in the hole and one day this pretty lady came in and smiled at me.

Walker:	Yeah?
Paul:	Yeah. You came in and you started to talk and what you said made sense and I listened and I started thinkin'. *Pause.* Are you still mad at me?
Walker:	No, Tommy, I'm not mad.
Paul:	It wasn't because I didn't trust you I didn't tell you.
Walker:	I know.
Paul:	You might not . . . like seeing me like this, but once I'm outa here, I won't have to be what I have to be here.
Walker:	Yeah.
Paul:	But you gotta understand everything I done makes up me—the good things, the bad things—I done things you wouldn't believe. I don't regret any of 'em. I'm not proud of 'em, but I don't regret 'em . . . I had nothin' and I made myself somethin'.
Walker:	What?
Paul:	Respected by people I know. *Pause.*
Walker:	We have to talk, Tommy.
Paul:	We're talkin' now, ain't we? . . . Hey, you know how things oughta be and I know how things are. Now you put those two things together, I think you got a pretty powerful thing happenin'. . . . Don't you?
Walker:	Maybe.
Paul:	That's you and me, Deed.
Pause.	
Paul:	What's the matter?
Walker:	Nothing.
Paul:	We been close.
Walker:	Yes.
Paul:	Real close. . . . What's the matter?
Walker:	We gotta talk.
Paul:	We're talkin'! *Pause.* Was everything bullshit therapy?

Walker: It's not as simple as that.

Pause.

Paul: You're tired.

Walker: I guess so.

Paul: Yeah, you're just tired. Why doncha try to sleep?

Walker: I don't want to sleep.

Paul: I'll look after things here, you sleep. *He sits her down in a chair, looks down at her. Pause.* I would never hurt you, Deed. *Pause. He moves behind the desk and sits.*

Hanzuk picks up the phone on the landing. Hangs it up and goes up the stairs.

McGowen enters the tier corridor. He waits for Hanzuk. The two of them join Wallace in his office.

While this is happening, Gillie gets up with his chicken and moves closer to Paul to share it with him. Pause.

Gillie: . . . Iran.

Paul: What?

Gillie: I bet Iran would take us. That crazy bugger'd take anyone. Make sure they try for Iran.

Pause. Neither of them feels much like eating the chicken.

Gillie: . . . I live so many places. . . . You live a lota places?

Paul: Yeah.

Gillie: You ever live in one of them homes?

Paul: Yeah.

Gillie: When she took us to welfare, she said it was just for a while, she'd be back. I remember that. And her hair. But she never came back . . . . Jesus, you shouldn't do that to poor little kids.

Paul: Maybe she tried, but she couldn't get back.

Gillie: You think so? . . . Yeah . . . She tried, but she couldn't get back. . . . Do you have a mum?

Paul: Yeah.

Gillie:	You remember your mum?
Paul:	I remember my gramma. I remember people always seemed to be dyin' . . . fallin' down drunk and freezin' to death, smokin' and sleepin' and burnin' to death, gettin' hit by a train, gettin' hit by a car, bein' in a car and hittin' a car. . . . I remember lookin' at my brothers and sisters and thinkin', Jesus, that is not gonna be me.
Gillie:	And I remember "Mr. Harry Sir" and the camp, what an asshole he was. Put on the gloves, him and me, everybody'd watch. He couldn't put me out, nosireeeee! *Laughs.* I could never land a punch, but he couldn't knock me out! I'd keep gettin' up and gettin' up and gettin' up! Shit, he'd be mad! *Pause.* Hate that son of a whore. *Pause.* Tommy?
Paul:	Yeah?
Gillie:	You remember how Desjardins used to scream in the hole? Used to say there was somethin' inside his head, somethin' drivin' him nuts?
Paul:	The hole drove him nuts.
Gillie:	I could hear me screamin' with him. Inside my head I could hear it.
Paul:	Yeah.
Gillie:	I don't wanna die in here.
McGowen:	Six men.
Hanzuk:	You got 'em.
Gillie:	We're gonna get on a plane and fly outa here. It's gonna be one of them silver planes leavin' a white trail across the sky, like you see from the yard.
Hanzuk:	I'd like to use my own piece, would that be alright?
McGowen:	Whatever you're comfortable with.
Gillie:	Whooooshh! . . . And we're gone.

Theme music.

BLACKOUT

ACT TWO

Theme music.

Lights up on Wallace behind his desk in the upper office.

Stocker is asleep in the inner office. Soholuk is awake.

Gillie and Paul appear to be dozing. Paul less so than Gillie. Walker stretches in her chair. Hanzuk is not at his usual post in the corridor/ landing area. Walker gets up to stretch her legs. She catches Soholuk's eye as she stands near the doorway to the inner office. A pause as they lock gazes.

Walker: . . . Tommy?

Paul: Mmmn?

Walker: I'm going in the office for a minute.

Paul: What for?

Walker: I want to . . . I want to see if they're alright. Gillie hurt him and maybe . . . I can do something.

Paul: OK, but make it fast.

Walker: Yeah. *She enters the inner office. Looks at Stocker.* Is he alright?

Soholuk: What do you think?

Walker: I asked a question, Frank.

Soholuk: The answer is no.

Walker: Can I—

Soholuk: No, you done enough already. Leave us alone.

Walker: We're all scared, Frank.

Soholuk: Get out. You don't belong in here.

Walker: I swear I didn't know anything about this.

Soholuk: You sure picked it up fast.

Walker: We can get changes made. He's drawin' attention to things, and when this hits the press—

Soholuk: Nobody gives a shit! Who do you think cares about them? And we'll make the headlines at noon, and at night they'll use us for garbage! This won't change a thing. He can't change a thing. And you know that, you bitch. In your gut, you know it.

Walker: Sometimes it's the struggle that counts, to struggle to keep on struggling.

Soholuk: For what?

Walker: A just cause!

Soholuk: Determined by who?

Walker: Yourself!

Soholuk: Ooh, we'd have a great kinda order then, wouldn't we.

Walker: What kinda order have we got now?

Soholuk: You're a lamb looking for a slaughter, Deed.

Walker: You gotta turn everything into some kinda head trip, don't you? You can't believe there's people willing to fight for things they're not gonna win!

Soholuk: Hallelujah.

Walker: It's all because their daddy left them when they were three, or their mommy didn't potty train them—you can't believe there's people willing to die for things they believe in because they believe in them!

Soholuk: Try for an overseas posting, Deed, I hear the Red Brigade's got openings.

Walker: My struggle's here, you asshole.

Soholuk: Be honest. It gave you some kinda honky liberal thrill screwing him in the office. You think that's a political act for christ's sake.

Walker: Can't you get it through your stupid head I did not fuck Tommy Paul!

Soholuk: You sit around sippin' your wine, playin' your reggae records, bobbin' your head and your ass, and singin' "everybody's cryin' out for peace—none of them is cryin' out for Justice"—Well, someone took you at your

	word, this is it, people are gonna die, this is real! So fuck off!
Walker:	There's more words to that song—"Everyone is cryin' out for Heaven; none of them is cryin' out to die."
Soholuk:	Dyin' for causes, that's your ticket, not mine. And not his [*Paul's*] either. There is an asshole here, Deed, and it's you. Now get outa here before I punch you in the mouth.
Paul:	Deed?
Walker:	Yeah. I'm comin'.

She returns to Paul in the outer office.

Benz enters the tier corridor and Wallace's office.

Benz:	There's a roomful of guards down the hall there with Hanzuk, now what the hell's goin' on?
Wallace:	Don't worry.
Benz:	I'm askin' a question!
Wallace:	If things flare up again, George wants someone prepared to go in. You can understand that.
Benz:	I don't understand anything.
Wallace:	He's not talkin' offensive action, he's talkin' reaction. There's a difference.
Benz:	Well I hope we all know what that is.
Wallace:	Come on, relax, take it easy, you want coffee?
Benz:	No.
Wallace:	*Reaching into a drawer of the desk.* How about . . .
Benz:	Where's Ev, does he—*Wallace holds up a scotch bottle.* What's this? Supplies for emergencies? *Wallace will pour them each a drink.*
Wallace:	I think this qualifies. . . . Straight?
Benz:	What else.
Wallace:	Better than nothing, eh?

Benz: Considerably better than nothing.

Wallace: A toast . . . "To Reform." *He drinks. Benz doesn't.*

Benz: You don't feel guilty drinkin' to that?

Wallace: Oh I don't know. What about you? Still hittin' the bottle?

Benz: *Laughs.* You bastard. *She knocks back her drink.*

Wallace: *Refills her glass.* Stoolie information's like electricity, Lena, it runs both ways. . . . Tired?

Benz: A bit . . . gettin' old.

Wallace: Here we are, two old warhorses. I work inside the system, you work outside, and neither of us matters a tinker's damn.

Benz: You said that, not me.

Wallace: We balance each other off. Nothing changes, only the faces.

Benz: I'm not that tired. Or old. You're tired.

Wallace: Honest. I'm honest.

Benz: Whatever.

Wallace: Well, you've been standing on street corners for damn near half a century, Lena, you tell me. Have things got better or worse?

Benz: Maybe you should sell shoes.

Wallace: And maybe you'd have accomplished more if you'd married a nice Jewish doctor and spent your time raising kids and funds for Hadassah.

Benz: I'd punch you out but you're not in my weight class. . . . Nothin' from Ottawa?

Wallace: Not yet.

Benz: You'd think they'd be faster.

Wallace: I snuck a look at your paper. [*The document on his desk.*]

Benz: "No comment?"

Wallace:	Hell, money and the most enlightened staff in the world could do bugger-all. The whole endeavour's wrong-headed, a vicious circle, do you ever feel that?
Benz:	You mean a downward spiral.
Wallace:	That's what I mean.
Benz:	No. I never feel that. *She pours herself another drink.*
Wallace:	*Smiles.* You're a sneaky broad, Lena.
Benz:	Practice.
Wallace:	We both should be good. *He holds up his glass which he has not refilled since his initial drink.* Here's to "Shoes"—a vastly underrated profession.

Chalmers enters from the tier corridor.

Chalmers:	What the hell's with the men with the guns?
Wallace:	*Puts away the scotch.* A back-up squad for protection.
Chalmers:	Protection—when did they move it in?
Benz:	When I came in they were settin' it up.
Chalmers:	Why weren't we informed?
Wallace:	It's a recent decision.
Chalmers:	If McGowen thinks he can rush them, he can't.
Wallace:	Alright.
Chalmers:	Not without risking the lives of Stocker, Soholuk, and Walker.

McGowen enters the office from the tier corridor. Hanzuk has followed McGowen onstage, but remains outside the office in the corridor. McGowen carries a piece of paper he gives to Wallace.

Chalmers:	What the hell's with this squad, George? . . . George?
McGowen:	We got word.
Benz:	And?
McGowen:	A helicopter'll land in the yard.
Chalmers:	They've got a flight out?

Wallace:	A runway's cleared at the International Airport, a government plane will take them from there.
Chalmers:	*Starts out.* Good, I'll—
Benz:	Hold it! Wait a minute.

Chalmers stops.

Wallace:	George'll oversee the transfer as far as the yard.
Benz:	I wanna know who's takin' them.
Wallace:	All I got here is procedure . . .
Benz:	Who's takin' them!
McGowen:	All your talk, Lena, and you don't believe any country would take em.
Benz:	I just want more information.
McGowen:	You got what they gave us.
Benz:	If you think I'm goin' back in on the strength of that— you got another think comin'! Now who's takin' them!
Wallace:	If that's to be your decision, we'll abide by it. *He signals to Hanzuk out in the corridor.*
Benz:	I said who's takin' them!

The speeches flow on top of each other as Hanzuk enters, grasps both of Benz's arms and manipulates her out of the office and down the tier corridor. Wallace follows them.

Chalmers:	Wait a minute.
Benz:	Leggo.
Wallace:	I'm sorry you feel this way—
Benz:	Hey.
Wallace:	But if you can't continue to act—
Benz:	I didn't say that.
Wallace:	Ev can take over.
Benz:	No!
Chalmers:	Wait a—

Benz, in Hanzuk's grip, and Wallace are going down the corridor and exiting offstage.

Benz: You wanna see me in court?

Wallace: Your decision again.

Benz: You're goose-steppin' me out!

Wallace: I'm escorting you to the gate.

Chalmers: What the hell—

Benz: *Faintly offstage.* Take your bloody hands off me!

Chalmers and McGowen are left alone in Wallace's office. McGowen sits in Wallace's chair behind the desk, and lights a cigarette.

Chalmers: What the hell are you people doing?

McGowen: Me? I'm havin' a smoke.

Chalmers: He's bootin' her out, that's what he's doin'.

McGowen stares at Chalmers but says nothing.

Chalmers: What's with this squad?

McGowen: A reaction squad.

Chalmers: And the plane?

McGowen: I just follow orders, Mr. Chalmers.

Chalmers: And the inquiry for Desjardins?

McGowen: That could be a problem.

Chalmers: Why's that?

McGowen: Desjardins' dead. He slit his wrists.

Chalmers: And your problem is what?

McGowen: Look, they send us these crazies, what can we do? We can't keep 'em general population, so we isolate 'em. That's what we do. And sometimes it happens. Suicide, top tier. Then you get an opportunist like Paul or like Benz, and they make us look bad. Guard's name in the paper, press harassin' his family—Can you understand our position?

Chalmers:	But a proper inquiry can reveal your position, can help you.
McGowen:	It doesn't work like that.
Chalmers:	Then you tell me how it does work. . . . Interesting paper. *Indicating the document on the desk.* I read in there of an inmate who strangled himself with a sheet. He had nothing to hang himself from, so he put it 'round his neck, and just pulled it as tight as he could. He died of slow strangulation. They say it took twenty minutes. The guards dragged him down the tier corridor by the sheet. The inmates of the cells stood and watched him go by . . . you see . . . that kind of incident makes me wonder. *Chalmers starts to leave the office.*
McGowen:	Would you like to know what makes me wonder, Mr. Chalmers? *Chalmers stops.* We got three inmates in here gettin' degrees, university degrees. Isn't that wonderful, eh? I served my country through France, Holland, right into Berlin with the tanks, and I can't afford to send my own boys to college. *Chalmers exits along the tier corridor.* Yeah, that kinda makes me wonder.

Chalmers walks to the top of the stairs. He stops there. Wallace enters the tier corridor. He catches sight of Chalmers. Chalmers does not see Wallace. Chalmers slowly starts down the stairs. He stops after a few steps. Pauses. Then goes back up the stairs. Wallace meets him.

Wallace:	Ev . . . Where're you going?
Chalmers:	I dunno.
Wallace:	What's the matter?
Chalmers:	Where's Lena?
Wallace:	We can't afford to take chances.
Chalmers:	She was right, you just goose-stepped her out.
Wallace:	She's a grand old lady, but she distorts things.
Chalmers:	I—
Wallace:	She antagonizes George, you can see that, and when she went in to speak to the prisoners, all hell broke loose, you were there.

Chalmers: Yes, but—

Wallace: You can't walk out on us now.

Chalmers: I dunno.

Wallace: Look, tomorrow this will be over for you . . . you'll have breakfast, drop the kids off at school . . . on Friday I'll see you down at the Y.

Chalmers: . . . I . . .

Wallace: But right now—*He grasps Chalmers' shoulder.* We need you in there.

Pause. Chalmers slowly starts down the stairs. He slowly walks down the corridor towards the outer office.

Wallace watches him till he gets to the foot of the stairs; then he returns along the tier corridor to his own office. He stops on seeing McGowen at his desk. McGowen moves from the desk and Wallace sits down behind it.

When Chalmers steps into the outer office, both Paul and Gillie leap from their relaxed semi-dozing into defensive positions, knives extended.

Paul: *On seeing it's Chalmers, relief.* Oh shit. *In explanation.* There's no Hanzuk yellin' in the corridor.

Chalmers: No.

Walker: Where's Lena?

Chalmers: I brought medication for Stocker. *Passes Paul a small bottle of medication, eye drops.*

Chalmers: Are they asleep?

Paul: I guess so.

Starts into the inner office with the drops.

Walker: Where's Lena?

Paul stops. Turns to look at Chalmers. An increase in tension. Pause.

Chalmers: OK . . . OK just hear me out, alright? . . . We were with Wallace. McGowen came in. . . . They got a procedure for a flight out.

Paul: We got a flight out! You hear that!

Walker: Hold on! What about Lena?

Chalmers:	Yeah . . . Lena wanted to know who was takin' you, they didn't have that information, only procedure—
Paul:	Go on.
Chalmers:	They had words, very few words. Next thing I knew they had her out the gate.
Paul:	They booted her out!
Chalmers:	Concentrate on the flight out!
Walker:	Where's Hanzuk?
Chalmers:	They've cleared the corridor, they want to know how you plan to come out.
Paul:	What about Desjardins?
Chalmers:	I give you my word I'll look into it. I'll get Joe on it, I'll do everything I can! What else can I say?
Paul:	I dunno. . . . Jesus.
Chalmers:	. . . Look . . . You're supposed to be smart—is this really the best move you can make?
Paul:	Lemme tell you somethin' . . . in the last four years I spent over eight hundred days in the hole, solitary, top tier, concrete vault where they bury you. Eleven by six foot coffin. Four solid walls. Six inch window in a steel door. Light in the ceilin' they never turn off. I shower wearing steel shackles and cuffs. If I'm lucky I shave twice a week in cold water. My toilet bowl is my sink. That's right, I gotta wash in the crapper. I gotta sleep with my head a foot from the crapper. They send me back to the hole, I'm dead . . . I'm crazy . . . or dead.
Walker:	Do you know why they kill themselves in the hole? To prove they're alive. To prove they got freedom of choice.
Paul:	To live, or to die. Some choice, eh? . . . Well, I got other choices! . . . We got a flight out?
Chalmers:	That's what the man says.
Soholuk:	*From the doorway to the inner office.* Hey, he's not good. His chest hurts, and his eye, the left eye looks hazy.

Paul indicates for Gillie to keep an eye on the corridor. He enters the inner office with the eye drops. Chalmers goes to follow him, Walker stops him.

Paul: Can you see?

Stocker: Bit blurry.

Paul hands the eye drops to Soholuk and watches him administer them to Stocker.

Walker: *Low and hurried.* Tell me again.

Chalmers: A helicopter's landing in the yard and flying them out. You out?

Walker: No destination?

Chalmers: They say all they got is procedure.

Walker: Is there a tactical squad?

Chalmers: Six men and Hanzuk oversee the transfer to the heli—

Walker: Who?

Chalmers: Eh?

Walker: Who's overseeing the transfer?

Chalmers: Hanzuk and six—

Walker: No, not Hanzuk.

Chalmers: Yeah.

Walker: Not Hanzuk!

Chalmers: What's the matter with Hanzuk?

Walker: It was Hanzuk's shift the night Desjardins died. They say he cut his wrists with a hunk of wire screening from the light. Have you ever seen one of those cells? Hell, there's no way he could have reached it, much less pry it loose. It stinks, the whole thing. You get Hanzuk offa that squad!

Chalmers starts to exit. Gillie steps in front of him, knife extended threatening.

Walker: It's OK Gillie.

Gillie steps back allowing Chalmers to exit. Chalmers quickly makes his way to Wallace's office.

Paul exits from the inner office as Chalmers leaves the outer office.

Paul: Where's he goin'!

Walker: To . . . tell Wallace you'll come out when the helicopter sets down . . . and you want to know where you're going.

Soholuk: You hear that?

Stocker: The government's flying them out.

Soholuk: Oh shit, where am I goin'? Who took 'em?

Chalmers bursts into Wallace's office.

Chalmers: Why Hanzuk!

McGowen: He's got the seniority.

Chalmers: Oh you got to do better than that! I've been talking to Walker. You haven't been honest with me and I want to know—Why Hanzuk!

McGowen: I don't answer to you or Walker!

Chalmers: Hanzuk hates Tommy Paul. There's a chance he's responsible for Desjardins' death! A decision's been made and I want to know who made it!

Wallace: Desjardins killed himself.

Chalmers: Why did you lie to me? Tell me it was internal, then it turns out Paul has a point about Desjardins, he has a point about solitary. They're torture cells, for christ's sake, described as such by a judge!

McGowen: It's a maximum pen, we need punitive isolation.

Wallace: Ev, what we're dealing with here is things as they are, not as we'd like them to be!

McGowen: Tommy Paul is a contract killer!

Chalmers: Alright. He was convicted. He was serving his time. Does his sentence mean "time"—plus ongoing physical and mental abuse. Is that what it means?

McGowen: I don't care what it means! Look, I have a job, I come in and I do it. And right now I got thirty minutes. In thirty minutes I want them out in the yard.

Chalmers: What about Hanzuk?

McGowen: Hanzuk's a good man. He has a job. And he does it. And right now, his job is head of the squad because he's quick and he's cool and when he shoots at something he hits it.

Chalmers: *To Wallace.* I'm requesting Hanzuk be removed from the squad.

Wallace: Now what kind of an administrator would I be if I over-ruled George who knows what he's doing better than I do? Security, custodial, is his bailiwick.

Chalmers: I want Hanzuk off!

Wallace: I'm sorry.

Chalmers: Jesus. *To himself.* What can I tell them?

McGowen: You tell them in thirty minutes to start down the corridor out to the yard.

Chalmers: When's the helicopter due?

Wallace: Thirty minutes.

Chalmers: Where are they going?

Wallace: We don't know.

Chalmers: I can't give them that and you know it!

McGowen: All you got to tell them is to start for the yard.

Chalmers: Is there a plane?

Wallace: What kind of question is that?

Chalmers: You're asking too much, too much of me, too much of them! I can't do it.

McGowen: Either you send them out—or else we go in.

Chalmers: No!

McGowen: If no one comes out, there's nothin' more to talk about.

Chalmers: Is there a plane?

McGowen: Yes there's a plane! Thirty minutes!

He exits along the tier corridor. Hanzuk enters the tier corridor. They meet. Hanzuk continues along the tier corridor to take up his position at the top of the stairs. McGowen exits offstage.

Chalmers: Have you got any words for them?

Wallace: Ev, try to understand my position. If I went around countermanding orders of George, do you know what would happen? Little things would start to go wrong. Minor infractions would grow. More charges written up. If security wants it can even arrange for a riot by doing nothing more than its job. Then administration looks bad. Inefficient. Administration is me. I walk a tightrope balancing security, rehab, and inmates. It's a tricky act.

Chalmers: Is that what I tell them? Hanzuk's on the squad because Mr. Wallace can't figure how to stop juggling three balls without dropping one?

Wallace: Tell them he's off, if you have to. They won't see him. The less tension the better.

Chalmers: Lie.

Wallace: If it makes the move smoother.

Chalmers: Are you lying to me?

Wallace: Come on, we got no time for that.

Chalmers: What do you know about Desjardins?

Wallace: He bled to death. Hanzuk found him at the end of his shift.

Chalmers: Is that the truth?

Wallace: Yes.

Chalmers: Do I believe you?

Wallace: Consider the implications if you don't. . . . So? *Pause.*

Chalmers: I want your word no move will be made by the squad unless violent action is initiated by Gillie and Paul. I want your word on that.

Wallace: You've got it.

Chalmers:	What's your word worth without George's?
Wallace:	I'll speak to George. *Pause. Chalmers starts to leave.*
Wallace:	Ev? *Chalmers stops.* . . . We've cleared out all personnel, the fewer people the better, so ah . . . stay in the office until after they get to the yard.

Pause. Chalmers leaves. He walks along the tier corridor to the stairs. Hanzuk, for the first time in the play, is wearing a holster and gun. Chalmers speaks to him as he passes.

Chalmers:	Hanzuk.

Hanzuk nods. Chalmers descends the stairs, stops. Pause. Looks back at Hanzuk.

Chalmers:	I hear you were on the night Desjardins died.
Hanzuk:	Yeah . . . but when I went in, when I first went in . . . he was already bled out.
Chalmers:	Oh?
Hanzuk:	Yeah . . . He was crazy. Always screamin'. He'd drive you crazy workin' the tier. Screamin' for his mother or Louis—that was his brother. . . . I got Paul to clean the wall and the floor. You got to do it right away or it smells. You get a lot of blood and it smells.
Chalmers:	How did he manage to do it?
Hanzuk:	How the hell do I know? Top tier you'd be surprised what they do. Why I seen 'em just keep runnin' their heads into the wall till they fracture their skulls—you want to kill yourself bad enough, you'll find a way. *Pause.* You know . . . when Walker first come here, I said, you're too nice a girl to be workin' in a place like this—and she laughed, and I laughed. You can't tell from lookin' at people .
Chalmers:	Carl—is it?
Hanzuk:	Yeah. Hanzuk. Carl Hanzuk. *He extends his hand, after a momentary pause Chalmers shakes it.* Guess it's pretty hard for you to understand this place, eh?
Chalmers:	Yeah.

Hanzuk:	Look . . . scar on the cheekbone, one on the chin? They, take razor blades, stick 'em in soap, you're walkin' along, someone throws a hunk a this soap at you. You don't know who did it, could a been anyone—all I am is a screw, eh? . . . You know what they say.
Chalmers:	No.
Hanzuk:	Well a screw's someone too lazy to work, and too dumb to steal—and look at them sayin' that about you. Well, there's more to my life than this place, you betcha. This isn't my life. You know I was a cop?
Chalmers:	No.
Hanzuk:	A good cop. I got a wife. I got a daughter, she's fourteen, real pretty. I also got an unlisted phone and I keep my address real quiet. One of these bastards gets released you don't know what's in his head, what's in people's heads, what they're thinkin' inside. . . . Listen, once I was standin' in line for a movie, standin' there with my wife, and a goof on parole walked by and spit in my face! . . . You know . . . I been here for eight years, servin' time in eight hour shifts. *Pause.* Sometimes . . . when Tommy Paul goes down for a session . . . . I'm out in the hall . . . it's not that I listen, it's like . . . time has stopped. I stand there, it's real quiet, like . . . on a machine that's recorded no noise. . . . Seems like the hall is filled with that kinda silence . . . . I just stand there . . . outside a her office. . . .

Pause. Hanzuk retreats a bit up the tier corridor. Chalmers, in the landing area, drops his head, a deep breath.

Gillie:	I'm feelin' good! I'm feelin' better and better! Hooooooooeeeeee! *Chalmers, from the landing area, is aware of Gillie's yells.* You hear me, Brothers! You hear me, South Wing! You hear me, Desjardins? We're walkin' out! We're sayin' bye-byes! We are goin' . . . where're we goin'?
Paul:	Wherever we're goin', it's gonna be home.
Gillie:	Yeah, I like that. I'm gonna boogie and booze and get one of them little glass jars with an airplane inside. . . .

	Hey, smile, Deed, it's almost over.
Walker:	It's almost all over.
Gillie:	*Talking to himself.* Yeah, gonna boogie, man, gonna boogie and booze.
Paul:	You nervous? Don't be. I'll keep it right at the neck, right at the ear, but don't worry, it's for show, that's all.
Gillie:	Hey . . . hey . . . do you know this . . . do you know this, Deed? *He hums snatches of "Danny Boy."* I know it! Yeah. It just come to me. Yeah. *He hums more of it.*
Walker:	"Danny Boy."
Gillie:	No, it's my mum's song . . . I think it's her song. Sure it is . . . I remember! . . . Come on, you dance and I'll sing. *He hums "Danny Boy."*
Paul:	You wanna dance . . . come on . . . make Gillie happy, it don't cost you nothin', come on.

Walker and Paul dance as Gillie hums. In the inner office, Soholuk looks at Stocker.

Soholuk:	Your lips are movin'.
Stocker:	Oh.
Soholuk:	So stop it, eh.
Stocker:	I beg your pardon?
Soholuk:	Churchill speeches, prayers, whatever you're doin'.
Stocker:	I'm sorry I—
Soholuk:	Yeah.
Stocker:	I'm just running things through in my head.
Soholuk:	Yeah.
Stocker:	I didn't realize I was—
Soholuk:	How about we just wait it out, eh?

Pause.

Stocker:	Did you know I—

Soholuk: No I don't know, I don't wanna know, I just wanna—look, man, it's me they're gonna—just leave me alone, eh? It's not fair! Nothin's fair! You spend your whole fuckin' life tryin' . . . it's not fair!

In the landing area, Chalmers checks his watch.

Stocker: I'm sorry.

Soholuk: Ah shut up, what would you know.

Chalmers moves down the corridor and enters the outer office. Gillie catches sight of him first. He stops his humming and simply stares at him. Walker and Paul turn to see him.

Chalmers: Time to go.

Paul: *No threat, simply a statement.* You been a while.

Chalmers: I've been talking to Wallace, getting things straight. We got a few minutes. They got some kinda schedule. . . . Is Stocker OK?

Paul: Check him out, Gillie, Deed.

Gillie moves into the inner office to check Stocker. Walker starts to follow him, but stops in the doorway to listen to Chalmers and Paul.

Paul: Where're we goin'?

Chalmers: They won't release it, but they've given their word a plane's comin' in, and a transfer squad's standing by.

Paul: No destination . . . what do you think?

Chalmers: I'll walk with you out to the yard.

Walker: Why?

Chalmers: I owe it.

Paul: You don't owe me nothin', I don't owe you nothin', I'm trustin' you, that's different.

Chalmers: I know what you're sayin'.

Paul: How much time have we got?

Chalmers: 'Bout ten minutes, then we start out.

In the inner office, Gillie prods Stocker to his feet, motions Soholuk to preceed Stocker.

Walker: Tommy?

Paul: Yeah?

Walker: You gotta think about this.

Paul: It's too late to start thinkin', I done all my thinkin'.

Walker: These things you don't know.

Paul: I know this is our chance.

Soholuk is in the doorway of the inner office listening. Stocker is behind him, Gillie behind Stocker. Sometime during the scene, Wallace, in his office, will get out the bottle of scotch and pour himself a drink.

Walker: Listen Tommy, what if Hanzuk's out there, on the squad?

Paul: A course he's on the squad! He'd give his eye teeth for the squad, it don't make no difference!

Walker: Tommy—

Paul: This is it, Deed.

Walker: We gotta talk! We gotta talk now!

Paul: We're not talkin', we're doin'!

Walker: What are we doin'?

Paul: Gettin' outa here!

Walker: Then what?

Paul: Be together, you and me!

Walker: That's not gonna happen, can't you understand that!

Paul: What're you gettin' at, say it!

Walker: I—

Soholuk: What's the matter, Deed, you run outa words?

Walker: Tommy, I—

Soholuk: You wanna know something funny, Tommy? Out on the street they're all talkin' about the chance of your cuttin' our throats—well, the joke's on you, man, 'cause she took you out months ago. Sure, you're dead, man, and she's been workin' the strings. You're her model

	prisoner, don't you know, prime example of the Walker rehabilitation method.
Paul:	What are you sayin'?
Soholuk:	People like her don't love people like you.
Paul:	What's he sayin'?
Soholuk:	Go on, Deed, we're all waitin' to hear it.
Gillie:	*Shoves Stocker out of the way, grabs Soholuk, knife at the throat.* Shaddup!!
Paul:	Deed?
Walker:	What?
Paul:	Do you love me?
Pause.	
Walker:	*Softly.* No.
Paul:	What?
Walker:	No . . . I . . . do love you, Tommy, but not in the way that you think.
Paul:	You love me as what.
Walker:	I love you as . . . as a person who's been . . . fucked up, and screwed around—but that's as far as it goes.
Paul:	*Screams.* Noooooo!!

He backhands Walker across the face. She falls to the floor, having spun around with the force of his blow so that she is face down. Paul kneels beside her, grabs her hair, yanks her head back, her neck exposed. His knife goes to her throat. He freezes. Pause.

Paul:	I love you.

He releases her. She falls forward. Gillie is frightened.

Pause. Then Chalmers gently takes Paul's arm, helps him up. Walker remains on the floor.

Gillie:	Tommy?
Paul:	. . . It's . . . it's OK. . . . it's OK, Gillie . . . it's alright . . . I mean . . . I want . . . And you . . . *A gesture towards*

Joe-Norman Shaw as Tommy Paul and Anne Wright as Dede Walker in the Stratford Festival production of *One Tiger to a Hill*, Stratford, Ontario, 1990.

Courtesy of the Stratford Festival Archives

> *Chalmers not complete . . . and . . . ah . . . hey . . . you know . . . it's better this way.*

Walker: Tommy I—

Paul: Don't say nothin'! There's nothin' to say! . . . It's OK— Gillie . . . hey . . . you know . . . I feel light, light as a bird. If I were a bird I wouldn't need wings, I'd just float over the wall.

Walker: Do you really feel that?

Paul: Sure. I was worried. For you, I was worried. Now there's just Gillie and me and I . . . I . . . You . . . got a pretty face, Deed, you got a kind face.

Walker: I'll go out with you just the same, just for show.

She holds out her hand. Paul pauses before he takes it, then brusquely, in a very quick movement he grabs her hand, yanks her to her feet, drops her hand quickly.

Paul: I'm gettin' itchy feet! Time to go! Time to go, Gillie, you hear that, time to go, Chalmers!

Hanzuk is standing in the tier corridor just upstage of the stairs. He stands parallel to the wall, his left shoulder down stage, his head turned to glance over that shoulder. Although we cannot see it, his right hand holds the gun.

McGowen enters unobtrusively. He is merely a shadow at the end of the tier corridor. We might see the glow of his cigarette.

Wallace sits at his desk with a drink in his hand.

All in a soft freeze.

Chalmers: We got . . . a couple of minutes.

Paul: Coupla minutes, coupla minutes, coupla . . . hey . . . you know McIver's cafe, the all-nighter cafe 'bout four blocks east a your office?

Chalmers: On the strip.

Paul: That's the one . . . I was standin' down there—a while back and this big black caddy pulls up, I told you this, Gillie. And this big black hooker hops out, man, she's sailin', people are partin' like the Red Sea. She comes up to the all-nighter cafe, someone opens the door, she never breaks step past the booths to the back where Jerry McIver is standin'. She sails up, sticks an ice pick in his gut, turns round, back past the booths, someone opens the door, hell, it mighta been me, the car's at the curb, she steps in—and she's gone. . . . Can . . . you . . . understand that?

Chalmers: Understand what?

Paul: I'm thinkin' . . . you can die . . . and all it is is a moment. . . . You're gonna walk out with us, eh?

Chalmers: Yeah.

Paul: You don't have to do that.

Chalmers: I want to.

Paul: I suppose . . . you got a wife and kids and a house.

Chalmers: Two kids.

Paul: I know there's a life out there different from mine.

Chalmers: Tommy—

Paul: I got choices, man!

Chalmers: Yes.

Paul: Well? . . . Come on, Gillie, let's go!

The electronic sound begins faintly and grows in volume during the following scene. There are no footsteps, gates, or rattling of keys, only a whining hum.

Paul: Let's go! Let's go! Check the hall. *Gillie does so.* Come on! *To Soholuk and Stocker.*

Soholuk: Look—

Paul: *Shoves him.* You with Gillie, Deed with me.

Soholuk: *To Chalmers.* Who's out there, eh?

Gillie: Real quiet, nobody there.

Paul: *Shoving Stocker into a chair.* Sit down and stay!

Soholuk: *Back to Paul.* Tommy you—

Paul: Shaddup! *Gillie grabs Soholuk, knife at the throat.* Hold him close and tight, Gillie, keep a good space between us, OK.

Gillie: Gotcha.

Paul: OK.

The electronic sound is just discernible.

Paul: Let's do it.

Chalmers steps out of the outer office. He is followed by Paul with Deed. Gillie waits a bit before following them. He is just into the corridor, Paul with Walker about centre stage, when Paul stops.

Paul: Wait a minute.

Chalmers: What is it?

Paul: Nothin' . . . Deed? . . . Hey Gillie? *He doesn't turn to look at Gillie. Walker is still held close and tight in front of him. Chalmers has turned to look back at Paul.*

Gillie: Yeah?

Paul: I changed my mind I want you to let Frank come up here, and you bring out Stocker.

The electronic sound is clearly heard and increasing in volume.

Gillie: Eh?

Paul: It's OK. We're gonna take Stocker and Frank with us. I want Deed goin' out with Chalmers . . . no sweat, man. . . . Frank, you come up here when I let Deed go.

Gillie: *Is confused.* I let him go now?

Paul: *Turns Walker around to look at her.* Go on, Deed.

Walker moves towards Chalmers. Paul turns back to look for Frank. Hanzuk takes a step to the top of the stairs, gun aimed down the corridor.

Gillie: Now?

Electronic sound loud. Hanzuk fires once. Paul turns, sees him, screams, and runs towards him.

Walker: *Screams. Nooooo! Nooooo!*

Hanzuk fires a second shot hitting Paul who falls. Gillie has released Soholuk and crouches like a child his hands over his ears. Soholuk has darted towards the outer office. They are in a soft freeze. Walker, on seeing Paul hit, runs from Chalmers towards Paul. As she reaches him she looks up at Hanzuk to see him recovering from the recoil of the second shot, and aiming at her.

Walker: Noooo!

Hanzuk fires. Walker falls close to Paul. The electronic sound is fading and gone. Chalmers stands staring down at Paul and Walker. Silence. Chalmers speaks to the audience.

Chalmers: I remember I stood there . . . looking down . . . and I thought . . . if Paul doesn't move the blood from his jaw will run into her hair . . . but he didn't move and neither did she. . . . What were the lies? . . . Is everything lies? . . . Tomorrow . . . I said . . . I will have breakfast . . . drop . . . the kids off at school . . . on Friday . . . I'll go to the Y. . . . *He weeps.*

BLACKOUT

Generations

Brian Paul as David Nurlin in the Alberta Theatre Projects production of
Generations, Calgary, Alberta, 1980.

Courtesy of the Glenbow Museum Archives

Production History

Generations was premiered by Alberta Theatre Projects, Calgary at the Canmore Opera House, 28 October 1980.

CAST

Charlie Running Dog	*Stephen Walsh*
Old Eddy Nurlin	*Stephen Hair*
David Nurlin	*Brian Paul*
Margaret Nurlin	*Doris Chillcott*
Alfred Nurlin	*Bob Aarron*
Young Eddy Nurlin	*Ric Reid*
Bonnie	*Marlane O'Brien*
Director	*Mark Schoenberg*
Stage Manager	*Bruce Kennedy*
Designer	*Richard Roberts*

ACKNOWLEDGEMENT

With thanks to Artistic Director Douglas Risk and General Manager Lucilee Wagner of Alberta Theatre Projects who commissioned this play.

CHARACTERS

Old Eddy Nurlin: a man in his late seventies. Thirty years ago he lost part of his left hand in a threshing machine.

Alfred Nurlin: Old Eddy's son. He is about fifty-six and married to

Margaret: who is three years older than her husband.

Young Eddy: Alfred's oldest son. He is in his mid-twenties.

David: two years younger than his brother, Young Eddy. David and

Bonnie: his girlfriend, are planning to marry.

Charlie Running Dog: aged eighty-one. Time and the elements have so conditioned and eroded his skin that he looks less like a Native Canadian, and more like some outcropping of arid land. Charlie is accompanied by an ugly, mangy dog whose age, if you multiplied it by seven, would be very close to Charlie's.

In a sense, **The Land** is a character revealed by the light and shadow it throws on the Nurlin's lives. It has many faces, but Old Eddy sees it most clearly when he stands in the heat of summer or the dead of winter in his Southern Alberta back section watching the sunrise, and looking right across the expanse of Saskatchewan all the way to Winnipeg.

SETTING

There should be some sense of the omniscient presence and mythic proportion of **The Land** in the design. DSL is the kitchen of the Nurlins' "New Place" which is what they call the house built in the fifties when Alfred and Margaret were married. It has all the usual accoutrements of a kitchen. The back door of the kitchen faces SR. It opens on a back veranda or porch which runs the width of the house. There is a pump in the yard. The prairie extends as far as the eye can see. Off SL lies the Nurlins' back section which is lying fallow. Extreme SR, in reality, some distance from the "New Place," a portion of the "Old Place" can be seen. This is the original homestead; it is extremely weathered, grey, tumbled, but still standing. It has the remnants of the porch, the steps, a couple of posts. The flooring of the exterior area, that is everything outside the kitchen and porch of the "New Place," resembles the packed dirt and yellow-brown vegetation of the West.

The first light on stage after the Blackout is the cold grey light before dawn. There is a faint sound of birds, life we cannot see. That cold grey light will change to rose, then a golden glow with the rising of the red ball of sun. It is very hot and dry. During the action of the play, the sun is slowly passing overhead, the earth is turning; this is reflected subtly in the changing patterns of light and shadow.

ACT ONE

Blackout. Cold grey light before sunrise. Charlie is standing near the Old Place, his back to the audience, his hands in his pockets, looking east. The dog is beside him. They are faint figures in the dim light. Old Eddy, not fully dressed, enters the kitchen. He does not turn on a light. He fills liberally the filter basket of an automatic coffee appliance with coffee. He fills the coffee pot with water, turns on the appliance, pours the water into the top, places the pot under the filter, and leaves the kitchen.

The light is changing prior to the sun making an appearance. Charlie coughs, spits, wipes his mouth with his hand, moves to the porch of the Old Place and sits. The dog follows him and lies down. Charlie will get out paper and tobacco and roll himself a cigarette.

David enters the kitchen. He does not turn on a light. He wears only his jeans. They ride low, he has no underwear on, no shirt, socks, or shoes. David opens the fridge door, takes out a large jar which once contained mayonnaise but now contains water. David drinks from the jar, leans on the fridge, rests his forehead on the cold interior. The sun is coming up. Old Eddy enters. He is dressed and tucking in his shirt. He does up his zipper. He is aware of David and David of him, but they don't greet each other. Their silence is born of ease. David takes another drink from the mayonnaise jar.

Old Eddy:	Hard night?
David:	Uh-huh.
Old Eddy:	You stick to a good rye like I tell yuh, yuh wouldn't be so dry in the mornin's.
David:	Yeah. *He takes another swig from the jar.*
Old Eddy:	Your mother sees yuh doin' that, she'll have your head.
David:	I wish someone would take it.
Old Eddy:	Yuh want some of this brew?
David:	Uh-uh.
Old Eddy:	Put hair on your chest.
David:	I got hair on my chest—on my teeth, on my tongue.
Old Eddy:	This'll remove it.

David:	I bet.
Old Eddy:	A good strong coffee sets a man up in the mornin'.
David:	Uh-uh.
Old Eddy:	Not that weak piss your mother makes.
David:	Your coffee takes the glaze off the mugs, Grampa. God knows what it does to your stomach.
Old Eddy:	Can't be any worse than what yuh was puttin' in it last night. Yuh know I seen a list of the chemicals—was a time yuh could count on your beer bein' pure. Not any more.
David:	It's not the quality of the beer I drink, Grampa—it's the quantity.
Old Eddy:	Yuh don't listen, that's your problem. Yuh should stick to a good rye.
David:	Right. *He squelches a burp.*
Old Eddy:	Ah, when I was your age yuh never seen me pulin' about after a night out.
David:	I'm not the man you were, Grampa.
Old Eddy:	That's the truth. Yuh know why?
David:	Why?
Old Eddy:	I drunk rye. A good rye.
David:	Young Eddy drinks rye.
Old Eddy:	Don't gimme that horseshit. I know what he drinks.
David:	What does he drink?
Old Eddy:	Scotch.
David:	Scotch?
Old Eddy:	Scotch.
David:	He don't drink it here.
Old Eddy:	We don't have it here.
David:	So how do you know he drinks scotch?

Old Eddy:	I read it.
David:	You read Eddy drinks scotch?
Old Eddy:	Some kinda survey—says lawyers drink scotch, doctors, professional people.
David:	You read it in the same magazine you read about beer?
Old Eddy:	*Maclean's*.
David:	You didn't read that in *Maclean's*.
Old Eddy:	Sure I did.
David:	They don't have stuff like that in *Maclean's*.
Old Eddy:	It was in some kinda ad.
David:	We buy *Maclean's* for the ads?
Old Eddy:	I didn't know it was an ad till I read it. *He gives David a cup of coffee.*
David:	An ad for what?
Old Eddy:	Scotch.

David smiles. Old Eddy smiles.

Old Eddy:	Besides, that's what he ordered the night we ate out.
David:	Yeah?
Old Eddy:	The fancy place. After the bar-enterin' ceremony. Yuh remember. Yuh was all talkin' up a storm 'bout the magnificent salad laid out. I couldn't see it myself. Anyways, I heard him, scotch, he says, to the dinky fella takin' the order. Hell, I says to myself, I says, just goes to show yuh—some things yuh read isn't lies . . . and I ordered a rye, a good rye, and yuh, meboy, yuh ordered a beer.
David:	I heard a joke last night, Grampa.
Old Eddy:	Now your mother, she ordered a rye, your father he ordered a rye, and Bonnie, she had some kinda coloured drink in one of them wine glasses with sugar she says it was stuck 'round the rim.

David:	Grampa.
Old Eddy:	A modern drink, yuh give 'em twice as much money for half the booze . . .
David:	You wanna hear this joke, Grampa?
Old Eddy:	Fire away.
David:	How is a politician like a church bell?
Old Eddy:	Yuh tell me.
David:	One peals from the steeple—the other steals from the people!

They laugh.

Old Eddy:	Here's one for yuh—do yuh know how Canada is like a cow?
David:	How is Canada like a cow, Grampa?
Old Eddy:	Well sir—she feeds off the West—she's milked dry by Ontario—and she shits on the Maritimes! *They laugh.* Yuh get it?
David:	I get it . . . well . . . I'm goin' to bed.
Old Eddy:	It's time yuh was up.
David:	I been up, now I'm goin' to bed.
Old Eddy:	Your mother'll root yuh out.
David:	I know.

He notices Old Eddy putting on his boots.

David:	Where're you goin'?
Old Eddy:	Up to the Old Place.
David:	Oh?
Old Eddy:	Gonna speak to Charlie 'bout them blockin' the irrigation water.
David:	Shit, Grampa, that's not gonna help.
Old Eddy:	Can't hurt.
David:	Look, every farmer 'round here agreed, you agreed to

	this meetin' tonight—wait till after the meetin' to see Charlie.
Old Eddy:	We don't want trouble.
David:	We already got trouble, and it's a hell of a lot more than water, no water. And it is not gonna do a damn bit a good talkin' to Charlie!
Old Eddy:	Yeah. Well. Yuh asked where I was goin' and that's where I'm goin'. *Yuh* was goin' to bed.
David:	I'm just tryin' to tell you—
Old Eddy:	So go why don't yuh!
David:	Save what you got to say to Charlie for the meetin' tonight!
Old Eddy:	When I was your age I been up for hours!
David:	Yeah . . . well . . . you drank a good rye. *An attempt to get back on a lighter footing.*
Old Eddy:	No goddamn money for rye! No time! I was out there workin' my ass off so's I could feed a family! So yuh, meboy, yuh get the hell to bed!
David:	Grampa, I—
Old Eddy:	I may be old—I'm not stupid!
David:	OK . . . OK. *He leaves the kitchen.*
Old Eddy:	Yet. *He finishes off his coffee. Ties his boots, makes a few minor adjustments to his clothing, and to the kitchen.* Speak to whoever I goddamn well please . . . don't need . . . I'm not dead yet either! . . . Don't know what work is . . . that's their problem . . .

He exits from the kitchen out the back door. He takes in the day like a dog, subtle sniff of the air, smallest swivel of the head taking in the environment. He misses nothing. He makes his way out of the yard, and over to the Old Place. He joins Charlie. Their greeting is more a matter of inaudible grunts, almost imperceptible movements of the head, shoulders, hands, as the two of them survey their surroundings much as Old Eddy did on exiting from the house.

| **Old Eddy:** | It's the heat. *Charlie looks at him.* I said, it's the heat! |

Charlie:	It's hot.
Old Eddy:	Not hot! Heat! I said, it's the heat! Makes the wires hum, can't yuh hear it?
Charlie:	Yuh come up here to tell me that?
Old Eddy:	You're gettin' old Charlie.
Charlie:	Eighty-one.
Old Eddy:	When yuh can't hear them wires hum in the heat, means the ears are goin'. *Pause.* Your ears are goin', Charlie.
Charlie:	Yuh come up here to tell me that?
Old Eddy:	No. *Pause.*
Charlie:	So . . . yuh come up here to tell me what?
Old Eddy:	When I'm in the fields yuh know, standin' there, I'm always listenin', listenin' for the hum . . . uuummmm-mmm . . . I hear her, and I say, I say, Eddy meboy, your ears are OK. That's what I say. . . . Now my eyes is another matter.
Charlie:	My eyes are fine.
Old Eddy:	I know that. *Pause.*
Charlie:	So yuh come to say what, Mr. Nurlin?
Old Eddy:	Now why do yuh call me that? Eddy, that's my name, Old Eddy Nurlin, what's the mister for? Yuh never called me that before.
Charlie:	Yuh come to say somethin'?
Old Eddy:	I thought yuh was supposed to be a gentle, quiet people. Patient!
Charlie:	Well, today some of us is busy.
Old Eddy:	Bullshit. Yuh been standin' up here for hours, yuh think I don't know that!
Charlie:	I never said *I* was busy. . . . I been waitin' for yuh.
Old Eddy:	*Grunts an acknowledgement of this fact. Pause.*

Charlie:	And then, eighty-one yuh don't need the sleep that yuh usta.
Old Eddy:	Your dog looks dead.
Charlie:	*Doesn't quite catch it; his ears are going.* That's right. *Old Eddy looks at him.* Eighty-one's so close to bein' dead, there's not a lot a difference 'tween bein' asleep and bein' awake, eh?
Old Eddy:	I don't know.
Charlie:	What?
Old Eddy:	I said I ain't eighty-one!
Charlie:	Damn close.
Old Eddy:	Not yet.
Charlie:	You'll see.
Old Eddy:	I said your dog looks dead.
Charlie:	*Glares at Old Eddy.* Well he ain't!
Old Eddy:	I said he *looks* dead, I didn't say he *was* dead!
Charlie:	Well he ain't!
Old Eddy:	Jesus Christ.
Charlie:	You'll see.

Pause.

Old Eddy:	Have yuh got a smoke? *Charlie removes ratty hand-rolled cigarette from behind his ear, gives it to Old Eddy.* Yuh got a light . . . I say yuh got a light!

Charlie gives him a light.

Old Eddy:	Now what I want to say is why the hell are yuh holdin' back the water.
Charlie:	Not been paid.
Old Eddy:	Yuh been paid, the government has paid yuh.
Charlie:	Council says not enough.
Old Eddy:	Look, yuh got—yuh made—this arrangement with

	the government to give us irrigation water from the reserve river, ain't that right now? Eh? And yuh agreed on a certain sum a money, yuh and them. To do that. Eh?
Charlie:	Not enough.
Old Eddy:	Yuh agreed!
Charlie:	Long time ago, Mr. Nurlin.
Old Eddy:	Now don't yuh call me that! The thing is yuh agreed and now yuh cut that water off, and we're the ones that's sufferin', not the government, the farmers! Why the hell're yuh takin' it out on us?
Charlie:	You're the only ones around.
Old Eddy:	Hit the government, not us!
Charlie:	The government don't use our water.
Old Eddy:	Goddamn it, Charlie!
Charlie:	Yuh keep right on yellin'. Council says the government don't hear us yellin', maybe they hear yuh.
Old Eddy:	That's not yuh talkin'.
Charlie:	No?
Old Eddy:	No, it's them others, the young ones.
Charlie:	Yuh got 'em too.
Old Eddy:	Listen Charlie. You're eighty-one, and I'm seventy-seven. Seventy-seven. Hell, everyone we know is dead. We go back a long ways. We got things in common.
Charlie:	Some things.
Old Eddy:	Yuh and me has stood and watched the top soil as far as yuh can see lift off in one big cloud and blow ten miles east. Don't that make us somethin'? Yuh and me, we killed a bottle in Medicine Hat the night the war ended, eh? Eh? Yuh seen me bury my wife and one of my boys, no doctor, no money, nothin' but guts and gumption to get yuh through the winter, and there's nothin' as cold as a prairie winter.

Charlie:	I hear yuh.
Old Eddy:	Yuh know Old Eddy Nurlin never asked nobody for nothin'. Stand on your own two feet, do what yuh got to, to survive, to live, to make somethin' grow, to build somethin'.
Charlie:	Seventy-seven is gettin' on.
Old Eddy:	You're goddamn right it is, and I come here to ask yuh to get your people to open up the dam. Hit the government direct, not through us, Charlie. Hell, yuh know there ain't a farmer 'round here can afford to lose this crop.
Charlie:	Nobody listens to an old man.
Old Eddy:	Now that's a lie. Yuh and me know that's a lie.

Old Eddy and Charlie will prepare to walk off together. The dog remains sleeping.

Charlie:	Maybe.
Old Eddy:	I remember yuh tellin' me—old men got a lot a pull. Yuh said that—and goddamn it, Charlie, you're old!
Charlie:	I told yuh that when I was young.

Pause.

| Charlie: | And then yuh see . . . could be I agree with Council. |

Pause.

Old Eddy:	Your goddamn dog *is* dead.
Charlie:	*Grunts a command.* Come.

The dog gets up and exits with Old Eddy and Charlie. Margaret enters the kitchen. She dumps out Old Eddy's coffee, makes fresh. Makes and butters toast.

Old Eddy:	One of these days he's gonna be.
Charlie:	Maybe.
Old Eddy:	Maybe? What the hell do yuh mean, maybe? Can't live forever.
Charlie:	Maybe.

The two of them fade out, drifting out of sight. Alfred enters the kitchen. He will go out on the porch taking in the day, then return to the kitchen, and have his breakfast.

Alfred: No rain in that air.

Margaret: Not a bit. . . . You want eggs?

Alfred: Nn-nn—where's David, he up and out?

Margaret: Still in bed, I took a peek on the way down. *Alfred looks at his watch.* I know. I'll holler in a minute. . . . Did you hear him last night?

Alfred: Hadda be deaf not to, he made one hell of a racket— you didn't hear him?

Margaret: *Smiles.* I heard him.

Alfred: Back door to bedroom he hits every wall in the house, and what he does on those stairs I dunno.

Margaret: It was that organizin' meetin' last night—and then he was seein' Bonnie.

Alfred: The beer parlour figures in somewhere.

Margaret: Bonnie don't go to the beer parlour.

Alfred: Mmmmn. *Pause.*

Margaret: She's a good girl. *Alfred stirs his coffee, drinks, eats.* I don't mean because she don't go to the beer parlour, I mean she's good for David. *Pause. Alfred eats.* She's a settlin' influence, and David needs that. *Alfred concentrates on his breakfast.* Are you listenin' to me?

Alfred: What?

Margaret: Did you hear a word I said?

Alfred: About what?

Margaret: Bonnie.

Alfred: I heard. *Back to breakfast.*

Margaret: What did I say?

Alfred: She's a good girl . . . she'll settle Davey.

Margaret:	Well?
Alfred:	Well what?
Margaret:	Well do you think I'm right?
Alfred:	Could be.
Margaret:	Alfred!
Alfred:	What?
Margaret:	Now do you think I'm right?
Alfred:	I dunno.
Margaret:	One of these days, Alfred, they'll be here, right at the door after breakfast.
Alfred:	Who?
Margaret:	The men in the little white coats, they'll be takin' me right off to Ponoka and it'll be your fault. You drive me crazy, Alfred.
Alfred:	I never sit easy with her.
Margaret:	Who?
Alfred:	Bonnie.
Margaret:	*Smiles.* I know.
Alfred:	I guess it's just me. *Margaret turns on the water to rinse dishes.* How's the pressure?
Margaret:	Low.
Alfred:	It's the well, coupla more days and that'll be it.
Margaret:	She's a smart girl.
Alfred:	Do you suppose that's it?
Margaret:	No I don't suppose that's it.
Alfred:	David can't feel it else he wouldn't be marryin' her—I mean you don't marry a woman you feel uncomfortable with. *Margaret smiles.* It's hard to forget she's a school teacher. I find myself foldin' my hands. Funny thing is, I usta sit easy—maybe it's her university trainin'.

Charmion King as Margaret Nurlin and Colin Fox as Alfred Nurlin in the
Tarragon Theatre producion of *Generations*, Toronto, Ontario, 1981.

Courtesy of Tarragon Theatre

Margaret:	Don't be silly. Young Eddy's a lawyer, and you sit easy with him.
Alfred:	That's family.
Margaret:	Well someday Bonnie'll be family.
Alfred:	Soberin' thought.
Margaret:	*Laughs, leans closer to Alfred.* You give her a chance, you'll like her again, she's a nice girl.

David enters dressed.

David:	You two at it again?
Alfred:	What's that?
David:	Slap and tickle in the kitchen, you're too old for that, Mum.
Margaret:	It's your father, he leads me on.
Alfred:	You're lookin' a bit ragged this mornin', Davey.
David:	I'm feelin' fine.
Margaret:	You eat some breakfast.
Alfred:	That musta been some meetin' last night.
David:	We got a bit done.
Alfred:	You woke your mother.
David:	Sorry 'bout that.
Margaret:	Did you see Bonnie?
David:	Nope.
Margaret:	Did you call her, tell her you weren't coming?
David:	Nope.
Margaret:	Da-vid!
David:	What?
Margaret:	You could have called.
David:	That's what she'll say alright.
Margaret:	And what'll you say?

David:	I got busy, we had a lotta things to discuss with this meetin' tonight—and right now—I gotta get on over to Sneider's.
Alfred:	That Sneider's a hothead, you watch him.
David:	Y-up. *Downs his coffee to leave.*
Margaret:	You eat and run you get stomach trouble.
David:	Uh-huh.
Margaret:	Ask your father.
David:	Gotta go.
Alfred:	David! . . . David!! *David stops in the yard, Alfred follows him out.* What's this meetin' this mornin' for?
David:	. . . Alternative action.

Old Eddy returns during the following scene, he listens to Alfred and David's argument.

Alfred:	What the hell's that?
David:	That's if we don't get some answers tonight.
Alfred:	Then what?
David:	Then what're we gonna do? This time we're serious, and we're gonna impress it on 'em with some kinda action.
Alfred:	Nobody mentioned this alternative business at any meetin' I was at.
David:	Look, we got the provincial member there tonight, we got a coupla Ottawa bastards and we got the media, we got a chance to make some kinda statement, and we're gonna make it.
Alfred:	Is it gonna open the dam—is it gonna get us water!?
David:	We're not talkin' water, what the hell, water! So the crop dies in the field, we lose money—shit, we can harvest it and sell it and lose money! That's the problem and gettin' reserve river water is not gonna solve it! *To Old Eddy.* What'd Charlie say?

Old Eddy:	Nothin' he can do.
David:	What'd I tell you.

Margaret is on the porch.

Alfred:	Now you listen, Davey—none of this altern—
David:	Think about it, will you! The Indians are usin' that water 'cause it's the only thing they got—well, we got somethin' we can use too.
Alfred:	What?
David:	The product of our labour for chrissakes!
Alfred:	I'm tellin' you—
David:	*On top of Alfred's line.* What the hell's wrong with—
Margaret:	David!! That's enough! *Pause.*
David:	I'm goin' to Snide's. *He starts off.*
Margaret:	David! . . . Eddy's comin' out today . . . he called last night when you were out.
David:	Yeah.
Margaret:	Will I ask Bonnie for supper?
David:	I don't care.
Margaret:	David.
David:	Yeah, sure, ask her.
Margaret:	Speak to your father. . . .
David:	. . . Yeah . . . Dad . . . I'm sorry . . . *Alfred nods, David leaves.* Won't be long, be right back.

Sound of the pickup truck, slam of door, engine starts, the truck pulls out. Margaret, Old Eddy, and Alfred return to the kitchen.

Margaret:	Bacon and eggs, Grampa?
Old Eddy:	Too hot . . . Young Eddy's comin' out?
Margaret:	For the weekend.
Old Eddy:	Mmm . . . Yup . . . Charlie says there's nothin' he can do.

Alfred:	No surprise.
Old Eddy:	Comin' back I walked over by the slough, took a look at the section . . . lookin' parched . . . only got a coupla more days.
Alfred:	It's dry alright.
Old Eddy:	That all yuh can say?
Margaret:	What do you expect him to say?
Old Eddy:	He could get up on his hind legs and fight.
Margaret:	Now don't you start.
Old Eddy:	I give my whole life to this place, built it outa nothin', ain't nothin' here I didn't give blood for.
Margaret:	He knows that.
Old Eddy:	Costs goin' up, prices outa whack, and now, goddamn it, no water 'cause a bunch of Indians are sittin' on the dam—what the hell're we gonna do about it, Alfred?
Alfred:	Have you and Davey been talkin'? What's he got up his sleeve with this Sneider?
Old Eddy:	I don't know nothin' 'bout Sneider, and I'm not sayin' Davey's right and I'm not sayin' he's wrong. I'm sayin' we can't sit and get picked off like a duck!
Alfred:	Well it's no good goin' off half-cocked.
Old Eddy:	What do yuh know, your heart was never in this.
Margaret:	Will the two of you stop it.
Old Eddy:	I can remember, always at me he was, he was gonna do this, he was gonna do that—the only thing he was never gonna do was carry on what I started.
Margaret:	He's here, isn't he?
Old Eddy:	Not by choice.
Margaret:	How can you say that?
Old Eddy:	It was the war—it was the killin' kept him here!
Alfred:	Papa, I—

Old Eddy:	Yuh think I'm old! Yuh think I forget! Always talkin' 'bout goin' places, goin' to the coast, goin' to Calgary, goin' to university—what yuh did was go to war, and yuh come back and yuh never talked 'bout goin' nowheres again!
Alfred:	I was a kid! I grew up!
Old Eddy:	Thank God for Davey! That's all I got to say, thank God for Davey! *He exits to the porch where he sits.*
Margaret:	Alfred? . . . Alfred . . . he's worried and he's old, that's all.
Alfred:	*Hits the table.* Goddamn! *His coffee spills.*
Margaret:	Oh Alfred . . . you feel better now?
Alfred:	*Softly.* Goddamn.
Margaret:	Go on, get the cloth.
Alfred:	Goddamn place. I sometimes wonder who owns who.
Margaret:	Here, I'll do it, you get ready to go.

She cleans up the spilled coffee. Alfred exits to the rest of the house for car keys, hat, etc. David enters, hot, dusty. He carries a gas filter, his hands are oily. He sits on the steps whacking dust off his jeans with his hat, wipes his forehead with his sleeve. Old Eddy watches.

Old Eddy:	That was quick.
David:	She died before I hit the highway.
Old Eddy:	Filter?
David:	Yup. Again.
Margaret:	*From the kitchen.* That you, David?
David:	Truck died. I'm gonna cut across the back section to Sneider's, gonna walk.
Margaret:	Your dad's goin' to the feedstore and I'm goin' shoppin', you want a lift?
David:	I'll walk.

Margaret exits to the rest of the house for her purse. Alfred joins David and old Eddy outside.

Alfred:	What is it?

Alfred: What is it?

David: Gas filter.

Alfred: Again?

David: Yeah—could you pick me up one from Jacky's?

Alfred: Right.

There is the distant rumble of thunder. The three men study the sky.

Alfred: It's passin' north.

Old Eddy: We won't get a drop.

David: Do you suppose Charlie was out doin' a rain dance for you, Grampa?

Old Eddy: If he did he's out by 'bout two hundred miles.

More rumbling of thunder.

David: Listen to it.

Old Eddy: Promises, promises, nothin' but promises.

Margaret exits from the kitchen ready for shopping.

Margaret: I'll leave a note for Bonnie, and we'll see you later. You comin' Grampa?

The note she sticks to the door falls down unnoticed. Alfred exits to the car. Sounds of the door closing and the car starting up.

Old Eddy: I'll walk a ways with Davey.

Margaret: Won't be long. *She exits.*

David: Don't forget the filter! And don't let him charge you! The last one's a piece a junk!

Sound of door, the car pulls away. Pause.

David: You comin'?

Old Eddy: Part ways.

David: Let's go.

They'll walk past the Old Place and eventually exit offstage.

Old Eddy: Yuh coulda got a ride.

David: Not the way he feels about Sneider.

Old Eddy: He's right. Young Sneider's a horse's patoot.

David: *Smiles.* I know.

Old Eddy: So's his father . . . and grandfather too. All horses' patoots.

David: Well, I guess it runs in the family.

Old Eddy: It don't run, it races.

David: Watch the rut.

Old Eddy: Yuh watch the rut, I been this way lots a times, I know this way. . . . Is this heat gonna break?

David: Dunno.

Old Eddy: . . . When I was your age, I usta walk out at night, that was when Edward, be your uncle if he lived, and your gramma was still alive.

David: Yeah? How old was she, Grampa?

Old Eddy: Be twenty-four on her birthday. . . . Got a smoke? *David gives him a cigarette. Old Eddy snaps the filter off and throws it away. The two of them smoke.* Yeah . . . she never got over Young Edward, 'cause he died hard yuh see, tryin' to breathe with the whoopin' cough. She nursed him, no hospital or nothin' and she just didn't have the strength after that. . . . He was . . . I think he was six, anyways that left me and Alfred. Your gramma was one pretty woman.

David: And how old was Dad then?

Old Eddy: I think he was . . . 'bout four . . . little tyke . . . yuh forget . . . anyways I'd walk out on that bit a rise, look around, I'd say—Eddy Nurlin, she's all yours, if you can keep her.

David: And you did.

Old Eddy: And I ain't losin' her now. . . . She's all yours . . . and your father's . . . and Young Eddy's, it's a legacy.

David: . . . Eddy'll be here today.

Old Eddy: How an honest man can be a lawyer I dunno.

Pause.

David: Oh say, Grampa . . . I ah read in *Maclean's*—they found out who was mutilatin' all the cattle. You read about that, eh? About someone cuttin' off their sex organs?

Old Eddy: Who was it?

David: Trudeau—he needs more pricks for his cabinet.

Old Eddy: *Laughs.* He's got enough pricks in his cabinet.

The two of them fade, drifting off.

Sounds of a car approaching, stopping, door slams. Young Eddy enters the yard. He enters the kitchen.

Young Eddy: Mum! *He enters the rest of his house, when he returns he no longer carries his small overnight bag. He steps out on the porch. He sees the note, picks it up, reads it, puts it in his pocket, steps out into the yard.*

Young Eddy: Halllooooo!

Bonnie enters the yard behind Young Eddy.

Bonnie: *A slight imitation.* Halloo.

Young Eddy: Hi Bonnie.

Bonnie: Eddy—[*Not animosity, curiosity*] What're you doin' here?

Young Eddy: Home for the weekend—well, for the day anyway.

Bonnie: Anyone home?

Young Eddy: Nope—but Mum left you a note. *He reads it.* Says gone to town, be right back.

He passes it to her. Looks at it over her shoulder as she reads it.

Bonnie: That's what is says alright. *She looks at him and moves away.*

Young Eddy: Found it on the porch, guess it ah . . . fell . . . down. *Smiles.*

Bonnie: Mmn.

Young Eddy:	So . . . how are things?
Bonnie:	Good . . . you?
Young Eddy:	Great, things are great.
Bonnie:	That's good.
Young Eddy:	It's been a while.
Bonnie:	Yeah. . . . *Checks watch.* Well, maybe I'll—
Young Eddy:	I didn't hear you drive up.
Bonnie:	Daddy dropped me off and I walked in.
Young Eddy:	So you're stuck, eh? Can't get away on me now.
Bonnie:	*Smiles.* You never give up.
Young Eddy:	Nope. You're looking good.
Bonnie:	*Laughs.* You're such a bullshitter, you know that?
Young Eddy:	Any truth to the rumour 'bout you and Davey? . . . lemme guess—more than rumour, less than truth, right?
Bonnie:	We're thinking about it.
Young Eddy:	Well, that's one of the things about comin' home, nothing ever changes.
Bonnie:	It might seem that way when you only visit.
Young Eddy:	How's Grampa?
Bonnie:	Pickin' on your dad with your mum runnin' interference.
Young Eddy:	What'd I tell you, same as ever. And Davey?
Bonnie:	You should hear him—guess you will, eh? He goes on and on about forming one of those farmers' groups like down in the States—get on the tractor, drive to Ottawa—can't you see it, thousands of tractors roaring along the Trans-Canada.
Young Eddy:	Dave in the forward tractor, hoe in hand ready for battle!
Bonnie:	Oh boy, Eddy, get him goin' and he'll never stop.

Young Eddy: Is that what bothers you? Hell, you know what he's like, ever since he was a kid, I mean how long have you known him, Bonnie?

Bonnie: Long as I can remember—you too.

Young Eddy: He's like a big kid, that's all—a big lovable—

Bonnie: There's sides to him you don't see.

Young Eddy: He flares up, he comes down just as fast, and he's never given Mum and Dad a bit of real trouble, not like me throwing a wrench into everyone's plans by taking up law.

Bonnie: What are you here for, Eddy? *Pause.*

Young Eddy: No reason . . . missed the place I suppose.

Bonnie: That's not it.

Young Eddy: Yeah. . . . Well, what the hell—but no tellin' anyone, eh, not till I've talked to the family.

Bonnie: Somethin' big?

Young Eddy: You can tell.

Bonnie: So go on.

Young Eddy: OK. I got this chance—to join a firm—no—not join—form. A coupla guys I went to school with, they've asked me to go in with them, to form our own firm—how about that, eh?

Bonnie: Don't Bell and Waller want to keep you on?

Young Eddy: That's not it—hell, I could stay with Bell and Waller, but this other's a real opportunity.

Bonnie: So what's the problem?

Young Eddy: The problem?

Bonnie: You must be here for some reason.

Young Eddy: I live here, it's my home. I can come home for a visit, can't I?

Bonnie: Sure, do whatever you want, you always do.

Young Eddy:	Come off it, Bonnie.
Bonnie:	You're always coming home waxing eloquent about the place, the sun rises, the sun sets, ain't nature grand, hit your father up for a loan, then off you go till the next time!
Young Eddy:	That's a lie!
Bonnie:	I keep asking myself—Eddy gets to be a lawyer, Dave gets to be a farmer—how come!
Young Eddy:	That's what he wants!
Bonnie:	How do you know? Who ever asked him?
Young Eddy:	Ever since he was a kid he wanted to farm!
Bonnie:	Who says?
Young Eddy:	I remember!
Bonnie:	Do you?
Young Eddy:	What the hell are you getting at?
Bonnie:	Why should Dave bother? Why should anyone bother! The land's worth a lot but you just lose money, go into debt when you work it. Why bust your heart, it doesn't make sense! *Pause.* Daddy sold out last year and moved to the Hat and plays Bingo and . . . I mean you got out and . . . well, Dave doesn't have to stay here and farm.
Young Eddy:	No. . . . I guess not.

Pause.

Bonnie:	I'm sorry, it's just . . .
Young Eddy:	Hey, it's alright, it's OK.
Bonnie:	No, it's not.

Sound of the truck pulling in, engine running, slam of door.

David:	*Offstage.* Thanks for the lift, Snide.

Sound of the truck pulling out.

David:	See you later! *He enters the yard.* Hi Eddy! How the hell are you! Got in early, eh? What the hell, no one

	got you a beer, go on Bonnie, get a couple a beer—you want a beer, eh?
Young Eddy:	Sure. You're lookin' good.
David:	Fit as a fiddle—you want a glass—hey Bon, bring Eddy a glass!
Young Eddy:	Bottle's OK.
David:	Never mind that glass, Bonnie, but chop chop with the beer, eh? Hey, did she tell you about the meetin' tonight? Hell of a good thing you're here, we could be needin' a smart lawyer.
Young Eddy:	What're you up to?
David:	*A small slap to the ass as he takes the beer from Bonnie.* How're you're doin', sweetie?
Bonnie:	You got lost last night?
David:	I got busy.
Bonnie:	You could have called.
David:	Next time I will. Hey listen Eddy, it's gonna be a humdinger tonight—first of all we got media types, and Stocker from Edmonton, and a dingbat from Native Affairs—that's for the dam business—and then to top her all off, a coupla Liberal interpreters for national agriculture—jesuus, wanna bet when they travel west they're wearin' bullet-proof vests—and earplugs?
Bonnie:	Maybe you should try voting Liberal.
David:	Maybe they should try listening.
Bonnie:	Maybe you should run for office, Dave.
David:	Maybe you should mark papers, Bonnie. Besides we already got a budding politician in Eddy here. It's true, isn't it, all lawyers turn into politicians 'stead a pumpkins stroke a midnight on their thirty-fifth birthday? *He laughs.* Sooooo . . . *Takes a drink of his beer.* How're things?
Young Eddy:	Fine. Things are fine. *Pause.*

Bonnie:	Eddy's had a change of plans.
David:	Yeah?
Young Eddy:	*A look to Bonnie, then,* Yeah. I ah . . . I'm thinking of not joining Bell and Waller, of maybe going in with a coupla other guys, to form our own firm.
David:	Hey, that's great, Eddy.
Bonnie:	But he's got a problem. What's the problem, Eddy?
Young Eddy:	No problem. I just came home to discuss it with my family. It's a big decision. *Smiles at David.* A career decision.
Bonnie:	Sure.
David:	What's the matter with you, I said I was sorry 'bout last night.
Bonnie:	It's not that.
David:	Then what the hell is it?
Bonnie:	You make me so damn mad.
Young Eddy:	Dave!
David:	Yeah?
Young Eddy:	Are you . . . happy doing this?
David:	Doin' what?
Young Eddy:	This. Staying here.
David:	What kinda question is that?
Young Eddy:	I'm just asking, that's all.
David:	Well I'm here, aren't I?
Bonnie:	That's not the question.
David:	You keep outa this.
Bonnie:	Simple question, Dave, do you want to spend the rest of your life—
David:	What's goin' on here? Did I miss somethin'? What the hell's goin' on?

Bonnie: Oh god, you make me so mad! You work and you work and for nothing! Look at the two of you! Him looking like a bloody lawyer with the weekend off— and you looking like a Dumb Farmer! *She slams into the house.*

David: *Looks at Eddy, a small smile.* Woooo-eeeeee! *Young Eddy smiles. Pause.* She's pissed off about last night . . . things are tough for her, she's teachin' at summer school, got a real class of rowdies—all the idiots who flunked last year. She worries about things.

Young Eddy: Yeah.

David: I want her to quit, get married, we'll have kids of our own she can scream at. . . . Have a boy, eh? Call him "Youngest Eddy," eh? *Smiles.*

Young Eddy: Yeah. . . . Dave?

David: What?

Pause

Young Eddy: You wanna walk?

David: Sure.

They will walk up to the Old Place.

Young Eddy: Old Charlie still alive?

David: Oh yeah, still hangs around the Old Place, Grampa says just down from the rise is where Charlie's mother's people used to camp . . . so . . . I guess he feels like he owns it in some kinda way.

Young Eddy: You know once when I was a kid up playin' around I came on the two of them, Charlie and Grampa, drunk as skunks sittin' on a coupla loose boards up here, sittin' in the shade of the house, and arguin' like hell. Old Eddy, Grampa, was sayin' the land was like some kind of monster a man had to wrestle and fight, and it was always throwing drought and frost and I don't know what at you—and you fought away like some kind of Greek hero I guess—and Charlie was sayin' no, no, it's like a woman, you gotta woo her and win

	her. And both of them drunk as skunks. I hid in the grass and I watched them. I'd never seen the two of them together like that before.
David:	They're funny alright.
Young Eddy:	Just pass each other in the Hat, give a kind of nod and keep on going. . . . Dave?
David:	Yeah?
Young Eddy:	Do you remember the night I told Dad I didn't want to go to Olds?
David:	You were scared.
Young Eddy:	Really scared. Nobody ever said to me, "Hey, Eddy, you gotta be a farmer!" but, I don't know, I felt it was kinda expected . . . is that what you feel?

A pause. David looks at the landscape rather than at Eddy. He doesn't answer.

Young Eddy:	You remember I said, I don't want to go to Olds, I don't want to go anywhere for anything like that, I'm just not interested. . . . You remember dad sat there, he didn't say anything, he just sat there running his finger over his knuckle like he does . . . for one awful moment I thought he might be gonna cry . . . and mum said, what do you want to do, and I said I don't know, go to university. *Pause.* Dave?
David:	Yeah?
Young Eddy:	Did you ever think . . . you might want to do something else, something different from what you're doin' now? *Pause.*
David:	I know what it was I wanted to tell you—Trudeau is walkin' along the street and he sees Clark carryin' this here duck and he hollers, "Where are you goin' with that turkey?" and Clark, he says, "Look, stupid, this is not a turkey!" and Trudeau says, "I am talkin' to the duck!" *He smiles.*
Young Eddy:	Come on, Dave.

Pause.

David: *Low.* Sometimes . . . when we're eatin' . . . I . . . look at their hands, Old Eddy's and Dad's. . . . They seem big. Too big. It's like something happens to the skin and the nails when you work with your hands . . . they get—worn, you know what I mean? Dad's hands are like that, mine'll be someday. *Gives Eddy a light touch on the arm, smiles.* Yours won't.

Young Eddy: Do you feel like you want to do something else?

David: What else would I do?

Young Eddy: Anything.

David: *Laughs.* Hell, Eddy, I'm a farmer! You're lookin' at one honest-to-goodness farmer, hayseed, cowlick and all! Yaaaaahhhhhooooooooo! *He throws his cap in the air.*

BLACKOUT

ACT TWO

Scene One

Bonnie is sitting at the kitchen table, her head in her hands. David enters the yard returning from the Old Place. Bonnie hears him on the porch. She lowers her head as if she were asleep. David enters the kitchen. He pulls a chair closer to her. Sits down, lifts a strand of hair and runs his fingers down it. She does not respond. He does it again.

David: *Softly.* Hey . . . *He blows in her ear.*

Bonnie: *Muffled, without lifting her head.* Don't do that.

David: *Softly.* It's your little Davey.

Bonnie: *Muffled.* Don't be stupid. *He blows in her ear.*

Bonnie: *Muffled.* Don't.

David: You like that. *He pulls his chair closer, clasps his hands together and places them around Bonnie. Whispers.* You know what, Bonnie—I'm gonna tell you a dirty joke.

Bonnie: No!

David: *Whispers.* Yes I am.

Bonnie: *Struggles.* No!

David: Gotcha captive—and I'm gonna tell you a dirty joke . . . you ready? Okey doke, once there was this here French fella from Tadoussac, eh? Only he's in Montreal and he gets a room in the Mount Royal Hotel—but by mistake the desk clerk gives him a room in which the former occupant, a beautiful woman has died, and is laid out waitin' to be picked up. *Bonnie looks at him, groans, and puts her head back down on the table.* . . . Are you listenin' Bonnie? Anyways this fella from Tadoussac goes up to the room, opens the door, and sees this here beautiful woman lyin' on the bed apparently asleep— so god, he jumps right in there and takes advantage of the situation. And in the mornin' as he's passin' the desk, the little clerk comes runnin' up to him and says "Ah messieur, I'm terribly sorry but I gif' you the wrong room there las' night, oh you must 'ave spent a terrible night," and the French fella from Tadoussac says, "What do you mean, messieur, there was a beautiful woman in my bed, I made luf all night, she was a bit cold and passive but—" "Messieur!" says the clerk, "she was not passive, she was dead!" and the fella from Tadoussac says, "Dead? I thought she was English!" *Bonnie lifts her head and looks at him.* Doncha like that joke? *Pause. He tilts his chair back, does a John Wayne voice.* I kicked Eddy's ass all the way back to Calgary.

Bonnie: Really.

David: Isn't that what you wanted?

Bonnie: No.

David: So what do you want?

Bonnie: What's best for you.

David: Well you gotta let me decide that, Bonnie.

Bonnie: But you . . .

David: What?

Bonnie: Nothing. What did you and Eddy really do?

David: Had a talk, and I came back to tell you I was sorry.

Bonnie: About what.

David: Last night, I shoulda phoned.

Bonnie: It's not that.

David: I woulda phoned honest, but the phone in the beer parlour was br-oh! *He clasps his hand over his mouth.* Broken—

Bonnie: I knew you were there.

David: Where?

Bonnie: You! *She hits him with the tea towel. He grabs it and pulls her closer, puts his arms around her.* Where's Eddy now?

David: Strollin' 'round the estate—fallin' in a gopher hole every second step.

Bonnie:	See, you do resent it.
David:	No, you resent it, I think it's funny.
Bonnie:	Be honest.
David:	You mean now?
Bonnie:	Yes.
David:	You want to know what I'm thinking?
Bonnie:	Yes.
David:	Really thinking deep down insi—
Bonnie:	Stop it.
David:	Let's get married.
Bonnie:	Why do I put up with you?
David:	You love me.
Bonnie:	Why? That's the question.
David:	I make you laugh.
Bonnie:	No.
David:	Yup.
Bonnie:	No, you make me mad.
David:	Same thing.
Bonnie:	No.
David:	Soooo . . . yes or no.
Bonnie:	Is that a proposal?
David:	A poetic proposal—soo . . . yes or nooo.
Bonnie:	I'm not laughing.
David:	Yes or—
Bonnie:	No!
David:	Great! Where and when?
Bonnie:	I'm not laughing.
David:	Sure you are, you're wearin' a smile upside down, I can see it.

Bonnie:	Be serious.
David:	OK. . . . I wanna get married. I wanna get married soon. Let's do it, eh? *Pause.* Do you remember the first time I asked you to marry me? You said yes. You always say yes in the end. The first time I did a better job of asking, more romantic, remember? I keep askin', you keep sayin' yes, but . . . we don't seem to move on from there, do we? I'm runnin' outa ways to ask you—funny, serious, romantic . . . desperate . . .
Bonnie:	The first time was in grade two, and I had a crush on Eddy.
David:	I wasn't countin' that time.
Bonnie:	Sometimes I wonder if that's what you see in me.
David:	What do you mean?
Bonnie:	That I liked Eddy, that Eddy and I—
David:	You be serious.
Bonnie:	What do you see in me, Davey?
David:	I always knew I was gonna marry you, that's all.
Bonnie:	Is it? . . . Well . . . maybe—that's what bothers me.
David:	What do you want me to say?
Bonnie:	I want you to look at yourself! You're not stupid, you're not insensitive to things but . . . it's like all your choices have been made for you and . . . sometimes you rant about this or that, but you keep right on going! You never ask why am I doing this, do I really want to do this! You ask how to do it, when to do it, and where to do it, you never ask why!
David:	I wanna marry you because I love you!
Bonnie:	I'm talking about a lot more than that! That's only part of it!

Pause. David gets a beer from the fridge and opens it.

Bonnie:	*Without anger, a simple statement.* You drink too much beer.

David is not angered by Bonnie's statement. He accepts it. He exits from the kitchen to the yard and takes a drink of his beer. After a moment Bonnie follows him out.

Bonnie: I love you Davey. I just want us to be happy.

Pause.

David: I . . . I dunno . . . I . . . I do resent Eddy comin' in and . . . he's my brother, I love him.

Bonnie: But don't you see, that doesn't mean you can't tell him how you feel.

David: I love this place.

Bonnie: You're tied to it, Davey, do you want to be?

David: I . . . I dunno.

Bonnie: Think about it.

David: Someone has to be.

Bonnie: Not if they don't want to be.

David: So what would they do if I wasn't here?

Bonnie: I don't know. . . . I guess they'd eventually sell it.

David: Oh for chrissake.

Bonnie: David—

David: This is my place, I belong here.

Bonnie: Only if you choose, David, it's not yours if someone else chooses for you.

David: Well maybe I chose it!

Bonnie: You should know if that's so.

David: I chose you, whether you think so or not!

Bonnie: Oh I can see what it is, I can see it so plain.

David: Now what the hell're you talkin' about?

Bonnie: It's all because of Old Eddy.

David: Shit, Bonnie.

Bonnie: He'd do anything for this place.

David:	He paid for it with his own flesh and blood. I won't have you sayin' anything 'bout Grampa.
Bonnie:	And now you're gonna pay, why can't you see that? You're gonna serve in Old Eddy's place when he dies—in Young Eddy's place—and our kids would be expected to do the same! I don't want that—this country uses people up and wears them out and throws them away! I saw it happen to my mum and dad, and it's not gonna happen to me!
David:	Your old man is a quitter, he gave up!
Bonnie:	And no one can say that of the Nurlins!
David:	You're damn right!
Bonnie:	Old Eddy Nurlin! He sacrificed his wife and his sons and now he'll sacrifice you to this bloody place! And you know it! And you're goin' right along with it! *Pause. She starts out of the yard.*
David:	You love me!
Bonnie:	Well sometimes love isn't enough! *She exits.*
David:	That's a lie!

After a moment he sits on the porch to finish his beer.

Old Eddy and Young Eddy enter by the Old Place. They each have a blade of grass. Old Eddy blows on his, producing a whistle clear and pure. Young Eddy keeps trying but only produces an abortive raspberry sound. He laughs.

Young Eddy:	I just can't do it . . . show me again . . . I used to be able.
Old Eddy:	Well now, it's as if you're gonna whistle, but yuh put your hands like this, and it's between 'em like that, and then what yuh do is . . . *He produces the whistle sound, Young Eddy another raspberry.* Not like that—like this. *Old Eddy a whistle, Young Eddy a raspberry.*
Old Eddy:	Well . . . some people got a talent, and some people don't.
Young Eddy:	You're right there.

As they settle for a sit at the Old Place, there is the sound of the car pulling in. While Old Eddy and Young Eddy continue their scene, David goes off to meet the car. Engine stops, slam of car doors. Margaret, Alfred and David enter with groceries. Alfred will toss the new gas filter to David, the two of them will exit from the kitchen into the yard and offstage, Margaret puts a few groceries away, then disappears into the house with toilet paper, tissue type items.

Old Eddy: Got a smoke?

Young Eddy: Nope.

Old Eddy: Oh. *Pause.* What's the time?

Young Eddy: I dunno. . . . Gettin' on.

Old Eddy: Where's your watch?

Young Eddy: I broke the crystal, it's in gettin' fixed.

Old Eddy: Oh . . . gotta keep an eye on the time, it can get away on yuh, and yuh know your mother, she ain't changed a bit.

Young Eddy: *Smiles.* I know.

Old Eddy: If your mother's got a fault, it's that she hates to keep a meal waitin', she won't have it.

Young Eddy: We got lots of time, Grampa.

Old Eddy: I been up here before and the time's got away.

Young Eddy: I was tellin' Davey . . . once I came up here to play, and I found you and Charlie ravin' on . . . I hid in the grass.

Old Eddy: Into our cups, were we?

Young Eddy: You could say that alright.

Old Eddy: The English say it's bad form to let a man drink alone—in that way me and Charlie thinks like the English.

Young Eddy: Did you often do that, you and Charlie?

Old Eddy: Hell no . . . only once in a while. Be more like today, yuh and me comin' on one another . . . I'd be out, he'd be out, sometimes we'd just stop a while together, sit on the steps, compare notes so to speak.

Young Eddy: I guess you're pretty good friends, eh?

Old Eddy: Who? Charlie and me? Hell no! He's an Indian!

Young Eddy: *Laughs.* Well, what are you then?

Old Eddy: I dunno . . . he's so goddamn old . . . and I'm gettin' there . . . the two of us has just been around the same place so long, if yuh know what I mean.

Young Eddy: You sure it's nothin' more than that, Grampa?

Old Eddy: It's like . . . well, like the night the war was ended, '45. I was goin' into the Hat with a bottle, gonna do some celebratin' for Alfred comin' through it alright—he'd be back, he'd be home—anyways I run into Charlie with his thumb stuck out on the highway. Come on, Charlie, I says, and he comes. I'm tellin' yuh we had a good time singin' and actin' foolish, and at the end of her all, I says we'll have another go when the boys get back 'cause Charlie's boy, he had gone too . . . and Charlie, he don't say nothin', we was just standin' there . . . *Laughs.* I think we was takin' a piss. . . . On the way home he tells me . . . Italy, four weeks before, at least that's what he heard, that's what they told him. . . . His boy wasn't comin' back, killed he was, right there in the Northern part of Italy, that's what they told Charlie . . .

Young Eddy: But you aren't friends.

Old Eddy: Hell no. . . . He knew the name of the town once, but a course he can't remember it now. He's gettin' old and the memory goes.

Young Eddy: I guess so.

Old Eddy: Thank god my own upper story's still there. . . . Course he's older than me. . . . Gimme a hand, I can't spring to like I usta. *Young Eddy helps him up.* The legs is the first to go.

Young Eddy: I never think of you as old, Grampa, you always seem the same.

Old Eddy: That's a hell of a thing to say to a man.

Young Eddy:	You've got a lot to be proud of, Grampa.
Old Eddy:	I know it.
Young Eddy:	Hey, Grampa.
Old Eddy:	What?
Young Eddy:	I . . . ah . . .
Old Eddy:	What?
Young Eddy:	There was something I wanted to ask you, something . . . important I wanted to talk about.
Old Eddy:	Well, I'm here, I'm listenin'.
Young Eddy:	Yeah . . . *Pause.*
Old Eddy:	Say Eddy, you like doin' this lawyer bit?
Young Eddy:	Yes I do, Grampa.
Old Eddy:	Well yuh know what I always say.
Young Eddy:	What?
Old Eddy:	A family can't accommodate one foolish bastard in it ain't worth a pinch a coon shit . . . long as the centre holds. And this here's the centre. Right here.
Young Eddy:	Yeah.
Old Eddy:	I though yuh was gonna ask me somethin'.
Young Eddy:	It'll keep.
Old Eddy:	Then what the hell're we waitin' for?
Young Eddy:	I dunno.
Old Eddy:	Your mother'll be hoppin'. Let's go . . . watch the rut.

As they walk down from the Old Place, Young Eddy blows on the blade of grass again. This time he gets a nice clear whistle from it.

Old Eddy:	Now yuh got it, now yuh got it, like this.

Both Eddys whistle back and forth on the grass. Alfred enters the yard with a pail. He begins to pump with no results.

Alfred:	Come on you beggar, don't go dry on us now. . . . You're early.

Young Eddy:	Got away early.
Alfred:	Good to see you.
Young Eddy:	Me too.
Alfred:	Real scorcher, eh, good to be outa the city.
Young Eddy:	Here, let me. *He takes over the pumping.*
Old Eddy:	Tap dry?
Alfred:	Thought I'd check it out.
Young Eddy:	You think there's anything down there?
Old Eddy:	There's water alright.
Young Eddy:	Here she comes, lots of water, just a matter of gettin' it up.
Old Eddy:	Question is, will there be water tomorrow.
Alfred:	That's good, I'll take it from there.

He takes the pail of water and exits.

Old Eddy:	She'll be dry tomorrow. *He and Young Eddy enter the kitchen.*
Young Eddy:	You want a glass of water? *Gets the glass out. Margaret bustles in to embrace Young Eddy.*
Margaret:	There you are! Oh Eddy! I got chicken, made a ton of potato salad, pie for you, lots of cold things.
Young Eddy:	Sounds great, Mom.
Old Eddy:	Say Eddy—what's your drink—when you're not drinkin' water?
Young Eddy:	Eh?
Old Eddy:	Do yuh drink a good . . . scotch?
Margaret:	Right now he'll have iced tea.
Old Eddy:	Scotch is it, Eddy?
Young Eddy:	Sometimes.
Old Eddy:	Would yuh say—most of the time?

Young Eddy: You could I suppose.

Old Eddy smiles a private smile.

Margaret: Tea, Grampa?

Old Eddy: Eh?

Margaret: You want tea?

Old Eddy: Tea?

Margaret: Iced tea.

Old Eddy: Proper tea.

Margaret: Do you want some?

Old Eddy: Is it on?

Margaret: I'll put it on.

Old Eddy: It's too hot for tea. . . . I think . . . I'll have me a lay-down . . . catch a coupla winks . . . have a lay-down. . . . *He exits into the rest of the house.*

Young Eddy: He's lookin' good.

Alfred enters.

Margaret: Tea, Alfred? I know. *She gets him a beer.* How about you Eddy?

Young Eddy: Tea's good. Iced tea.

Margaret: He's funny, isn't he. But you know most days he's fine, grabs a coupla winks in the afternoon and—well, you saw him—always out, always goin' somewhere.

Alfred: Get him and Dave onto politics, and look out.

Margaret: Always at your father, come on Alfred do this, come on Alfred do that. And if it weren't for your father injectin' a bit of common sense every once in a while, I don't know where we'd be. Oh Eddy! *She embraces him.* It's good to see you, Eddy.

Young Eddy: You too, Mum.

Margaret: Yes it is. *She holds him at arm's length looking at*

> *him. . . . Well . . . Would the two of you get out of here? I got work to do!*

The two men move to the porch. Margaret works in the kitchen but doesn't miss a word through the screen door.

Alfred: You have a visit with Dave?

Young Eddy: Yeah, we were talkin' a bit.

Alfred: That's good.

Young Eddy: Do you suppose he likes farming?

Alfred: Who?

Young Eddy: Dave.

Alfred: Ever since he was little—like some kids and firemen.

Young Eddy: I guess so.

Alfred: Why do you ask?

Young Eddy: Just . . . wonderin'.

Margaret: What're you saying?

Young Eddy: Nothing. . . . I was just thinking . . . we got this place, and it's pretty big. What would you do if nobody wanted to keep on?

Margaret: What do you mean?

Alfred: David does.

Young Eddy: I know. I was just wondering.

Margaret goes back to preparing the meal. Pause.

Young Eddy: Dad?

Alfred: Mmn.

Young Eddy: What do you suppose Grampa would've said if you'd told him you weren't gonna farm?

Alfred: He'd of said I was crazy.

Young Eddy: A course it would've been different for you, I mean than it was for me. There was no one else to carry on but you, your brother had died.

Alfred: That's right.

Margaret drifts back to the door to listen.

Young Eddy: There was only Grampa and you.

Alfred: That's right . . . we lived in the Old Place, him and me . . . then, when your mother and me married, we built this place.

Margaret: *Coming out on the porch with a bowl of food.* Your father took me out on a blind date, Eddy, first time he came home on leave. He didn't know it, but I set my cap for him. Some day same thing'll happen to you.

Young Eddy: *Smiles.* You think so?

Margaret: Oh yes, some lucky girl is gonna snatch you right up. This bachelor state is just an interim state. . . . We went out . . . how many years, Alfred?

Alfred: . . . Married in '53.

Margaret: Well, I guess it depends if you count that first date. You know I knit him every pattern in the beehive knittin' book, didn't I, Alfred? I was makin' myself indispensable. I knit argyle socks, stripes, curlin' rocks, golf clubs, diamonds, heads a horses, sheaves a wheat—then I moved into sleeveless pullovers and started again: argyles, stripes, curlin' rocks . . . *Gives Alfred a bit of the food.* . . . Too much salt?

Alfred: Mm-mm.

Margaret: And you know what it took? In '52 Old Eddy lost part of his hand in the threshin' machine, and the next thing—your father is doin' some serious courtin'! *Teasing* . . . Eddy, I think your father married me so I could do what Old Eddy with one hand couldn't do. I mean, all that knittin' had proved I was nimble and I persevered, an important thing on a farm. Isn't that right, Alfred?

She smiles at him. There is a warm feeling between them whether her reasoning is correct or not. He puts his arm around her.

Alfred: You know Eddy, beside the bed your mother's got a whole library a Harlequin romances all written by women with unlikely names—and have they got a lot to answer for.

Margaret shoves another spoonful in his mouth.

Margaret: Not enough salt?

Alfred: Just right.

Margaret returns to the kitchen where she will add more salt.

Margaret: One of these weekends, Eddy, you'll bring a friend home, a female friend.

Young Eddy: Maybe. . . . I guess what I was tryin' to say was . . . do you think you'd have had a right to your own life if you hadn't wanted to farm—to do what you wanted. If you hadn't wanted to be part of all this.

Alfred: I dunno.

Young Eddy: Like me, in a way.

Alfred: I dunno.

Margaret: Your father's always done what he wanted, haven't you, Alfred?

Young Eddy: I was thinking of Davey.

Pause.

Margaret: But . . . David loves the place, maybe loves it too much. Why do you talk about Davey?

Young Eddy: No reason.

Faint ring of phone. Margaret goes to answer it.

Young Eddy: Dad? I had a special reason for coming out this weekend.

Alfred: Oh?

Young Eddy: I wanted to talk to you about something important.

Alfred: I'm listenin'.

Young Eddy: It's ah . . . it's this. You know how excited I was when I got taken on by Bell and Waller?

Alfred: Can't forget that.

Young Eddy: We talked about it being a great opportunity and all that. You remember how I went on, eh?

Alfred: I remember.

Young Eddy: There was the possibility of them asking me to stay on when the year was up, after my bar exams.

Alfred: Uh-huh.

Young Eddy: Well, that's what's happened, they've asked me to stay on.

Alfred: That's wonderful, Eddy.

Young Eddy: Yeah.

Pause.

Alfred: What's the trouble?

Young Eddy: Well . . .

Alfred: Isn't that what you wanted?

Young Eddy: I know how much you've done, how much everyone's done.

Alfred: You don't want to keep on?

Young Eddy: But I want to be fair—to you and—to David.

Alfred: Just say what you have to.

Young Eddy: OK . . . I got this chance to buy into a firm. I want to do it but I need money and I don't have that kind of cash. What I want to ask is—can you help me?

Alfred: Ready cash.

Young Eddy: That's right.

Alfred: That's . . . hard for us to come by right now . . . you know it's tied up.

Young Eddy: Some day you'd be leaving me something—and the way I see it right now's when I need it.

Alfred: But I—

Young Eddy: Can you understand that?

Alfred: I—

Young Eddy: Maybe you can't.

Alfred: I know how you feel.

Young Eddy: No you don't.

Alfred: Right now's a bad time, that's all.

Young Eddy: Look, if Dave weren't to keep on, wouldn't that change things?

Alfred: But he is.

Young Eddy: We could sell a section, what about that?

Alfred: Sell?

Young Eddy: Only a section.

Alfred: No!

Young Eddy: Why not?

Alfred: We can't do that!

Young Eddy: Why not?

Alfred: It wouldn't be right!

Young Eddy: What the hell do you mean, it wouldn't be right?

Alfred: Be stupid to sell anything now.

Young Eddy: But now's when I need it.

Alfred: Who do you think's gonna buy it?

Young Eddy: Hell, the way the Hat's gonna grow, anyone might!

Alfred: No!

Young Eddy: It's what I want to do! It's important!

Alfred: No!

Young Eddy: Look, I'm not like you! . . . This opportunity's the most important thing in my life. . . . This place might've been alright for you and for Grampa, but it's not the same thing for us.

Alfred: Who are you talkin' about?

Young Eddy: Me—and David too maybe. You should think about that—I love the place but, hell, it's not my whole life. Nor his.

Alfred: Davey can speak for himself.

Young Eddy: I don't want to fight. I don't want to argue. I just want you to try and understand . . . if you just sold a section.

Margaret: *At the doorway.* What is it?

Young Eddy: . . . Nothin', mum. Tell you later. . . . One good thing about a bachelor, they're real handy in the kitchen so put me to work. Must be something I can do.

Margaret: *As the two of them exit to the rest of the house.* You can help me in the dinin' room.

Young Eddy: Okey doke.

Alfred stands in the yard looking towards the horizon. Sound of the truck pulling into the yard. David enters. Approaches his father. Looks in the same direction as his father, looks at his father, back at the horizon.

David: What do you see?

Alfred: Nothin'.

David: What do you wanna see?

Alfred: Nothin'.

David: Well, that's what you're seein'.

Alfred: Thinkin'.

David: Oh . . . Does it help?

Alfred: What?

David: Lookin' at nothin'. *Alfred looks at him.* In case I should want to do some thinkin' some day. *Gives his father a playful punch on the arm and starts for the house.*

Alfred: Dave?

David: Yeah.

Alfred: Did you . . . catch up with Bonnie?

David: I checked out the hall for tonight.

Stephen Ouimette as David Nurlin and Colin Fox as Alfred Nurlin in the Tarragon Theatre production of *Generations*, Toronto, Ontario, 1981.

Courtesy of Tarragon Theatre

Alfred:	Truck runnin' OK?
David:	More bother than it's worth—Snide's got one he's willin' to sell, you should take a look at it.
Alfred:	What's that Sneider got up his sleeve?
David:	He's dry—and he's startin' to hurt. No different than us. Maybe this time we plan to do somethin' about it.
Alfred:	To do what?
David:	Look we been carryin' the East on our back for so god-damn long they think we're the horse and they're the rider. Now you can't tell me that isn't so?
Alfred:	What're these plans?
David:	Don't worry, I know what I'm doin'.
Alfred:	You watch—
David:	Sneider, he's a hothead, yup got it, will do. *On his way into the house.*
Alfred:	Davey?
David:	Ah-huh.
Alfred:	I was talkin' to Eddy.
David:	Yeah?
Alfred:	He was talkin' about this firm thing. Have you heard about that?
David:	Yeah.
Alfred:	He mentioned it, eh?
David:	Yeah, it came up.
Alfred:	I was wonderin' how you felt about that.
David:	What's to feel about?
Alfred:	Well, I wouldn't feel right movin' on my own.
David:	Yeah?
Alfred:	Do you think I should go over to the bank or should—

David:	The bank—what for?
Alfred:	Well he needs cash and—
David:	Cash?
Alfred:	You didn't talk about that?
David:	Where the hell're we gonna get cash?
Alfred:	The bank or—
David:	What?
Alfred:	He's talkin about sellin' a piece.
David:	Sellin' a piece?
Alfred:	He says—
David:	Shit, why don't we just burn it! Let her go in one big swoop! *Pause.* I'm sorry . . . spend my whole life sayin' I'm sorry . . . it's just, I dunno, I feel we oughta be doin' better—why aren't we?
Alfred:	We do alright.
David:	We just get by every year. Some years are better, some years are worse but it's always something. How can you spend your whole life like that, and then say we do alright?
Alfred:	I got two fine boys and we've never gone hungry.
David:	That's not what I'm talkin' about—two fine boys and never gone hungry—what's that got to do with the price of farm machinery or crop insurance?
Alfred:	What're you sayin'? Are you sayin' you think we should quit?
David:	No!
Alfred:	Then what're you sayin'?
David:	I don't know what I'm sayin'! . . . I'm sayin' . . . we gotta remember one thing . . . my grampa came over in the hold of a ship in 1908 . . . and he worked his butt off from the time he was seven . . . and we got something worthwhile here!

Alfred:	But—if, someday, you weren't to keep on, there'd be no reason to keep it together.
David:	Now what're you sayin'?
Alfred:	. . . It hardly seems fair to Eddy if—
David:	Fair? You wanna talk fair! What's fair about Eddy and the whole fuckin' city sittin' drinkin' scotch and feedin' their faces while we bust our ass to put food on their tables! Two-thirds of the goddamn world dies of starvation and the farmer's low man on the totem pole! You wanna talk fair!
Alfred:	That's the way things are!
David:	I don't like it!
Alfred:	You can't change it!
David:	Who says I can't change it!
Alfred:	Davey—
David:	This time you're gonna tell Eddy no.
Alfred:	I know I give in to Eddy. I know that.
David:	Not this time. We're not sellin' a piece and we're not takin' no more loans out for Eddy.
Alfred:	I see myself in Eddy, him doin' things I mighta done, but—
David:	You say No!
Alfred:	I wanna ask you a question, Davey, and I want a straight answer.
David:	What the hell is it now?
Alfred:	Do you feel stuck here, Davey? Do you hate this place?
David:	Do you?
Alfred:	Not any more.
David:	I don't believe that.
Alfred:	What?

David:	That you ever hated the place. I don't believe that.
Alfred:	I'm talkin' about you. What're your plans?
David:	There's a meetin' tonight. I'll be at it!
Alfred:	Long-range plans.
David:	Jesus christ, is everyone gonna ask me that question today?
Alfred:	Do you think you'll be farmin' after Grampa dies?
David:	Who put that idea into your head?
Alfred:	I'm only askin'.
David:	Was it Eddy?
Alfred:	A straight answer, Davey.
David:	It was wasn't it? And wouldn't that suit him just fine eh? Whole place is gonna go anyways, we may as well start sellin' her now—sure, gets Eddy his money and everything!
Alfred:	I'm thinkin' about you, what you want!
David:	Bullshit! *He starts for the house.* Eddy! Eddy!
Alfred:	*Following him.* Davey.
David:	*Enters the kitchen.* Eddy!

Young Eddy, Margaret following him, meets David in the kitchen.

David:	I want you to listen and I want you to listen real good! See! I'm here! I'm stayin' here! And you can take your goddamn law firm and shove it!
Margaret:	Davey—
David:	This's between Eddy and me! *To Eddy.* You got that!
Young Eddy:	Hey look Dave—
David:	You got it? I don't wanna hear any more of this maybe Davey wants to do that, maybe Davey wants to do this shit—I don't want you talkin' to no one about that!
Young Eddy:	I was only trying to—

Old Eddy enters the kitchen.

David: It'd work out just right for you, wouldn't it?

Young Eddy: Look, I—

David: You don't give a shit for this place!

Young Eddy: That's not true!

David: Sure, sell a piece here, sell a piece there!

Old Eddy: Nobody's sellin' nothin'! What the hell're yuh talkin' 'bout?

David: That's right! Nobody's sellin' nothin'!

Old Eddy: What the hell's goin' on?

Pause.

Young Eddy: I got a chance to form a company, Grampa, my own company. *Pause.*

Old Eddy: Go on.

Young Eddy: I asked Dad if he could raise some cash; I need some cash, Grampa.

Old Eddy: Alfred? *Pause.*

Young Eddy: I feel the way you do about the place, Grampa . . . it . . . just seemed the easiest way . . . to sell a parcel of land, that's all.

Old Eddy stares at Young Eddy. His gaze moves to Alfred. He looks away from both of them. He blinks his eyes several times and then exits from the kitchen. He slowly starts out of the yard. Alfred moves to follow Old Eddy.

David: *Stops him brusquely.* No!

David follows Old Eddy. The rest of the family remain in the kitchen motionless. They say nothing. Old Eddy, after walking a piece, stands alone studying the horizon. David joins him. After a moment David lowers his head. Old Eddy turns to look at him. Pause.

Old Eddy: What the hell's wrong with yuh?

David: I got somethin' caught in my throat.

Pause.

Old Eddy: Yuh wanna hear a joke?

David shakes his head no.

Old Eddy: I asked yuh if yuh wanna hear a joke!

David lifts his head to look at his grandfather.

Old Eddy: . . . It goes like this. *Pause* . . . It's not too good a joke . . . but it's the only one I can remember right now . . . *A rather long pause.*

David: Grampa?

Old Eddy: What. *Pause.*

David: Some people say there ain't no hell. If they've never farmed how can they tell? *Pause.*

Old Eddy: What's that supposed to be?

David: It's a quotation from *Reader's Digest.*

Old Eddy: Who said it?

David: Anonymous.

Old Eddy: They quote him a lot.

David: *Smiles.* That's a joke, Grampa.

Old Eddy: I know . . . I made it. *Pause. He studies the landscape, he looks at David.* You wanna walk . . . no talkin', just walk. *David nods.* Alright then. Let's walk.

They exit offstage.

BLACKOUT

ACT TWO

Scene Two

Later the same day. Although it is not yet dark outside, the exterior has an evening shade. The kitchen light is on. Some empty dishes sit about. Young Eddy, Alfred, Margaret and Bonnie have just finished eating in the dining room. A soft murmur from Alfred and Young Eddy can be heard from that room as Margaret and Bonnie enter the kitchen carrying dishes.

Margaret:	You stay and chat, Bonnie, I'll do this.
Bonnie:	That's alright—what'll I do with the leftovers?
Margaret:	Stick 'em in the fridge. Davey'll be hungry when he gets back, Grampa too.
Bonnie:	Not like either of them to miss a meal.
Margaret:	No.
Young Eddy:	*Off.* You're not doin' dishes now, are you?
Margaret:	We're just gonna stack 'em.
Young Eddy:	*Pokes his head in the door.* Make sure that's all you do.
Margaret:	You and your father get ready, we're runnin' late here.
Young Eddy:	*Offstage.* She says to get ready.
Alfred:	*Pokes his head in the door.* What about Davey and Pa?
Margaret:	Can't afford to wait any longer—the meetin'll be over 'fore we get there, now you get a move on.
Alfred:	What about you?
Margaret:	It'll take me no time at all, but you change those pants and your white shirt's hangin' in the closet. Get goin' the two of you! . . . I don't know where they'd be without me proddin' them on.
Bonnie:	Don't you ever get tired of it?
Margaret:	Of what?
Bonnie:	Prodding them on. *Margaret looks at Bonnie, doesn't*

reply to the question. The two of them clean up for a bit.

Margaret: Now—you sit down and have a coffee, I'll finish up, I know where it goes.

Bonnie: You're always busy.

Margaret: Got a lot to do.

Bonnie: You're always . . .

Margaret: What?

Bonnie: Nothing.

Margaret: Did you and Davey straighten out last night?

Bonnie: Oh . . .

Margaret: He's a good boy, Bonnie, you just got to have patience.

Bonnie: He's not a boy.

Margaret: They're all boys at heart. That's why they need proddin' and managin' and someone seein' to things.

Bonnie: I don't believe that.

Margaret: It's got nothin' to do with *believin'*. It just *is*.

Bonnie: No.

Margaret: You'll see.

Bonnie: Why weren't they at supper? *Pause. Margaret gives no indication she has heard her, almost a pointed ignoring.* Because of Young Eddy?

Margaret: No . . . no, they just got . . . busy somewhere.

Bonnie: What about Eddy? . . . He needs money, doesn't he? . . . Does he want to sell?

Margaret: Well, I . . . it's something we have to talk about.

Bonnie: We?

Margaret: Alfred and I.

Bonnie: What do you think? You must have some opinion on the subject. When you sit down to talk, you and

	Alfred, what're you going to say?
Margaret:	I don't know.
Bonnie:	I know. You're going to agree with whatever Alfred says. No matter how you feel you're going to agree with whatever the "men" in the family decide.
Margaret:	I often do.
Bonnie:	You always do. I've never seen you once disagree— how do you do that?
Margaret:	Do what?
Bonnie:	Always be here . . . cooking and cleaning and agreeing . . . how do you do that? Don't you get tired of doing that? *Pause.* I . . . could never do that, you see. I could never . . . I don't want to do that.
Margaret:	You just don't know your own mind.
Bonnie:	At least I have one . . . I didn't mean that.
Margaret:	Oh . . . you probably did . . . I always thought . . . we liked one another.
Bonnie:	We do.
Margaret:	I suppose you see me . . . in a very particular way.
Bonnie:	I admire you, I—
Margaret:	Do you?
Bonnie:	No . . . I don't. I . . . marvel at you . . . I don't admire you. I marvel at . . . how you can submerge yourself in all this. Be nothing but . . . an extension of this. . . . I would not want that to happen to me.
Margaret:	I don't feel *submerged*—I am *tired* on occasion.
Bonnie:	I'm afraid of that happening to me.
Margaret:	Why?
Bonnie:	Why? . . . Because . . . I don't want . . . to lose *myself*.
Margaret:	Lose *yourself*? Lose yourself. . . . And what would you know about loss? . . . It's true I might not have a mind, but I do have a memory, and I remember the thirties. I

remember us all huddled 'round the radio hopin' for somethin' to get us through the next day, and what did we get? Bennett babblin' about managin' money, when none of us had any money to manage. Oh yes, the Nurlins were lucky, they hung on to this place but some of us, we weren't so lucky. . . . My father, first he lost his livestock, then his faith, and in the end the bank took what was left, so we moved to the Hat and lived hand-to-mouth, god knows how. . . . When I met Alfred Nurlin, and he asked me to marry him, I knew I had a chance to be part of something again. . . . And you talk about losin' yourself? Are you so special, so fine, so wonderful, there's nothin' bigger worth bein' part of? . . . Good. . . . You be whole then, be complete, be self-sufficient. And you'll be alone. And in the end, you'll be lonely.

Bonnie: There's worse things than lonely.

Margaret: Are there?

Bonnie: Yes.

Margaret: I don't know what *they* are.

Young Eddy: *Enters the kitchen.* You ready?

Margaret nods and exits from the kitchen. Young Eddy scrutinizes Bonnie who looks down at the pan which is in front of her on the table. She looks up at Eddy.

Bonnie: Pineapple squares.

Young Eddy: She makes 'em every time I come home.

Bonnie: Yes she does. *She gets up and puts them away in the fridge.*

Young Eddy: What's the matter?

Bonnie: . . . Do you ever feel guilty about leaving the farm?

Young Eddy: . . . No.

Bonnie: Do you ever feel guilty about asking them to sell?

Young Eddy: . . . No. *Pause.* Are you sure you don't want to come to this hoohah?

Bonnie: Yeah.

Young Eddy:	I'm just gonna pop in and pop out—Nurlin solidarity, eh? Are you gonna be here when I get back?
Bonnie:	I don't know.
Young Eddy:	I might not see you before I leave then.
Bonnie:	Maybe not.
Young Eddy:	You got my number in Calgary though, in case you get in? I gave it to you, didn't I?
Bonnie:	Yeah.
Young Eddy:	Don't lose it.

Alfred enters the kitchen. He stops with a look to Young Eddy and Bonnie sensing a certain something in the atmosphere. A pause. Young Eddy speaks with a feigned informality.

Young Eddy:	Are you going to wait for Davey then?
Bonnie:	I guess I will. For a while.
Young Eddy:	You ready, Dad?
Alfred:	Yup. . . . No sign of 'em yet?
Young Eddy:	Maybe they plan on coming over on their own.
Alfred:	You don't know your grampa. He's set on the Nurlins makin' an entrance en masse.
Young Eddy:	Well it's gettin' late, I'll get my jacket and give a holler to Mum. *He exits leaving Alfred and Bonnie alone. Alfred steps out on the porch, then returns to the kitchen where he stands awkwardly aware of being alone with Bonnie. She begins to get out school papers to mark. Alfred clears his throat. Bonnie looks at him.*
Bonnie:	Sorry?
Alfred:	What?
Bonnie:	I didn't hear what you said.
Alfred:	Oh. *Terrible pause as Bonnie looks at him expectantly.* . . . School doin' OK?
Bonnie:	Alright.

Terrible pause as Alfred looks at her trying to come up with some other

Bob Aarron as Alfred Nurlin, Doris Chillcott as Margaret Nurlin, and
Ric Reid as Young Eddy Nurlin in the Alberta Theatre Projects
production of *Generations,* Calgary, Alberta, 1980.

Courtesy of the Glenbow Museum Archives

conversational gambit. Great relief from Alfred as Margaret and Young Eddy enter. Alfred escapes to the yard.

Young Eddy: Gotta hurry, Mum.

Margaret: Now are you sure you don't wanna come, Bonnie?

Bonnie smiles and nods her head.

Young Eddy: See you later, Bonnie.

Margaret: You make sure you wait for us, Davey'll want you to wait.

Young Eddy: She'll wait, come on, Mum. *They start out.*

Alfred: Now where the hell are they?

Young Eddy: They'll meet us there, Dad.

Alfred: No.

Margaret: You know Davey won't miss it.

Alfred: I'll wait.

Margaret: It's gettin' late, Alfred.

Alfred: You take your mother, Eddy, I'll meet you there.

Young Eddy: Grampa and Davey'll ride over with Sneider.

Alfred: You two go on.

Margaret: Come on, Eddy, I know that tone. *She and Eddy exit.* It's a waste of time talkin'. We'll see you there, Alfred!

Sound of the car starting up and pulling away. It's getting darker. Bonnie comes to the porch door and looks out.

Bonnie: Do you think they'll show up?

Alfred: I dunno . . . most likely not. . . . Should wait just the same.

Flash of lightning, rumble of thunder. Bonnie exits to look at the sky.

Alfred: Look at that.

Bonnie: Happenin' somewhere.

Alfred: Heat lightnin'.

Flash of lightning, rumble of thunder.

Bonnie:	It reminds me of summers when I was a kid . . . I used to be scared of the lightning.
Alfred:	Yup.
Bonnie:	I used to be scared of . . . I think I was born in the wrong place . . . I should've been born in . . . oh, I don't know . . . New Brunswick. Have you ever been there?
Alfred:	Nope.
Bonnie:	It's . . . domesticated there. I mean, little trees and little hills and little towns—like you laid out a province on one of those boards you get for an electric train set . . . little phoney trees and bridges and towns. It's like Munchkin Land—but you can relate to it. That's where I should've been born. *Alfred smiles.* I mean here, I've always been afraid of the spaces. How can one person relate to the prairies? Maybe that's the trouble.
Alfred:	They make you feel small alright.
Bonnie:	Useless.
Alfred:	Not useless . . . unimportant maybe.
Pause.	
Bonnie:	It's funny . . . I've come and gone here ever since I was . . . But I don't feel as if I . . . know you at all.
Alfred:	Not much to know.
Bonnie:	Have you ever . . .
Alfred:	What?
Bonnie:	I don't know. Just . . . wondering . . . things.
Alfred:	Yup . . . Yup . . . I never seen much of this country. Only this place and around.
Bonnie:	But you were overseas.
Alfred:	Oh yes . . . seen a bit a things there . . . signed up in '42. Alls I wanted to do was see the world and kill Germans. . . . Was a crack shot. *Smiles.* Shootin' gophers probably did it. Had those little crossed rifles

on my shoulder, yellow they was . . . maybe not . . . I remember the first man I seen wearing a chain 'round his neck with all these here gold rings he took off the dead . . . I remember . . . a Dutch girl they had in a shack . . . and my sergeant said come on Al, what the hell, may be the last piece a tail you ever get . . . I shouldn't be tellin' you that. . . . I come home in '45, fall it was . . . the place seemed different. Didn't seem such a bad place to be at all. I'd seen enough. *Pause.*

Bonnie: *Softly.* You'll be missing your meeting.

Alfred: Yup. *Pause.* I guess I should go alright.

Bonnie: Davey'll be there.

Alfred: Yup. *He gets up to go.* I hear you and Davey'll be settin' a date. *Something in Bonnie's look makes him hurry on to a new subject.* Well if they show up, you tell 'em I waited.

Alfred hurries off. It's possible to see a figure in the shadows of the Old Place. He draws on a cigarette. Alfred turns just before going offstage. The figure at the Old Place would appear to be observing Alfred. Alfred feels as if he is being observed but can see no one. Bonnie enters the kitchen and settles down to marking her papers. Alfred, undecided for a moment, hesitates, then exits offstage. Sound of the car leaving. Old Eddy steps out from the Old Place and makes his way through the yard to the house.

Bonnie: *Hearing Old Eddy on the porch.* Davey?

Old Eddy continues into the kitchen, giving Bonnie a brief glance. He gets out a pint of rye and a glass. He is about to pour himself a shot when he looks at Bonnie and offers the bottle.

Bonnie: No thanks.

Old Eddy pours himself a drink, knocks it back. Pours himself a second which he will drink more slowly.

Bonnie: . . . Alfred waited. *Pause.* But he left. *Pause.* Where's Davey?

Old Eddy: At the meetin'.

Bonnie: You didn't go? *Old Eddy takes a drink of his rye.* Would you . . . like something to eat?

Old Eddy:	I et.
Bonnie:	Oh.
Old Eddy:	We went into the Hat and we et.
Bonnie:	Oh.
Old Eddy:	Frank's cafe. Have yuh ever et there?
Bonnie:	No.
Old Eddy:	Make sure yuh don't.

Bonnie smiles and returns to her papers.

Old Eddy:	How's your father likin' the Hat?
Bonnie:	Oh he gets along.
Old Eddy:	He had a nice piece a property here, too bad he lost it.
Bonnie:	He didn't lose it. He sold it. *Pause.* Why didn't you go to the meeting?
Old Eddy:	I been here since 1908. I heard all them speeches before.
Bonnie:	You'll be missed.
Old Eddy:	Mm. *Pause.*
Bonnie:	Mr. Nurlin . . . are you going to sell Eddy's section?
Old Eddy:	What section?
Bonnie:	. . . What . . . what would come down to Eddy.
Old Eddy:	Yuh mean when I'm dead.
Bonnie:	*A bit awkward.* Yes.
Old Eddy:	Yuh might not've noticed. I ain't dead yet.
Bonnie:	Maybe I spoke out of turn.
Old Eddy:	And when I go, what I'm leavin' is land, not money.
Bonnie:	What about Eddy?
Old Eddy:	He's a smart fella. A smart fella can always make money, and a helluva lot easier than I come by this place.

Bonnie:	Times change.
Old Eddy:	That's just somethin' people say to get what they want. Real things, things that count, they never change.
Bonnie:	You're wrong.
Old Eddy:	What the hell would yuh know.
Bonnie:	Because you're old doesn't mean you're right.
Old Eddy:	If you're worried about Eddy, I'll tell yuh—he'll find a way.
Bonnie:	It's not Eddy I'm worried about.

Faint sound of car pulling in.

Old Eddy:	And I'll tell yuh somethin' else. To be a farmer yuh got to have a soft spot 'bout the size of a quarter in your brain, and yuh gotta have a strip 'bout this wide a iron in your soul. Yuh don't have that winnin' combination, yuh gonna spend your whole life runnin' scared in this place. . . . Yuh don't have it, yuh keep away from my Davey.
Young Eddy:	*Enters the kitchen.* Where the hell were you, Grampa?
Old Eddy:	Mmmn?
Young Eddy:	You missed a meetin' and a half—correction. You missed half a meetin'. *He gets a beer from the fridge.*
Old Eddy:	Yeah?
Bonnie:	What happened?
Young Eddy:	Those silly government bastards! Everyone's firin' questions at them, and all they can talk about's the next election. Christ, people're standin' on chairs yellin' and screamin' and the next thing I know, all hell breaks loose.
Bonnie:	Where's Davey?
Young Eddy:	The whole hall empties, everyone out the door. I'm left standin' at the back starin' across about two hundred wooden chairs at the three-piece bonkies who are still sittin' there starin' at me.

Old Eddy:	Where's your father?
Young Eddy:	I dunno. Everyone was tearin' on over to Sneider's. Shit, it's a mob scene, there's reporters and a TV crew—something's up, Grampa.
Bonnie:	Where's Davey?
Young Eddy:	Him and Sneider are smack dab in the middle of it.
Old Eddy:	Come on. *He starts out the door.*
Young Eddy:	Shit, Grampa, I got a beer.
Old Eddy:	Dump the goddamn beer and come on!

They're met by Alfred running as they come out the door.

Alfred:	Eddy! Eddy! Jesus christ!
Old Eddy:	What is it?
Alfred:	The bastards! They've fired the fields down at Sneider's, and at Randall's they got livestock culled, bunch a calves and some pigs and they slaughtered them!

Faint sound of a prairie fire. Smoke and a glow growing ever so slowly. Volume of fire will build.

Bonnie:	Where's David?
Alfred:	Jesus, I told him! It's that goddamn Sneider, it's all his idea! What the hell's wrong with 'em!
Young Eddy:	Look!

They're aware of the red glow, the smoke, the sound.

Alfred:	Oh jesus jesus, the stupid bugger—he's fired the back section.
Young Eddy:	Come on! They're tryin' to turn it! Come on!

Alfred and Young Eddy run off towards the fire. It's gotten fairly dark now. Old Eddy follows them, but quite a bit behind, both from age and shock. The roar of the fire is fairly loud. He stands for a moment watching the approaching fire. David runs on. He is still flushed with the excitement, the exaltation of his actions.

Old Eddy:	*Roars.* Davey!!

David stops. As he turns to see his grandfather his "high" drains away.

Old Eddy: I'm gonna kill yuh!!

David says nothing. Old Eddy approaches him and gives him a large backhanded slap across the face.

Old Eddy: Yuh stupid son of a bitch!! What the hell do yuh think you're doin'?!

Old Eddy hits David again.

Old Eddy: Fight, yuh son of a whore! Fight!

David lifts his hands to protect himself against Old Eddy's assault. Old Eddy fights David in earnest. He curses David as he does so. There is the faint rumble of thunder and flashes of lightning. David, after a number of blows, begins to try and defend himself, eventually to hit back to stop Old Eddy long enough to contain him. Thunder and lightning grow. Rain begins to fall. As the rain drenches Old Eddy and David, they begin to succumb to fatigue, the fire too is quenched, the crackle and glow dying away. At last Old Eddy falls to the ground. David is swaying but still upright. Pause. David offers his hand to his grandfather.

Old Eddy: Get away from me. *He struggles to his feet and eyes David.* Yuh got anything to say for yourself?

David: I made a mistake.

Old Eddy: Don't do it again.

Old Eddy walks off not too steadily. David watches. He then enters the house past Bonnie who is still in the doorway from where she has watched the fight. Bonnie gets a washcloth, goes to press it to David's eye. He takes it from her, throws it in the sink. Pause.

Bonnie: You know something, Davey? You've got a soft spot the size of a quarter in your brain.

David: Only a quarter.

Bonnie: What did you think you were doing?

David: Shut up. I want you to shut up and listen.

Bonnie: Dav—

David: Shut up—I'm gonna talk and then you can say what you want, OK? . . . I'm not smart like Eddy and I'm not smart like you and I don't give a shit! . . . I can rail and I can fight against all kinda things, but I know *one thing*, alright? *Out there* . . . is . . . something—I know it. Out there . . . is a feelin' . . . you don't get other places. Other places it's hidden in all the dinky scenery, but on the *prairies* it's just there. A *power*. Can you understand that?

Bonnie: I—

David: I don't care if you understand it or not, I under-stand it! Sure I could do some stupid job some-where else, but when I'm standin' out there . . . well . . . there's just somethin' 'bout a person standin' there on the prairies, everything else stripped away. It makes things simple. *Pause.* So . . . Bonnie . . . you do whatever you want. You can't hack it, you get the hell out.

Pause.

Bonnie: You are stupid.

David: I know it. I said it.

Bonnie: All this is going, can't you see that?

David: I don't give a shit. I'm here now!

Bonnie: Do you think Eddy'll give up?

David: I can handle Eddy.

Bonnie: Who do you think you are?

David: *He smiles.* I'm the salt of the earth. Who are you?

Bonnie: You're crazy.

David: Who are you?

Bonnie: You make me laugh.

David: Who are you!?

Bonnie: I don't know!

David: Well if you find out—you let me know.

Bonnie exits. David listens and hears the sound of her car pulling away.

He goes to the fridge and gets out a beer. Opens it. Takes a drink and exits to the rest of the house.

Lights dim out on the house.

Faint light of dawn on the Old Place. Old Eddy and Charlie make their way on stage to the Old Place. The dog accompanies them and lies down.

Old Eddy: Scorched.

Charlie: But still standin'.

Old Eddy: She'd of have gone if it weren't for that rain.

Charlie: Yuh think so?

Old Eddy: Beat the shit outa him—not too old for that.

Charlie: Inside—I don't feel so old.

Old Eddy: Charlie?

Charlie: Yeah?

Old Eddy: The night she died . . . I come out to that rise. . . . Lost Edward the oldest that winter, their mother in the spring. Only Alfred and me, and Alfred little more than a baby. . . . All night I stood there on the rise.

Charlie: I seen yuh.

Old Eddy: I was thinkin'. . . . When the sun come up, I looked Her straight in the face. And I thought, Look at me, yuh Old Bitch! Look at me! Eddy Nurlin! I'm here! I'm still here!

Charlie: I watched yuh.

Old Eddy: I knew yuh was watchin'.

Charlie: I know.

Old Eddy: We're still here, Charlie. Hell, we'll always be here.

The sun starts to come up.

BLACKOUT

Whiskey Six Cadenza

Wally McSween as Mr. Big, Lee Royce as Mama George, and
Rebecca Starr as Leah in the Studio Theatre production
of *Whiskey Six Cadenza*, Edmonton, Alberta, 1985.

"Whiskey Six," 1985, 90-80-148, Studio Theatre Fonds, University of Alberta Archives.

Production History

Whiskey Six Cadenza was premiered at Theatre Calgary 10 February 1983 with the title *Whiskey Six*.

CAST

Mr. Big	*Robert Benson*
Mama George	*Joyce Gordon*
Leah	*Kim Horsman*
Johnny Farley	*Robert Metcalfe*
Mrs. Farley	*Rita Howell*
Cec Farley	*Barney O'Sullivan*
Will Farley	*Duval Lang*
William Windsor	*Stephen Hair*
Dolly Daniel	*Jacquie Presly*
Gompers	*Earl Michael Reid*
Old Sump	*David Marriage*
Widow Popovitch	*Rita Howell*
Constable	*Duval Lang*

Director	*Rick McNair*
Designer	*Terry Gunvordahl*
Costume Designer	*Sheila Richardson Lee*
Composer	*Allan Rae*
Stage Manager	*Rick Rinder*

ACKNOWLEDGEMENT

With thanks to Artistic Director Rick McNair of Theatre Calgary who commissioned this play.

CHARACTERS

Mr. Big: a man in his sixties
Mama George: his wife of about the same age
Leah: last name unknown: girl in her late teens
Johnny Farley: young man about twenty
Mrs. Farley: Johnny's mother
Cec Farley: a miner and Johnny's father
Will Farley: a miner and Johnny's older brother
William Windsor: AKA Bill the Brit, member of the Prohibition Police
Dolly Danielle: Will's girlfriend, same age as Leah
Gompers: an employee of Mr. Big
Old Sump: elderly miner
Widow Popovitch: older woman (double with Mrs. Farley)
Constable: seen, no lines (double with Will)
Voice of the Trainman
Blairmore Marching Band are shadows only.

TIME

Act One: the fall of 1919
Act Two: the spring of 1920

PLACE

The Crowsnest Pass, straddling the Alberta/British Columbia border and the Canada/US border.

PLAYWRIGHT'S NOTE

The opening and closing dance sequence and voice-overs, as well as the stage directions referring to the refracted, fragmented images, reflect production components of the Theatre Calgary premiere. These, plus the gossamer depiction of the Crowsnest Pass, are options which not every production need choose to exercise. I think of them as strong indicators of the play's ambiance, and nothing more or less than that. Terry Gunvordahl's wonderful set did many things, not the least of which was the creation of Will's ghost on stage with, and yet not with, Dolly sitting and dancing in Act Two.

ACT ONE

The front of the stage is filled by a gossamer depiction of the Crowsnest Pass. The view is of an open expanse of rolling foothills with mountains as misty peaks. We are looking westward. Nestled in a crook of the landscape, the smudgy and vague outline of a small, distant town that might-have-been, Blairmore. All is as if seen through a soft rain. The light grows on the gossamer depiction so that the image is well-established. A plaintive note is heard, repeated and faint, from a player piano. Light builds behind the image, exposing it as no more than a grey, dusty, cobwebby affair much as a spider might spin in the entrance of an abandoned mine-shaft. The cobweb parts. We see what was formerly obscured, the player piano playing, as well as skeletal bits and pieces of the town of Blairmore, primarily a Farley area and the Alberta Hotel area. In the Alberta Hotel, a chair is knocked over. Images and figures often appear fractured, refracted, fragmented. Behind the town, surrounding it, is the gossamer depiction of the rolling hills, the misty mountains, but seen from a different perspective—from what was once the main street of Blairmore. The landscape extends into the infinite, giving an impression of viewing eternity through a glass, a telescope, a microscope, a kaleidoscope.

The music from the player piano quickens in tempo slightly, growing in volume. The figures, now complete, now fractured, refracted images, of Mr. Big and Leah, Will and Dolly, Cec and Mrs. Farley, Gompers and Mama George dance; Old Sump dances alone. Occasionally they change partners. Bill the Brit watches, dancing with no one. Johnny is absent.

Voice-overs are heard, they sound like the wind, blowing softly, stirring tumbleweeds, increasing, and dying.

Mr. Big: *Voice-over.* And around . . . and around . . . and around . . .

Leah: *Voice-over.* My head . . .

Mr. Big: *Voice-over.* And around . . .

Leah: *Voice-over.* It's whirling . . .

Mr. Big: *Voice-over.* And around . . .

Mrs. Farley: *Voice-over.* And dip . . .

Mr. Big: *Voice-over.* T'gether . . .

Dolly: *Voice-over.* And out . . .

Will: Voice-over. And 'round . . .

Mama George: Voice-over. Ohhhhhhhh . . .

All: Voice-over. Ohhhhhhhh . . .

Leah: Voice-over. Whirrrrl . . .

Gompers: Voice-over. And dip . . .

Dolly: Voice-over. Whirrrrrrl . . .

Mrs. Farley: Voice-over. Ohhhhhh . . .

Cec: Voice-over. And out . . .

Mr. Big: Voice-over. And out . . . and 'round . . . and 'round . . .
                     and out . . . and 'round . . . and out . . .

Leah: Voice-over, faint as the image of Mr. Big and Leah is the
                     last to fade from view. . . . And . . .dip. . . .

*Silence. Lights fade to black as a small round green light alone in blackout
grows in brightness. Blast of train whistle followed by sound of distant but
approaching train. Green light changes to red light. Headlight of train
shines directly into audience. It grows in size to the sounds of the train as
it draws nearer, slows down, and stops at station. Steam from the engine
floats in front of headlight.*

Trainman: Voice-over. Blairmore! Blairmore! Is that it? . . . No
                     more for Blairmore?

Sound of train increases as it readies to pull out.

Trainman: Voice-over. Board! All Aboard!!

*Sound of the train pulling out. Its headlight grows brighter, brighter, blind-
ingly bright and larger as the train departs as if through the audience.
Sound fades with the departing train. The stage is left in darkness except
for the residual steam from the engine, and the red light. The red light
turns green. Faint whistle from train.*

In the drifting steam the faint figures of Mr. Big, Leah, Gompers, in one grouping; Johnny, by himself, can be made out. They have gotten off the train. Johnny passes	**Mrs. Farley:** *In darkness, sings.* Somebody's boy's in temptation Away from the shelter of home, Far from a mother's protection

billfold to Mr. Big. Mr. Big, Gompers, Leah exit, with Mr. Big and Leah stopping to exchange a backward glance with Johnny, who watches them depart. He stands a moment in thought, takes a deep breath, glances towards home and Mrs. Farley.

Johnny draws closer to Mrs. Farley, watching her, listening.

And weary and sad and alone.

There are pitfalls oh in plenty
Awaiting his soul to destroy,
Oh voter speak out at election,
And help to save somebody's boy!

Light slowly builds on her.

Somebody's boy may be your boy,
His eyes just the same shade of blue,
Someday your tears may be falling—
The breweries don't care if they do.

'Tis theirs to ruin and trample,
To crush out all hope and all joy.

Mrs. Farley:	*Glances down at her song book. She speaks to herself in an absent-minded way.* Praise the Lord . . . ame. . . . *She catches sight of Johnny; she can't believe her eyes.* Johnny? . . . Johnny? . . . John-ny! You're home. You are home, you're home!
Johnny:	That's it.
Mrs. Farley:	And just look at you. . . . Oh you've grown!
Johnny:	I have.
Mrs. Farley:	But you're thin.
Johnny:	I am.
Mrs. Farley:	You've got so big, and you've got so skinny. . . . Now did you never eat?
Johnny:	I ate.
Mrs. Farley:	And why are you standin' there? Aren't you comin' in, aren't you even gonna sit even?
Johnny:	I'm in, Mum.
Mrs. Farley:	Well sit then.
Johnny:	Gonna stand a bit.

Mrs. Farley:	Oh I did miss you, Johnny—and I prayed for you, yes I did, I just love you and miss you so much, thank the Lord, thank you Lord for . . .and now I'm gonna cry.
Johnny:	Don't cry.
Mrs. Farley:	Don't you be lookin' at me cryin', don't you be doin' that. You could be sittin', you could be lookin' like you're gonna stay a while—did you never eat?
Johnny:	I ate, Mum.
Mrs. Farley:	You never wrote.
Johnny:	I wrote.
Mrs. Farley:	Not proper letters, not continuin'-like letters, not every week you didn't.
Johnny:	No.
Mrs. Farley:	You never wrote like you should.
Johnny:	No.
Mrs. Farley:	Like you promised.
Johnny:	I had nothin' much to write about.
Mrs. Farley:	You coulda wrote about that.
Johnny:	Ah-huh.
Mrs. Farley:	It woulda been somethin'.
Johnny:	I know, I just didn't get down to doin' it, that's all.
Mrs. Farley:	Not even to tell us you were comin'.
Pause.	
Johnny:	Where's Pop?
Mrs. Farley:	At the mine—and William—same shift. *Her attention drifts from Johnny for a moment. He watches her. She looks at him. . . .* You've not come back, are you?
Johnny:	Guess they'll be surprised to see me, eh?
Mrs. Farley:	You've not come back? I mean it's just for a visit, eh Johnny?

Johnny:	So, ah, how are they, Will and Pop?
Mrs. Farley:	Your father's coughin' and spittin' and dyin'—but still workin'.
Johnny:	I don't want you to start in on that, Mum.
Mrs. Farley:	I as'ed you a question—are you come back?
Johnny:	I tried, I did try, Mum, but I . . .
Mrs. Farley:	You tried!
Johnny:	If you'd listen . . .

Faint blast from a mine whistle.

Mrs. Farley:	Don't need no listenin'! Him who can't write a letter is tellin' me to listen? You listen, Johnny! You . . .
Johnny:	Don't cry.
Mrs. Farley:	And haven't I the right?
Johnny:	There weren't no jobs east.
Mrs. Farley:	If you cared nothin' for me, you should care somethin' for yourself. Why are you come back?
Johnny:	Do you think I wanna work in the colliery?
Mrs. Farley:	There's your father dyin' of the lungs; there's William who'll end up just the same—if he don't go like his brothers Teddy and Robert, workin' the same shift . . .
Johnny:	I remember.
Mrs. Farley:	The two of 'em, your brothers too, Johnny, caught and crushed and chokin' to death when the air give out. One hundred and eighty-nine dead at Hillcrest— now did they die for nothin', Johnny?
Johnny:	You know it's not what I want but I got no choice, Mum!

Cec enters black from the mine.

Mrs. Farley:	There he is! There! Now is that what you wanna be? Look at him! The black worked right through the skin and the blood and the heart and the lungs and the brain! That's not a man, Johnny, that's a thing, a

utensil belonging to Dominion Colliery! *Exits.* Can't even tie his shoe without spittin' a clot.

Pause.

Johnny: 'Lo Pop.

Cec: You're taller.

The two regard each other. There seems to be a desire on their part to embrace in greeting but some other subtle but stronger force prevents them. Cec busies himself with removing his black work clothes.

Cec: Yup, 'bout what? Two inches?

Johnny: Dunno. Maybe.

Cec: They says you's supposed to stop 'bout eighteen.

Johnny: Musta been that eastern air.

Cec: Robert now, he grew some after that, and he never had a tetch a eastern air. He thrived on dust, that Robert did.

Johnny watches his father undressing. Silence for a moment. His father looks at him. Awkward silence between them for a second before Johnny speaks.

Johnny: Where's Will?

Cec: Out back throwin' some water on hisself outa the pump. Got hisself a girl and she don't mind the callused hand, but she surely don't care for the black. Gonna scrub the skin right off he is, and not do a damn bitta good. *He laughs.*

Will enters looking dampish. He and Cec will change their clothes during the scene. Will sees Johnny.

Will: Well je-sus.

Johnny: God damn.

Will: Well je-sus god damn and holy shit, what're you doin' here, boy?

Johnny: What the hell does it look like, boy?

Will: It looks like my baby brother! Arrrrrrrrrr!! *He bellows*

	and holds out his arms. He and Johnny embrace. What the hell are you doin' here?
Cec:	*Feeling considerably more at ease now that he's no longer alone with Johnny.* He heered a rumour all the way back in Tronna, he heered some fella out here in Dominion Colliery got a foolproof way to get the black off so's he come to see.
Will:	Just like huggin' a picket offa fence, boy, you're all straight lines and angles.
Cec:	I told him that rumour's all horseshit, can't nobody get the black off.
Will:	You seen Mum?
Johnny:	Ah-huh.
Cec:	Oh he seen her all right.
Johnny:	Yeah.
Cec:	And she give it to him, good and proper.
Will:	Are you come back then?
Johnny:	I ah . . .
Cec:	Well there he is standin' there ain't he? The favourite is come home.

Johnny looks at him, saying nothing.

Will:	That's right, Johnny?
Johnny:	I guess so.
Cec:	And she don't like it, not a bit.
Will:	*To Johnny.* Hey.
Cec:	Ain't no escaping the mines.
Will:	Buck up, me buckeroo.
Johnny:	Yeah.
Cec:	Filled his head, she did, but it comes down to the same in the end. And didn't I say it when you left, boy? Didn't I say it?

Will:	Ain't the end a the earth.
Johnny:	No.
Cec:	Shoulda heard her, Will. Held his father up as a bad example she did. Here I was, nothin' but a damn utensil, wasn't that what she said, Johnny? No better than a spoon, only worse, 'cause I'm coughin' up the clots on the shoes, Will . . . and don't you be laughin' 'cause the same thing is gonna happen to you! Only worse! That's what she says, boy, your mother says it. *He laughs.*
Will:	Hell, I thrive on the dust.
Johnny:	Like Robert and Teddy did?
Cec:	Now that's your mother in you, that is. *He gathers up the clothing and exits with it.*
Will:	Hey.
Johnny:	Nothin' changes.
Will:	Don't pay him no mind. He's glad to see you, he just can't say it.
Johnny:	Sure.
Will:	And you him—so why the hell can't you say somethin'?
Johnny:	I will.
Will:	It's real good to see you, boy, welcome home. *They embrace. Will whispers.* The mines ain't the end a the earth, boy.

Cec re-enters with clean clothes for himself and Will. Cec is not so particular about removing the black as Will.

Cec:	She's pourin' over the good book lookin' for helpful verse.
Will:	You wanna see somethin' fine?
Cec:	What?
Will:	Look at that. *Holds out a hand.* I still got the cal-luses . . . but . . .

Cec:	What?
Will:	White.
Johnny:	Red.
Cec:	*Examines Will's hand.* What the hell you use on that?
Will:	Lye.
Cec:	Lye?
Will:	I used the lye and the bleach.
Cec:	Jesus christ, Will, that hand's gonna rot.
Will:	But you can't see the black now can you?
Cec:	You didn't use no lye on that?
Will:	Sure I did. *He winks at Johnny.*
Cec:	*Catches him.* Ha! He's always merry-makin', this one. This boy'll be laughin' when he's lyin' in bed coughin' his lungs into a hankie he'll be laughin'.
Will:	I'd bawl if I thought it'd help.
Johnny:	Pop says you got a girl.
Cec:	He even give her a picture.
Will:	I got girls up to my armpits.
Johnny:	A particular girl.
Cec:	Go on Will, you tell him.
Will:	Could have.
Cec:	Tell him her name.
Will:	You watch it.
Cec:	It's Dolly.
Will:	Tread carefully there.
Cec:	Dolly Danielle.
Johnny:	A Frenchie?
Cec:	A bohunk.
Will:	A blonde.

Cec:	You remember the Yakimchuks?
Johnny:	Ah-huh.
Cec:	Well this here's the one that used to be Polly.
Johnny:	Polly Yakimchuck?
Cec:	And . . .
Will:	I'll take it from there.
Johnny:	Polly with the braids all 'round the head?
Will:	Uh-huh.
Johnny:	Legs like matchsticks and knees like grapefruit?
Cec:	Them grapefruits' moved up a bit.
Will:	*Warning.* Uh-uh.
Cec:	And she don't like the black.

Will makes a motion as if to hit his father.

Cec:	Eeeehhhhh would you hit an old man, would you hit your father there Will?
Will:	You betcha.
Johnny:	How did Polly Yakimchuk get to be Dolly Danielle?
Cec:	She went to Tronna.
Will:	I'll take it from there. It's like this, Johnny boy. She's like you, kinda like you, for this girl's got a particular hatred for coal. It's true she don't like the black, and what she don't like even more is the thought of the men crawlin' thro' seamy little spaces in the bowels a the earth, and more than that, is the ponies.
Johnny:	She don't like the colliery ponies?
Will:	You don't want to get her talkin' 'bout them ponies, Johnny.
Cec:	That's the truth.
Will:	It brings her to tears.
Cec:	And it bores you to tears.

Rita Howell as Mrs. Farley, Barney O'Sullivan as Cec Farley, Robert
Metcalfe as Johnny Farley, and Duval Lang as Will Farley in the Theatre
Calgary production of *Whiskey Six*, Calgary, Alberta, 1983.

Will: She's a sensitive girl.

Cec: Tell him 'bout changin' her name.

Will: I'm gettin' to that.

Cec: Only a bohunk'd think a French name's a step up in the world.

Will: Shut up, do you hear?

Cec: Ohhh, no jokin' 'bout Dolly Danielle.

Will: To make a long story short, she goes to Tronna, she comes back from Tronna, and while in Tronna, she changes her name.

Pause.

Johnny: Is that it?

Will: Pretty well it, *Pause.* You see it kinda makes her feel like she didn't come from here, like she kinda chose here 'stead of endin' up here.

Johnny: Oh.

Will: She's a sensitive girl.

Cec: Is that what she told you?

Will: I can see that for myself.

Cec: Lemme look at you—right enough—you got a thin layer of dust right over them eyeballs.

Will: You old . . .

Mrs. Farley: *Offstage and faint, singing.* Somebody's boy's in temptation. *Going flat.* Away from the shelter of—

Johnny, Will and Cec listen for a moment.

Johnny: I was hopin' she'd got over rampagin' for Temperance.	**Mrs. Farley:** Away from the shelter— Shelter of— offf . . .
Cec: She needs a cause to keep goin'.	Away from the shelter of home, Far from a mother's protection,
Will: She'd have a man so	And weary and sad *Flat again*

240   Whiskey Six Cadenza

dry you'd have to prime him to spit.

Cec: She's in a state, she is.

Will: You can tell 'cause her throat tightens up—

Cec: Resultin' in that . . . She'll move into the hymnary next.

Cec: What'd I tell you?

and alone,
Alone,
Alooone.
There are pitfalls oh in plenty *Flat*
ty ty plenty,
Pitfalls oh in plenty,
Awaiting his soul to destroy. *Flat*
Oh voter speak out at election.
And vote to save somebody's boy.

With renewed vigor.

Mine eyes have seen the glory
Of the coming of the Lord.
He is stamping out the vintage
Where the grapes of wrath are

Creeping in is the sound of a marching band, building in volume.

Johnny: Still prayer meetings on Wednesday and service on Sunday?

Cec: And temperence on Thursday.

The marching band is fairly loud.

Will: Like clockwork.

Cec: I thank the Lord she more or less give up on us.

Will: She ain't intercedin' on our behalf no more. If we're to be saved it'll be by the direct intervention a the . . . the Lord.

Mrs. Farley:

He is loosening the Vengeance
Of His terrible swift Sword.

Mrs. Farley:

His Truth goes marching on.
Glory, glory, Hallelujah!
Glory, glory, Hallelujah!
Glory, glory, Hallelujah!
His truth goes marching on!

The sound of the marching band is quite loud, fragmented images of trumpets, trombones, light glancing off brass instruments. Finally, Mrs. Farley can no longer be heard, only the marching band.

Will: . . . Hisself . . . What the hell is that?

Cec: It's . . . it's the Blairmore marchin' band!

Will: Key-rist! Had me worried.

Cec: This ain't no practice night.

Will: So what the hell's it out for?

The marching band is outside the house, still playing.

Cec: It's stopped outside.

Will: Front a the house.

Cec: Here comes Old Sump—he ain't no band man.

Will: And Gompers, ain't that Mr. Big's man Gompers?

Old Sump, followed by Gompers, approaches the house.

Old Sump: Cec! Cec, you home t'ere, Cec!

Cec: Pray to God your mother don't see Gompers comin' here.

Old Sump: Cec!

Will: He'll have to smite her ears as well as her eyes.

Old Sump: Cec!

Will: Whata you want, Sump?

Cec: *Whispers.* What the hell you doin' here, Gompers?

Old Sump: Come for Johnny.

Will: For Johnny?

Cec: Eh?

Old Sump: *To Johnny.* I wanna shake your hand.

Cec: What the hell for?

Old Sump: 'E's a 'ero, 'e is.

Will: He's a what?

The band is continuing to play outside the house.

Cec:	*Yelling.* Hey! Could you play somethin' soft—and maybe religious?
Gompers:	Come on.
Johnny:	Wait a sec.
Gompers:	He says bring you, I bring you.
Johnny:	Who?
Gompers:	Mr. Big.
Johnny:	Who?
Will:	He's the rumrunner, Johnny.
Cec:	What is happenin' here?
Will:	Damned if I know.
Old Sump:	Up you go. *They lift Johnny onto their shoulders.*
Will:	Where're you goin'?
Old Sump:	T'Alberta Hotel, you're invited!
Cec:	What the hell—
Will:	How come?
Old Sump:	'E's a 'ero!

He nearly drops Johnny.

Gompers:	Suuuummp!!
Old Sump:	Oh t'at was close, t'at was.
Cec:	The Alberta Hotel?
Gompers:	Mr. Big!
Old Sump:	At t'Alberta Hotel! Are you comin'?

Old Sump, Gompers and Johnny exit. The sound of the marching band and the glint of instruments fade.

Mrs. Farley:	*Offstage and faint.* Johnny?
Will:	Why'd the rumrunner send Gompers to bring him?

Mr. Big, dimly lit but light growing, draws himself a beer at the Alberta Hotel. Mama George wipes the bar. Leah hums softly, pushing back a strand of hair. Leah activates the player piano, which plays in the background.

Mrs. Farley: *Offstage, faint.* Johnny!

Cec: There'll be booze.

Will: At the Alberta Hotel.

Mrs. Farley: *Offstage, faint.* Johnny!

Will & Cec: We're comin'! *They exit.*

Scene shifts to the Alberta Hotel.

Mr. Big: You'll see, Mama, just wait till you see him.

Mama George: But to give him your wallet . . .

Mr. Big: It was that or lose it to a pair of American thieves.

Mama George: It coulda been stolen by him.

Mr. Big: You haven't seen him, Mama.

Mama George: That's true.

Mrs. Farley: *Offstage, faint.* Johnny!

Mr. Big: Now if I'd had a son . . .

Leah: 'Stead of a daughter?

Mr. Big: 'Long with a daughter. . . . This boy's got character, Leah, same as you've got character.

Mama George bustles offstage.

Leah: *Smiles.* Character.

Mr. Big: And I am a judge of character. That 'bility to judge is not somethin' you cultivate, it's somethin' you're born with. Now the first time I saw you I knew right here. *He touches his heart.* Same thing with him. And that's why I passed him my wallet. You see I could tell just by lookin' at him—soon as I looked at him—somethin' like you, the first time I laid eyes on you. Can't you remember the first time I laid eyes on you?

Leah: What kinda character could I have had at eleven?

Mr. Big:	Whata you mean?
Leah:	I mean I was only eleven.
Mr. Big:	Go on.
Leah:	I mean what kinda character could you see in me at the age of eleven?
Mr. Big:	I could discern your potential to love, and to be loved, to be honest, to be loyal, to trust, to be worthy of trust, to . . .
Leah:	All that at the age of eleven?
Mr. Big:	Was I wrong?

Mama George re-enters with food for the party.

Mr. Big:	Eh Mama, whata you say?
Mama George:	Mmmn?
Mr. Big:	I was talkin' 'bout Leah.
Mama George:	Judge a character, that's what I heard.
Mr. Big:	Was I right about Leah?
Mama George:	Sounded more like a litany for a dog than a daughter.
Mr. Big:	A chosen daughter.
Leah:	Mama's right, Mr. Big.
Mr. Big:	And I chose her because a my great capacity for judgin' character.
Leah:	You felt sorry for me.
Mr. Big:	Well anybody would've, but that wasn't it.
Leah:	Now look—Mama's feedin' seventeen cats in the kitchen.
Mama George:	Never in the kitchen.
Leah:	From the kitchen, in the back, you know what I mean, and where did they come from?
Mr. Big:	I know what you're sayin' but that isn't it either.
Leah:	So how's a man who can't pass a mewling cat to side-

step a cryin' kid?

Mr. Big: But you were not cryin'! That's one of the first things I noticed.

Leah: I was cryin'.

Mr. Big: Inside you were cryin'—cryin' out—not a tears kinda cry but a passionate suffusion that . . .

Leah: *Laughs.* Oh Mr. Big, what stories!

Mr. Big: It's true.

Mama George: He believes it.

Mr. Big: And another thing! . . . No shadow. Here's this scrawny little girl-child walkin' along without castin' a shadow.

Leah: It was rainin', Mr. Big.

Mr. Big: For you! For me there was a radiance all around you, and it was comin' from you. From you, Leah. And I didn't stop for more than a . . . it coulda been a hundred years, or a second, or no time at all! Like an instantaneous gatherin' up, like God descendin' to take his Chosen up into heaven in a fiery chariot!

Leah: Are you God, Mr. Big?

Mr. Big: At that moment, I was. Invincible, Leah.

Mama George: He was.

Mr. Big: And when I come home, I said, Mama, look Mama.

Mama George: I thought it'd be a ring with a real diamond in it like the pearls that he gave me before.

Mr. Big: That you keep in the box.

Mama George: I look silly wearin' those kinda things.

Mr. Big: But it weren't none a those things. It was somethin' more precious. The most valuable thing I could give her . . . that I never gave her before.

Pause.

Leah: It gets better every time you tell it. . . . What was it

	really like?
Mr. Big:	Can't you remember?
Leah:	No.
Mr. Big:	It was just like I said.
Leah:	*Smiles.* You.
Mr. Big:	And this boy the same. Not exactly the same, but a certain kinda sameness. That's why I passed him my wallet.
Mama George:	Didn't I tell you it's risky travellin' by train?
Leah:	'Specially when you're carryin' cash.
Mr. Big:	Six thousand dollars! I could tell just by lookin' at him not a dime'd be missin'.
Mama George:	Next time you take the MacLaughlin.
Mr. Big:	What . . . and have the Brit stuck to my bumper from here right into Lethbridge?
Mama George:	The poor man.
Mr. Big:	Bill the Brit a poor man?
Mama George:	He's just doin' his job.
Mr. Big:	We will be outa business the day he starts doin' his job.
Mama George:	I still say . . .
Mr. Big:	Mama George listen! Are we agreed I'm a great judge a character?

Mama smiles.

Mr. Big:	Agreed. Well, when I peruse Sergeant William Windsor, known to some as Bill the Brit . . .
Leah:	*Savouring the word.* Pah-ruuse.
Mr. Big:	Read, scan or study.
Leah:	I know.
Mr. Big:	Now when I peruse Sergeant William Windsor a the Prohibition Police . . . there's a void. A vacuum. The

man has no character.

Leah: Everyone has some sorta character.

Mr. Big: Not Bill.

Leah: Despicable maybe but . . .

Fragmented image of William Windsor, aka Bill the Brit, is first seen. Bill approaches the Alberta Hotel, observing it before entering.

Mr. Big: The first time, Leah, I saw William Windsor . . .

Leah: Was he castin' a shadow?

Mr. Big: Sur-rounded by shadow—and imprinted on him comin' was the western hemisphere, and on him goin' the eastern!

Leah: What?

Mr. Big: If you split him down the middle, you'd have a map a the world—predominantly covered in red . . . The Empiah!

Leah: *Laughs.* Oh.

Mr. Big: And all a those red parts were throbbin', this angry red pulsin' and throbbin'!

Leah: Sounds awful.

Mr. Big: It was like lookin' at a movin' planet a boils.

Leah: Make him stop.

Mama George: Now who could do that?

Mr. Big: Honduras and Hong Kong!

Leah: What about 'em?

Mr. Big: Strategically located, and hideously hued!

Bill the Brit enters. He looks more like a Boy Scout than a policeman.

Mr. Big: Aahhh, Sergeant Windsor.

Bill: What?

Mr. Big: A pleasure I'm sure.

Bill: Ah-huh. . . . Which bloody tap have you got runnin'

	today?
Mr. Big:	Beg pardon?
Bill:	I said, is it the two per cent beer you're pourin' . . . or the hard stuff?
Mr. Big:	Two per cent's legal tender, Sergeant Windsor. . . .
Bill:	Mmmn.
Mr. Big:	But if you're lookin' for a drink a bootleg liquor, you better go elsewhere.
Bill:	What?
Mr. Big:	I said, this is a law-abidin' establishment.
Bill:	You're a wily old dog . . . but I'm on to your scent.
Mr. Big:	Do you think I'd have it otherwise, Mr. Windsor?
Bill:	Sergeant Windsor to you—and you bloody well would, if you could.
Mr. Big:	So . . . is it the sarsaparilla . . . or the two per cent legal brew you've a thirst for?
Bill:	I'll take . . . *He considers. . . .* the tap on the right. . . . *Leah draws him a glass. He observes closely. . .* Now the left. . . .

He watches intently. Leah glances at Mr. Big, then draws a second glass for Bill, and gives them both to him. He tastes first the one, then the other. He's disappointed as both are legal drafts. He continues to drink from both.

Mr. Big:	Tell me . . . do ah . . . two glasses of two per cent legal beer constitute four per cent beer, hence an indictable offense?
Bill:	You're workin' somethin' with those taps—and don't you think I don't know it.
Mr. Big:	Ohhh, never have I underestimated your perspicacity, Sergeant Windsor.

Leah stifles a giggle.

| **Bill:** | Mmmm. *Drinks his beer.* |
| **Mr. Big:** | Shall I take a liberty? |

Bill:	*Mmn?*
Mr. Big:	I'd like to ask you something.
Bill:	*Suspicious.* What's that?
Mr. Big:	Well . . . there you sit . . .
Bill:	Mmn.
Mr. Big:	A member of the rulin' class . . .

Bill slowly nods his head in quiet assent.

Mr. Big:	Stalwart a the British Empire . . .
Bill:	Right.
Mr. Big:	Steeped in Raleigh, Drake, and Clive . . .
Bill:	India.
Mr. Big:	Correct. Trafalgar, Waterloo, Bleinheim.

Bill lifts his glass in a silent toast to the noble fallen.

Mr. Big:	And here you sit, isolated in a colonial outpost, surrounded by Ruthenians, Silesians, Bukovinans, Austrians, Russians, Galicians, Moldavians . . . and Irish . . .
Bill:	British subjects.
Mr. Big:	But didja know the classification Canadian-born's been accepted in this year's census?
Bill:	Same thing—British subjects.
Mr. Big:	True . . . I suppose.
Pause.	
Bill:	Was that the question?
Mr. Big:	Mmn?
Bill:	The liberty you were takin' to ask . . .
Mr. Big:	Ah yes. Here, 'tis you must bear the mantle a British decency—Justice! Fair play and pluck! Eh Sergeant Windsor?
Bill:	Is that the question?

Mr. Big:	You stand lone against the sky preserving the prairies and British civilization from the inroads of barbarism!
Bill:	Right.
Mr. Big:	Would I lie? And what I want to ask is this. How is it that the plebiscite, with the Drys urgin' "YES TO PROHIBITION," the electoral slogan of the Wets was "BE BRITISH, VOTE NO TO PROHOBITION?"

Pause.

Bill:	You think you got me, don't you?
Mr. Big:	Caught in a conundrum, Sergeant Windsor?
Bill:	I'm not nowhere but here. . . . Stuck in Blairmore and dealin' with the likes of you.
Mr. Big:	Did you yourself vote in the plebiscite? Oh, forgive me. To address such a question to you.
Bill:	You're bloody right.
Mr. Big:	This obsession with the bloody . . .
Bill:	What obsession are you talkin' about?
Mr. Big:	Does it come with the Empire?
Bill:	That's something you'll never know.
Mr. Big:	But to return to the question at hand. . . . Of course you voted! It would be un-British not to! How did you vote? . . . And that's the question.
Bill:	That's nobody's business but my own.
Mr. Big:	Ahhh.
Bill:	And if you had any sense a the basics a democracy, you wouldn't ask!
Mr. Big:	Therefore I extrapolate: you're British therefore you voted and being British you voted No. No to Prohibition!
Bill:	You don't know how I voted.
Mr. Big:	The slogan Sergeant Windsor, "BE BRITISH AND VOTE NO." Would you cast aside your heritage for Yes?

Bill:	No . . .
Mr. Big:	Ah!
Bill:	But . . .
Mr. Big:	Could the slogan be erroneous in its assumption a the British character?
Bill:	In some . . . .
Mr. Big:	Would this cast doubt on the veracity of all British comment?
Bill:	No.
Mr. Big:	Published accounts a valiant struggles against the knavish conspiracies a Latin Popes!
Bill:	Oh.
Mr. Big:	I'm talkin' dates, William Windsor, can even these be trusted!
Bill:	What are you saying?
Mr. Big:	I'm speakin' a dissimulated information regardin' the nefarious activity a benighted savages in Africa, Asia, the Americas, and Anglo-Saxon efforts to overcome the same!
Bill:	What the bloody hell are you talkin' about?
Mr. Big:	*Sings.*
	Rule Brittania.
	Brittania rule the waves!
	Did you vote dry to preserve your job, William Windsor, or did you vote Wet—Yes or No—and even now as you sit here sippin' my legal draft, are you engaged in the activity a policin' an unjust and damnable law that you yourself voted against!? *Pause.* Aaaahhh . . . what it must do to your soul, William Windsor.

Pause.

Bill:	Which of the mongrel races do you originate from?
Mr. Big:	Canadian, sir.

Pause. Bill looks at Leah.

Bill:	What's she doin' here?
Mr. Big:	She lives here.
Bill:	No women.
Mr. Big:	In their livin' room?
Bill:	What livin' room?
Mr. Big:	This livin' room.
Bill:	What livin' room?
Mr. Big:	Perhaps not your kinda livin' room, but the Alberta Hotel is our home, Mama's and Leah's and mine, and such as it is, this is our livin' room.
Bill:	No operatin' a business from your livin' room. I could charge you for that!
Mr. Big:	A business?
Bill:	You're sellin' beer, aren't you?
Mr. Big:	Did you pay for your beer?

Pause.

Bill:	I could get a score a people to swear they bought beer in this room.
Mr. Big:	On those occasions I am runnin' a business . . . and should you ever catch Leah or Mama on the premises, of course they must be charged.
Bill:	You can't run a business one minute, and a livin' room the next.
Mr. Big:	You've presented irrefutable proof that I do.
Bill:	But you can't.
Mr. Big:	But I do.
Bill:	What I'm sayin' is there's a law against it!
Mr. Big:	Ahhhhh. *Accepting Bill's statement.* What law would that be?

Pause. Bill gets up to leave.

Mr. Big:	Sergeant Windsor? . . . Has the local constabulary

	apprehended the two responsible for the holdup on today's train outa Lethbridge?
Bill:	Why do you ask?
Mr. Big:	Well my good man, I was a passenger on the same, and I lost forty dollars to the tip of a gun.
Bill:	Forty dollars?
Mr. Big:	Correct, sir.
Bill:	Mmm.
Mr. Big:	Have . . .
Bill:	We caught 'em crossin' the border.
Mr. Big:	I see.
Bill:	Story has it they're American rumrunners, come up and paid a big man in these parts for a load a booze. Six thousand dollars worth.
Mr. Big:	What a sum.
Bill:	And they hoped to steal it back offa that man on the train he was takin'. A double-cross you could say.
Mr. Big:	And were they in possession a six thousand dollars?

Bill shakes his head.

Mr. Big:	Their "big man" musta travelled some other route.
Bill:	*Nods his head.* Suure.

Sound of the marching band approaching. Glint of light on brass. Fractured images. Eventually the figure of Johnny appears on the shoulders of Will and Gompers, accompanied by Cec, Dolly, and an exhausted Old Sump.

Mr. Big:	Six thousand dollars . . . and I thought it a tragedy to lose forty-five.
Bill:	Forty-five?
Mr. Big:	*Smiles.* Forty in bills, and five dollars in change, forty-five in all. Approximate.
Bill:	Approximate.

Mr. Big:	Ah, listen . . . I'm plannin' a wee celebration—in our livin' room, this evenin'. Would you care to join us, Sergeant Windsor?
Bill:	Celebratin' what?
Mr. Big:	I'm extendin' an invite.
Old Sump:	*From outside.* Are we t'ere t'en?
Will:	Jesus, Johnny, think light.
Widow Popovitch:	*Running on to join them.* Vait! Vait! Ve should make d'entrance togetter.

Bill starts to leave.

Mr. Big:	Maybe later? . . . Any time.
Dolly:	Leah!

Martial music galore. As Bill steps out of the Alberta Hotel to view the motley herd, Old Sump cuts the sound from the band. A brief squawk from a horn instrument. Mr. Big laughs. Dolly rushes to Leah.

Dolly:	Wait till you see him.
Leah:	Who?
Dolly:	His brother.
Leah:	I've already seen him.
Dolly:	You have?
Leah:	Uh-huh.
Dolly:	A best friend is someone you don't hide nothin' from.
Leah:	Here they come.

The crowd rushes in as Mr. Big greets them and Mama pours drinks.

Mr. Big:	Good man, Gompers. A precise delivery. . . . And Will Farley, beast a burden to your brother . . . and what a brother.
Will:	How do.
Old Sump:	*To the offstage band.* Thanks for the hot air, now bugger off.

Mr. Big:	Get your man a whiskey, Dolly. He's earned it. *To Johnny.* Don't go, boy. Here, beside me, right here beside me.
Will:	*Whispers.* Hey, Johnny?
Dolly:	Come on, Will. *She yanks him over to the bar.*
Mr. Big:	You've a fine son, Mr. Farley, I wish I'd the same. I envy you this boy.
Cec:	How'd him and you . . .
Mr. Big:	He's got potential. . . . We'll drink to that, if your good wife doesn't . . .
Cec:	What she don't know won't hurt her.
Mr. Big:	Nicely put.
Dolly:	*Holds up a glass.* For you, Cec!
Cec:	I'm acomin'!
Mr. Big:	And Widow Popovitch, a pleasure, Widow.
Widow:	Why don't you haf dat Leah help vit da mama?
Mr. Big:	But she's helping with me.
Widow:	And den I vould not haf d'opportunity to do so, eh? *She laughs and moves to help Mama at the bar.* Mama, look at dese hands, dey are crying out, put dem to vork!
Mr. Big:	And Sump.
Old Sump:	Ah-huh.
Mr. Big:	Have you survived the Frank Slide and both minin' disasters a 1914 to succumb on my step to simple exhaustion?
Old Sump:	I'll revive wit' a drink.
Mr. Big:	A drink for Old Sump!
Old Sump:	T'boy looks lean enuff but 'e still wears on you after a mile.

The Widow gives him a drink and he drains it.

Old Sump:	I feel me 'strengt' comin' back . . . not *totally* back . . .
Mr. Big:	Another, my friend?
Old Sump:	I t'ink it would help.

Dolly and Leah in one conversation, Mr. Big and Johnny in another.

Mr. Big:	Now let me get a good look at you, boy.
Dolly:	Well?
Leah:	Well what?
Johnny:	What do you see?
Dolly:	Well, what do you think?
Leah:	'Bout what?
Johnny:	What is it?
Dolly:	Tell me.
Leah:	You mean him?
Mr. Big:	I see a fine lad. .
Dolly:	He's not as cute as his brother.
Mr. Big:	A lad to be proud of.
Leah:	You think not?
Dolly:	Not half so cute.
Johnny:	You can't tell that from lookin'.
Leah:	No?
Dolly:	No.
Johnny:	Can you?
Mr. Big:	Some can—and some can't.
Johnny:	Oh.
Leah:	Is so.
Mr. Big:	I can.
Leah:	And nicer too. . . . Here you are. *Hands him a drink.*

Johnny:	Thanks.
Mr. Big:	It's an elegant distillation.
Will:	Hey Johnny, there's things you been keepin' from us boy.
Mr. Big:	All in good time, eh, Johnny?
Will:	Me and the old man, we was wonderin' how the two a you . . .
Mr. Big:	And a notable tale it is, Will.
Will:	Yeah?
Mr. Big:	But first lubrication . . .
Old Sump:	Can I have a t'ird, t'en?
Mr. Big:	You not only can, you must!
Old Sump:	T'ose are t'words t'at bind me to you. *He's off for a third drink.*
Johnny:	And second?
Mr. Big:	Illumination.
Will:	Illumination—you got that, Johnny?
Johnny:	Ah-huh.
Will:	Well—Pop and me'll just keep workin' on the lubricatin' part. . . . Johnny?
Johnny:	In a minute.
Leah:	Do you want me to get you another?
Johnny:	I ain't hardly touched this one yet—but thanks all the same.
Mr. Big:	I owe you, young man.
Johnny:	You don't owe me nothin'.
Mr. Big:	But I do. You did me a service.
Johnny:	Wasn't much.
Mr. Big:	And when a service is done, a debt is incurred . . . you'd agree?

Johnny:	I guess . . . in general . . . yes, I'd agree.

Mr. Big smiles.

Johnny:	Did I say somethin' funny?
Mr. Big:	I'm a judge a character, Johnny—and I liked the way you handled that query.
Johnny:	You did?

Mr. Big nods.

Johnny:	It don't necessarily mean that I agree you owe me.
Mr. Big:	I understand what you meant.
Johnny:	And if you did owe me, which you don't, the booze for Pop and Will—and myself—and the general celebration and all, well, that's more than paid off the debt. Which you don't owe me. If you get what I mean.
Mr. Big:	I do. Precisely.
Johnny:	Good.
Mr. Big:	And the perambulation that I arranged with the marchin' band, you don't mention that?
Johnny:	Well, to tell you the truth, I been ridin' that train straight out from Tronna, and what them Pullman benches started, them bony shoulders finished. My be-hind's so raw you could. . . . Oh . . . I beg your pardon, Miss.
Mr. Big:	My daughter, Leah.
Johnny:	Nice to meetcha. *He stares at Leah.*
Mr. Big:	You were sayin'?
Johnny:	Mn? . . . Oh. Nothin'. . . . Just . . . nothin'.
Mr. Big:	I'm int'rested, boy.
Johnny:	I . . . I ain't got nothin' else to say, I don't think.
Mr. Big:	So . . . home from Toronto . . . for a visit?
Johnny:	No, I come back you could say.
Mr. Big:	Couldn't find work.

Johnny:	That's it.
Mr. Big:	How'd you pay for your ticket?
Johnny:	I . . .

He looks down at his hands. Pause. Mr. Big squeezes his shoulder.

Mr. Big:	It's all right. You're a good boy. I can tell.
Johnny:	I tried.
Mr. Big:	I know.
Johnny:	I walked them streets applyin' for jobs a dog wouldn't take . . . worse than the mines.
Mr. Big:	You think so?
Johnny:	No. Not worse than the mines, but you see . . . I could never get nothin' steady and now the soldiers is back and nothin' steady for them and . . .
Mr. Big:	And what?
Johnny:	And . . . I give up. That's what I done. I give up. Ain't got no choice. I had to come back.
Mr. Big:	You been over to the colliery?
Johnny:	Not yet.
Mr. Big:	But those are your plans.
Johnny:	There ain't nothin' else but the mines.
Mr. Big:	And are you lookin' forward to that?

Johnny stares at Mr. Big. He says nothing. Mr. Big leans closer to him.

Mr. Big:	There's a radiance 'round you, boy, and those with eyes can see it.
Johnny:	*Smiles.* That's 'cause I ain't got the black from the mine yet. Any radiance Pop had is all gone, and Will's is just peekin' through in spots.
Mr. Big:	I'm talkin' incandescence, boy . . .
Johnny:	Yeah?
Mr. Big:	Look at Leah.

Johnny:	Ah-huh.
Mr. Big:	Can you see it?

Johnny looks at Leah, tilts his head, squints his eyes a bit, looks at Mr. Big, back at Leah. Leah smiles.

Leah:	Sometimes he just talks like that.
Johnny:	Ah-huh.
Mr. Big:	Can you see it?
Johnny:	Aah . . .
Mr. Big:	Can you?
Johnny:	Bit maybe.
Mr. Big:	Same thing with you. I can see it. A luminous aura. That's how I knew I could trust you. . . . I'm a man a influence, Johnny. Do you know what I'm sayin'?
Johnny:	No.
Mr. Big:	I'm talkin' gainful employment, and a position right here, by my side. Like a son, Johnny.

Mr. Big moves away from Johnny to address the gathering. Leah touches Johnny's arm.

Leah:	You'll get used to him. He's just kinda like that.
Johnny:	*Nods his head.* Yeah. Okay.
Mr. Big:	Ladies and gentlemen!

The player piano begins playing very softly of its own accord. It provides an accompaniment to Mr. Big's speech.

Mr. Big:	Ladies and gents of the flourishin' city of Blairmore!
Cec:	City you says!
Mr. Big:	Says city I do! For the future is as clear to me as the past! Destiny calls to Blairmore. . . .
Will:	Ooooooooo-eeeeeeeeee!
Mr. Big:	Oooooooooo-eeeeeeeeee! And this tiny town will feed and fatten on the efforts a citizens such as ourselves to achieve one day a state a such metropolity

	it'll make Tronna no more than a cow pie, and its environs nothin' but road apples!
Old Sump:	Watch where you step, oooooo-eeeeee!
Widow:	And vere vill you place in da scheme a tings den?
Mr. Big:	Where fortune and destiny dictate.

A round of applause.

Mr. Big:	But tonight is not one dedicated to paeans a future exploits, no matter how well deserved and inevitable they be. Tonight I speak of a courageous deed executed by this young man here!

The player piano grows a bit in volume with appropriate music as Mr. Big sets his "train cars" with a couple of chairs. The others, at first reluctantly, but then with growing enjoyment, play the roles he assigns.

By the time The Widow enters as the conductor there is much fun and games; it is no longer necessary for Mr. Big to direct or assign. Everyone is into it.

Mr. Big:	Picture . . . if you will . . . the interior of the railway car from Lethbridge. . . . This seat here . . . and here . . . and here. . . . And here . . . sits Johnny, gingerly but alert, fourteen days on the rails from the mysterious east, but within sight and smell a home and mother. . . . Forgive me, Mrs. Farley! To mention your name in these surroundings is to render less than your due, which is prodigious for producing such a boy as Johnny.
	And here . . . a lady with a dark brow and piercin' eyes and a countenance to turn the hens off their nest for a fornight. Now Dolly, it's a challenge to your art a make-believe. And by her side a child. . . . *Places Will in chair next to her.* . . . with little of the cute and cunning ways of children. But rather the sad inheritor of all those traits least amiable and features most repulsive from both maternal and paternal lineage. Coupled with these, a voice like a rasp and in possession of a small drum. To even contemplate, much less act upon, the intention of inflicting this tot on one's fellow man in an enclosed space. . . . Ah truly there are

things answerable only when the dead awaken.

. . . And here . . . my Leah . . . and close at hand, my Gompers ever faithful, ever watchful, ever . . . ever Gompers.

And myself.

Well outa Lethbridge.

The sound and motion of the train begin among those on it. It picks up speed.

Mr. Big: Past Pincher Creek. . . . Into the Crowsnest. . . . Past picturesque log cabins cut from virgin lodgepole pine. . . . When suddenly from the end a the car . . .

Widow: *Enters the train car swaying to the motion of the train.* Blairmore! Blairmore! Next stop Blairm. . . . Dat child's a menace, ma'am.

Cec and Old Sump enter the train car. Old Sump has a gun he's got from behind the bar.

Widow: Blairmore! Nice trip, Mr. . . .

Cec: Everybody calm and nobody gits hurt!

Dolly: Aaaahhhhhh!

Old Sump: *To Gompers.* Don't try nothin' funny.

Widow: Da safety a da passenge . . .

Old Sump: Shaddup or I ventilate t'chest!

Dolly: Aaaaaahhhhh!

Mr. Big stands up with his wallet behind his back. Johnny plucks it out of his hand and shoves it into the back of his pants under his jacket. They never stop responding to the train's motion.

Cec: *To Dolly.* Your money or your grapefruit!

The child, Will, bites his arm.

Cec: Ahh! Git this kid off! Leggo!

Old Sump: You! *To Mr. Big.* I want da wallet!

Cec: Help! *As Dolly and Will beat at him.*

Old Sump snatches a billfold Mr. Big offers.

Old Sump: Come on, let's go!

Cec: Help!

Gompers makes a grab for Old Sump. Old Sump gives him a whack with the gun.

Gompers: Ouch! Hey!

Old Sump grabs Cec. They make their way to the end of the train car. Dolly, Will, The Widow and Gompers advance on them with murmurs of protest.

Old Sump: Back! Back! Don't make me fire! Back! Ready, Floyd?

Cec nods. Old Sump fires three real shots in the air as Cec opens the "door." The two of them jump supposedly from the train, rolling as they hit the dirt. Dolly, Will, The Widow, even Gompers, break out of character as they realize the shots are real.

Will: Holy shit!

Cec: Je-sus, Sump, whata you got there?

Old Sump: T'bar gun.

Cec: That's some real, that is.

Old Sump: Didn't t'ink it'd hurt none.

Johnny returns Mr. Big's wallet to him. Mr. Big puts his arm around Johnny's shoulders.

Mr. Big: Thank you, Johnny.

Johnny nods, accepting his thanks.

Dolly: I was scared.

Mr. Big: In a tight corner, you're a man I'd have at my back.

Widow: Dis ear, dere is notin' dere, maybe not ever again.

Old Sump: Eh?

Will: She says you bust one a her ear drums.

Old Sump: Half a what you hear ain't wort' listenin' to anyways.

They all get fresh drinks.

Mr. Big: For you. *Gives a drink to Johnny.*

Cec: You hear that, Popovitch?

Widow: Vit dis ear I hear it. Vit dis, notin'.

Bill appears on the run.

Gompers: Then stand to the other side a Sump. *He turns her bad ear
towards Old Sump.* That way you'll not miss a thing.

A roar of laughter. Bill rushes into the Alberta Hotel.

Bill: All right everyone! Hold it!

They obey.

Mr. Big: Delighted you could join us, Sergeant.

Bill: I heard somethin'.

Mr. Big: Convivial folks rejoicing!

Bill: Sounded more like a shot.

Widow: Oo vas shot?

Will: Somebody shot?

Old Sump: Murder!

Cec: Help, police!

Bill: Hold it!

Mr. Big: This is surely distressing news . . . have you appre-
hended the villain?

Bill: I know the villain all right.

Mr. Big: Quick work.

Bill: I've got him 'tween a rock and a hard place.

Mr. Big: Congratulations.

Bill: I'm impounding the contents . . .

Mr. Big: A toast . . .

Bill: . . . a the glasses!

Mr. Big: . . . to Sergeant Windsor!

Bill: Hold it!

They down the contents of their glasses as Bill makes a futile attempt to grab a glass or two for evidence.

Bill: You! Hey! Come on there!

Bill gets Dolly's empty glass. Several of the company are repressing their reaction to downing overproof whiskey in one gulp. Bill runs his finger around the inside of Dolly's glass. The Widow plucks the glass from his hand as he tastes his finger.

Mr. Big: My god, man, I'd no idea you craved it so.

Bill: Whiskey.

Bill grabs Leah's glass. He runs his finger around the glass.

Mr. Big: A beer for Bill the Brit!

Bill: Sarsaparilla.

Mr. Big: Profuse apologies, sir.

Mr. Big presents Bill with a glass of legal two per cent brew. Mama has switched the taps. All get a two per cent beer which they sip with little satisfaction and some discomfort.

Bill: Two per cent.

Mr. Big: A legal draft.

Bill: I had the evidence right here. *He holds up his finger.*

Widow: *Grabbing Bill's finger and giving it a suck.* Mmmmn—sch!

Bill: Ah, you revoltin' old . . .

Cec: Hey!

Old Sump: T'at's enuff!

Bill: But she . . .

Cec: Watch it!

Bill: What the bloody hell . . .

Mr. Big: Bear with the rustics.

Bill: It's your doin'.

Mr. Big: Oh no. It's a Canadian custom—like kissing the hand of a king.

Rita Howell as Widow Popovitch, David Marriage as Old Sump, Stephen Hair as William Windsor, and Duval Lang as Constable in the Theatre Calgary production of *Whiskey Six*, Calgary, Alberta, 1983.

Courtesy of Theatre Calgary

Will: He's right.

Will grabs Dolly's hand, gives a quick kissy suck to her finger.

Cec: I do it myself.

Old Sump: Every time we meets t'members of t'colliery head office, we all does it!

Will, Dolly, Old Sump, The Widow, and Cec start a mad round of quick kiss/suck of any and all fingers, dropping curtseys and murmurs of obeisance or patronage. Johnny and Leah are amused. Johnny takes Leah's hand. He pauses, then kisses the back of it. She smiles at him. Mama George notices. Mr. Big does not.

Mr. Big: It's a mark of respect.

Several make grabs for Bill's hand. He tries to shake them off, nevertheless several succeed in quick kissy sucks.

Bill: Get away! Get away there! Aaaahh! Get away!

Car headlights flash on the window, two short, one long honk from a car horn. Mr. Big and Gompers exchange a look.

Will: It can't be!

Old Sump: But it is!

Bill: What is?

The headlights are extinguished.

Dolly: Didn't you hear it?

They rush to peer in the opposite direction to that of the car.

Cec: Oh no!

Widow: Vight here in Blairmore!

Bill: What is it?

Dolly: Didn't you hear it?

Will: Look!

Bill: Where?

Dolly: There.

Cec: Oh my god.

Old Sump:	It's t'em.
Bill:	Who is it?
Dolly:	Didn't you see 'em?
Will:	And tomorrow is pay day.
Cec:	Today is pay day!
Bill:	Who is it!
Old Sump:	Why it's t' . . . *at a loss.*
Cec:	It's the . . .
Dolly:	It can't be . . .
Will:	That gang from Montana . . . two honks and a toot!
Old Sump:	T'ey're headin' for t'colliery office.
Will:	They're after the payroll!
Cec:	Help, police!
Bill:	If this is some kinda ruse.
Mr. Big:	Are we to inform Manager Wheatley a Dominion Colliery you thought it not worth checkin' out?

Pause.

Will:	A workin' man could lose his job for that kinda oversight.

Pause. Bill exits on the run. The company laughs.

Mr. Big:	Switch the taps, Mama.
Mama George:	The whole buncha you ought to be ashamed.
Mr. Big:	*Checking outside.* Poor man, eh Mama?

Car lights flash on, off.

Will:	He only got five horses and three cars.
Cec:	To patrol all Southern Alberta.

Gompers draws on gloves.

Widow:	He vill vun all d'way to d'colliery.
Old Sump:	'uffin' and puffin'.

Mr. Big: *Prepared to leave.* A drink to the man's dedication. A *proper* drink, Mama.

Mama switches the taps, pours the drinks.

Mr. Big: Excuse us my friends.

Old Sump: You'll be back, t'en?

Mr. Big: In a while.

Gompers stands ready to go.

Mr. Big: Remember . . . celebrate—enjoy—else my wrath'll fall directly on you. . . . You Sump and Will and Cec . . . Dolly, Widow, Johnny . . . Mama too . . . and Leah, even you!

Old Sump: We swears to celebrate.

Several: Amen!

Mr. Big and Gompers exit in the direction of the car.

Old Sump: Now—as I was sayin'—t'legal draft tastes just like bunny pee.

Will: And when'd you drink that, Sump?

Leah, with a look to Johnny, drifts over towards the piano. Johnny follows.

Old Sump: Be you buried four days you drink most anyt'ing.

Dolly: Where'd you get the bunnies?

Old Sump: Was your own piss you drunk, but we likes to call it bunny pee.

Will: Bunny pee?

Old Sump: T'ere's ladies present.

Will: Bunny pee?

Old Sump: T'beer tastes like piss.

Will: Ah-huh.

Old Sump: So's I was lookin' for a genteel way a sayin' t'at.

Johnny: You was sayin' . . . he's always like that?

Leah: Who?

Johnny: Him. Mr. Big.

Leah: Most always.

A single note on the piano, low, hardly distinguishable as such, could almost be the sigh of the wind, a stirring of the heart, a ting of a glass from the bar. There are four rough groupings: Johnny and Leah apart from the others, Will and Dolly not so much so, Cec and Old Sump in close proximity but not with The Widow and Mama. The note, and sometimes a couple of notes, repeat on the piano at intervals during the following. Lights move back and forth across the figures picking out first this grouping, then that, a fluid dance of soft light with the voices, the piano, the people.

Will: You're not upset by that, are you?

Dolly: By what?

Will: "Piss."

Dolly: I heard it before.

Will: That's good.

Widow: I'm vatchin' dem, Mama. You vatch vit me.

Leah: Do you wanna stand or do you wanna sit?

Johnny: What do you want?

Leah sits. Johnny sits.

Will: God but you're pretty.

Dolly looks away.

Will: I mean it.

Old Sump: I'm t'inkin', Cec, didja know t'at? Didja know what I'm t'inkin'?

Cec: 'Bout piss?

Old Sump: In a way. I was t'inkin' t'at t'Lord said to me t'ree times—no, m'boy, don't wantcha. . . . Worked in t'mines all me life, and I never got no lungs t'at I know of, and t'ere you be losin' boys right and left . . .

Cec: And they was good boys too.

Old Sump: T'at t'ey were.

Cec:	Teddy named after her father, and Robert strong as a bull.
Old Sump:	Didn't do him no good when it come to it.
Cec:	No sir.
Old Sump:	T'ere ain't none of it makes a helluva lot a sense . . . didja ever t'ink t'at?
Cec:	Nope.
Old Sump:	Just as well. Don't do to dwell on 't.
Will:	Look at my hands, Dolly.
Dolly:	You got nice hands.
Will:	You wanna know what I used on 'em? . . . I used the lye, and the bleach.
Dolly:	Really?
Will:	Uh-huh.
Dolly:	I don't think that would be good for you.
Will:	I do it for you. It stings like hell, eats the skin right off, that's why it's so red.
Dolly:	Do you think you should?
Will:	I don't give a damn if it hurts. I do it for you.
Dolly:	I wouldn't want you to do something that wasn't good for you because a me.
Will:	It's 'cause I know you don't like the black . . . have you still got that picture I give you?

Dolly nods.

Johnny:	I can see you're not a great one for talkin'.
Will:	Lemme hold your hand, Dolly.
Leah:	If I've got somethin' to say, then I say it.
Johnny:	Ah.
Leah:	Besides, you're not so talky yourself.
Johnny:	I toldja I been away for a while on my own. . . . You

	get to talkin' more to yourself when that happens.
Leah:	With Mr. Big, it's hard to keep up.
Johnny:	My mum's a big talker—a course not like him—she's more a your . . . ordinary talker.
Widow:	Dey're talkin'.
Mama George:	Mmn. *Assent; she's noticed.*
Widow:	I said dey're talkin', da two a dem, look at dem talkin'.
Mama George:	I heard ya.
Leah:	Are you gonna take that job?
Johnny:	What job?
Leah:	The job that he offered you.
Johnny:	He just said employment.
Leah:	Workin' for him.
Johnny:	He said a bunch a stuff, a person don't know what he means and what he don't mean. *Johnny looks over towards his father, who is quite drunk.*
Cec:	Too good for the mines, filled his head with garbage. *Cec and Johnny catch each other's gaze. . . .* Good enough for Will, good enough for me.
Johnny:	*Back to Leah.* What's he do, 'sides talk?
Leah:	*Gets up.* Lotsa things.
Johnny:	What'd I be doin'?
Leah:	What he told you.
Cec:	*Staggers to his feet, bursts into song.*

My father was a miner,
My mother she is dead,
And I am just an orphan child,
No place to lay my head. . . .

Old Sump:	*Joins Cec in song.*

All thro' this world I wander,
They drive me from their doors,

The two of them precariously prepare to exit for home.

> Someday I'll find a welcome
> On Heaven's golden shore!

They're out the door.

> Now if to me you'll listen,
> I'll tell you a story . . .

Resounding crash as Cec falls, dragging Old Sump with him.

Old Sump: Popovitch!

Cec: Christ.

Widow: I go.

Cec: Popovitch!

Will: I'll see to 'em.

Widow: You go vit your Dolly. I valk dem up and down and den home.

Old Sump: Popovitch!

Widow: When you're not'in' to no one, you're dead. Dey keep me alive. *She joins Old Sump and Cec, moving them off.* You break my ear den you call for Popovitch! Get up! Get up! Get going! Popovitch vill drive you like pigs!

The Widow, Old Sump, and Cec disappear from sight, an oblique image flashes and they're gone. Will and Dolly prepare to leave. Johnny looks at Leah, who's standing.

Johnny: Where're you goin'?

Leah: To bed.

Johnny: Stay.

Will: *With his arm around Dolly.* You comin' Johnny?

Johnny: Go on, I'll catch up.

Dolly: Good night.

Leah: 'Night Dolly, 'night Will.

Will and Dolly exit from the Alberta Hotel. Will is whistling. They stop. Will kisses Dolly. They make their way off, Will whistling.

Johnny sits watching Mama and Leah restore a bit of order. Mama tidies. Leah looks as if she might leave.

The reflected and softly blurred image of Dolly and Will kissing. Will's whistling heard faintly from offstage. The image fades. Whistling continues, growing fainter for slightly longer.

Johnny: Do you gotta go right now?

Leah: Why?

Johnny: I thought maybe we, you and me, we could . . . sit and talk.

Leah: What do you want to talk about?

Johnny shrugs.

Mama George: Went thro' a whole keg, imagine that. *She places a small light so it may be seen outside.* Course it doesn't take long, fact it takes a lot less than a body'd think. Just the same, I'm always surprised. . . . He's taken to you.

Johnny: Oh?

Mama George: Yes he has. Ask her. She'll tell you.

Johnny: I will.

Mama George: If you need tellin'. And do you know who she is?

Johnny: I think so.

Mama George: A chosen daughter. . . . And now who'd you be?

Johnny: Me?

Mama George: Ah-huh.

Johnny: Johnny Farley.

Mama George: You're a fine lookin' boy all right.

Johnny: Who're you?

Mama George: Mama George. With or without incandescence, a body'd be lookin' twice at you, eh, Leah?

Leah: Looks aren't everything.

Johnny: Are you related to him?

Leah:	Mama George is Mrs. Big . . . course we don't call her that.
Mama George:	There can only be one Big in a family.
Johnny:	That ain't his real name—Mr. Big.
Mama George:	His chosen name, that's what it is.
Johnny:	Mr. George, is that his real name?
Mama George:	Glasses, glasses, more glasses . . . the two of you stay, I'll see to these. *She exits with glasses to be washed.*

Pause as Johnny and Leah eye each other.

Johnny:	So . . . is it George?
Leah:	Does it matter?
Johnny:	No. . . . What's your last name then?
Leah:	Unknown.
Johnny:	What?
Leah:	Last name unknown.
Johnny:	I thought you was their daughter.
Leah:	Their . . .
Johnny:	Chosen daughter, ah-huh. . . .
Leah:	What're you thinkin'?
Johnny:	Nothin'.
Leah:	You must be thinkin' somethin'.
Johnny:	No.
Leah:	What're you thinkin' you don't wanna tell me?
Johnny:	Nothin'.
Leah:	I'd tell you if you asked me.
Johnny:	What're you thinkin'?
Leah:	I'm thinkin' . . . you are better lookin' than your brother.
Johnny:	We wasn't even talkin' 'bout that.

Leah:	I know.
Johnny:	You wasn't livin' here when I left.
Leah:	No.
Johnny:	Did I tell you I went to Tronna?
Leah:	Dolly went to Tronna.
Johnny:	I heard.
Leah:	She said it was awful.
Johnny:	She's right.
Leah:	She had to do awful things. And then she came back here even though her mum was already dead and her dad died after she left and there weren't none of her family left, she still came here. . . . Why do you think she did that?
Johnny:	I guess it was home.
Leah:	With nobody left.
Johnny:	A place can be home, the sky and the hills.
Leah:	I'm lucky.
Johnny:	How's that?
Leah:	'Cause that will never happen to me.
Johnny:	What?
Leah:	What happened to Dolly in Tronna. It coulda happened to me but it won't . . . and do you know why?
Johnny:	Why?
Leah:	'Cause he gathered me up, like God descendin' to take his Chosen up into Heaven in a fiery chariot! *Johnny is staring at her. She stops and looks at him.* And the same thing can happen to you, if you let him.

Pause. Johnny leans over and kisses her. Pause. He kisses her again. These are little kisses, not passionate ones.

Leah:	You shouldn't do that.
Johnny:	Why not?

| Leah: | Because. |

They sit in silence.

| Leah: | D . . . |
| Johnny: | Don't talk. |

They sit in silence.

Leah:	We gotta talk sometime.
Johnny:	It's a nice place, this. I feel good sittin' here. Feel right sittin' here.
Leah:	If it weren't for him and Mama, I wouldn't have anyone.
Johnny:	You'd have me.
Leah:	You just met me.
Johnny:	But it don't feel that way, does it.
Leah:	I feel funny, that's all.
Johnny:	I feel . . . like I . . . like I knowed you—and him—for a hundred years, don't you feel like that?
Leah:	I dunno.
Johnny:	Say you do. I knowed you do. I said it 'cause I knew you could feel what I was feelin'. I wasn't afraid to say it.
Leah:	I am.

Johnny stares at her.

| Johnny: | I . . . |

Leah gets up and starts to leave.

Johnny:	Leah! . . .
Leah:	What?
Johnny:	Do you think I should take this job?
Leah:	It's up to you.
Johnny:	Do you want me to?

Leah: I dunno.

Johnny: Either you do or you don't.

Leah: Well I don't then.

Johnny: You're lyin'.

Leah: Well I do then.

Johnny: Well I will then.

Leah: All right then. *Leah starts off.*

Johnny: Leah!

Leah: What?

Johnny: I just wanted to look at you before you left.

Leah: Well?

Johnny: You look real nice.

She starts to exit.

Johnny: Leah!

Leah: What?

She stops and turns to him.

Johnny: Good night.

Leah: *Looks severe for a moment, then smiles.* Good night. *She exits.*

Johnny: *Watches her go, then softly.* Ooooooooo-eeeeeeeeee. Oo-ee. *He slowly looks around at his surroundings. He walks to where Mr. Big formerly stood, strikes a pose reminiscent of Mr. Big's. He speaks softly.* Ladies and gents a the flourishin' city a Blairmore . . . *He laughs.* Says city I do. *Pause. Serious again, he goes to the bar. He pours a glass from the tap.*

Mr. Big and Gompers approach the Alberta Hotel.

Johnny: Like a son . . . like a father . . .

Mr. Big: Is the count right?

Gompers: Yes sir.

Johnny takes a large swig from the glass. He spews it out. Mr. Big and Gompers enter the hotel. The light is dim; they are unaware of Johnny, who watches them. They busy themselves with lowering two kegs from the rafters.

Mr. Big: I want you in the forward car with the goods. I'll be right behind. Now remember, any sign a the Brit, and go like hell for the border.

Gompers: Which border?

Mr. Big: Any border you got a hope in hell a crossin' 'fore he catches up. And praise the Lord for the Whiskey Six. *Their focus is on their work.* . . . It's been my experience . . . a little prayer . . . never hurt . . .

A clink of glass from Johnny. Mr. Big and Gompers tense, turning to scan the bar. Gompers makes a move. Mr. Big places a hand on his arm.

Johnny: . . . It's me.

Mr. Big: *Relaxing, nods to Gompers to continue.* Ah, so it is. *He moves to Johnny at the bar as Gompers works.*

Mr. Big: Mama set the lamp, I thought . . . *Runs a finger through the spewed drink.* Did she switch the taps? What you do is . . . replace the glass on the shelf to the left a your knee if you'd care for an illegal draft or a whiskey . . .

Outside the Alberta Hotel, slightly distorted, is a fractured image of Bill in uniform, a bit more formal than his original scoutish uniform. Bill himself appears in the shadows observing the hotel. A stir in the shadows behind him. After a moment we see that a second figure is there—Mrs. Farley. Bill turns to whisper to Mrs. Farley. Mrs. Farley nods. Bill seems to assure her. The two of them gaze at the Alberta Hotel. Mrs. Farley scurries off.

Johnny moves to the glass, looks at Mr. Big, then pours another drink from the tap. He tastes it, looks at Mr. Big, and laughs.

Mr. Big: Bit better?

Johnny: Lot better.

Mr. Big: Now that's a secret, boy . . . not a word, even to Gompers.

Johnny:	What's a . . . what's a Whiskey Six?
Mr. Big:	Six cylinder MacLaughlin, fastest car on the road. A most seductive vehicle. *He blows out the lamp, and looks out onto the street, he can see Bill the Brit.* Do you drive, Johnny?
Johnny:	I could learn.

Gompers looks out the window onto the street with Mr. Big. Mr. Big continues his conversation with Johnny. The two kegs are ready to be moved out.

Mr. Big:	Do you believe . . . it criminal to eat a cucumber sandwich, Johnny?
Johnny:	No.
Mr. Big:	Nor is it a crime to drink a beer. . . . Prohibition will never last, boy.
Johnny:	It won't, eh.
Mr. Big:	For it's based on a lie.

Bill the Brit gives up and exits from his post of observation. Mr. Big nods to Gompers who moves to the kegs. Mr. Big turns to Johnny.

Mr. Big:	And a lie cannot endure.
Johnny:	Where do you want that?
Mr. Big:	Edge of the bar for now.

A groan of effort from Gompers. Mr. Big and Johnny move to help him.

The kegs are awkward to move. They work in silence for a second except for the slight sound of exertion. Light is fading on the Alberta Hotel.

Johnny:	Jesus.
Mr. Big:	All right?
Johnny:	I never knew booze was so heavy.

Mrs. Farley:

In darkness.

And in the midst of the seven candlesticks one like unto the Son of Man clothed with a garment . . . and girt 'round . . . a golden girdle. *Light begins to build on Mrs. Farley. She reads from a book.* His head and hairs were white like wool, white as snow and his eyes were as a flame of

| **Mr. Big:** | Tell me, Johnny. Can you keep a man sober thro' coercion a law? Can a man be made moral by threatin' punishment? Now what are your thoughts on this, Johnny? | fire, and his voice as the sound of many waters and he had in his right hand seven stars and out of his mouth a two-edged sword and his countenance was as the sun shineth in its strength, and when I saw him I fell at his feet as if dead. |

The Alberta Hotel disappears in darkness.

Mrs. Farley: And he laid his right hand upon me saying fear not. . . . I am the First and the Last, I am he that liveth and was dead and behold I am alive evermore . . . and have . . .

Sound of Johnny whistling offstage.

Mrs. Farley: The keys . . . *She shuts the book.* . . . of hell and of death . . .

Whistling grows in volume slightly. Johnny stops whistling, doesn't sneak in, but enters quietly. He stops on seeing his mother.

Mrs. Farley: . . . Do you know what time it is?

Johnny: 'Bout twenty past.

Mrs. Farley: Past what?

Johnny: Five.

Mrs. Farley: In the afternoon, Johnny.

Johnny: I know what you're gonna say.

Mrs. Farley: How could you . . . when I don't know myself.

Johnny: Why don't you just say it.

Pause.

Mrs. Farley: When your father got in, it was light.

Johnny: Yeah.

Mrs. Farley: And William, he was later than that.

Johnny:	We had a kinda celebration, Mum.
Mrs. Farley:	Both of 'em still weavin' when they left for work.
Johnny:	I helped a fella out on the train up from Leth . . .
Mrs. Farley:	I know it! I may be the last to know it, it bein' all over Blairmore, but someone, outa the goodness a their soul, or the pleasure they get from sorrowin', someone did tell me, so I do know!
Johnny:	. . . Anyways . . . the fella thanked me by havin' a do.

Pause.

Mrs. Farley:	I'd a thought you'd be out and over with your father and William.
Johnny:	That's a funny thing for you to be sayin'.
Mrs. Farley:	I'd a thought you'd be over applyin'.
Johnny:	You know how we both feel 'bout me workin' the colliery.
Mrs. Farley:	Good enough for your father and William.
Johnny:	No it's not.
Mrs. Farley:	It's them workin' there this minute pays for supper tonight, and don't you forget it!
Johnny:	What's got into you?
Mrs. Farley:	Nothin'!
Johnny:	Then what's wrong?
Mrs. Farley:	You tell me.
Johnny:	Wasn't it you three years ago beggin' me to leave this place? Wasn't it you cryin', "Not the colliery, Johnny! Not the mines!" From the time I was little, you whisperin' and beggin' and cryin', "Get out, get away, go? Fly away, Johnny!" Wasn't that you?
Mrs. Farley:	But you come back and . . .
Johnny:	I had no stomach for starvin' and freezin' and bein' alone.
Mrs. Farley:	Better that than . . .

Johnny:	Than what?
Mrs. Farley:	I love you, Johnny.
Johnny:	I don't need no colliery now.
Mrs. Farley:	You was always my favourite, always.
Johnny:	I said I don't need no colliery, I got somethin' else.
Mrs. Farley:	I don't want to hear it.
Johnny:	The fella over at the Alberta Hotel offered me somethin' and I'm thinkin' a takin' it.
Mrs. Farley:	No.
Johnny:	That's why I'm so late gettin' in; I give him a hand last night.
Mrs. Farley:	Johnny.
Johnny:	So I don't have to work at the colliery.
Mrs. Farley:	You'll make me a laughin' stock, you know that!
Johnny:	Is that all you care about?
Mrs. Farley:	I care about you! I tell you I love you and you never listen!
Johnny:	You only love me when I do what you want!
Mrs. Farley:	Wouldn't you fight if you saw a person you loved goin' wrong?
Johnny:	It's not a crime for a man to drink liquor or sell it!
Mrs. Farley:	There's the law, and them that breaks it is criminal.
Johnny:	Well then Mum, the whole bleedin' country's criminal—them that works in the mines, them that owns the mines, the lawyers, the judge, and who's to say the god damn Prime Minister don't have a wine when he chats with the King?
Mrs. Farley:	And them that sells it is worse than them that drinks it!
Johnny:	Why don't you fight what drives Pop to drink instead a the drink?
Mrs. Farley:	You are not workin' for that man, Johnny.

Johnny:	I'm thinkin' a doin' that. I'm tellin' you straight that's what I'm thinkin'.
Mrs. Farley:	Do you know what he is?
Johnny:	He's a fella offered me a job.
Mrs. Farley:	Offa the train from nobody knows where.
Johnny:	Have you made that a crime?
Mrs. Farley:	And his wife . . .
Johnny:	Don't . . .
Mrs. Farley:	Never speakin' to no one . . .
Johnny:	Mum . . .
Mrs. Farley:	Whose only friend is a Jew . . .
Johnny:	Shaddup!
Mrs. Farley:	And you know why his wife's so quiet? 'Cause right in that Alberta Hotel, the same roof, the same bed, her husband is keepin' a whore!
Johnny:	What are you talkin' about?
Mrs. Farley:	Young enough to be his daughter.
Johnny:	I don't believe you!

Pause.

Mrs. Farley:	I been sittin' here steelin' myself to say it. You want nothin' to do with her. Or him.

Sound of faint blast from mine whistle; they don't appear to hear it.

Johnny:	You're lyin'.
Mrs. Farley:	Why would I lie?
Johnny:	You'd lie 'cause . . . 'cause you'd rather see me dyin' for a livin' in the mines, than workin' in the clean, pure air for a rumrunner.

Sound of a second blast from the mine whistle. This time Johnny and his mother do hear it and realize it is the second blast they've heard. Mama George, Mr. Big, and Leah appear on stage.

Johnny:	. . . That ain't the end a the shift.

Mrs. Farley's lips begin to move slowly and silently. Sound of a third blast. Gompers appears, then Bill, and finally Dolly.

Johnny: That ain't the end a the shift!

Sound of a fourth blast, as Cec and Old Sump enter the house.

Cec: Mum.

Johnny: What happened?

Old Sump: Weren't not'in', Johnny . . . a piece a timber . . . t'bracin . . . it just shifted like.

Johnny: Weren't nothin'.

Old Sump: Not a bit a rock fell, just t'at one piece a timber, it just shifted like, 'gainst t'wall, t'at was all. . . . And it caught 'im.

Johnny: Will?

Old Sump: He jumped . . . but he weren't fast enuff.

Cec: Mum.

Old Sump: We got 'im out. We got 'im up. He died when we 'it t'surface.

Pause. Johnny starts to leave.

Mrs. Farley: Johnny? . . . Where're you goin'?

Johnny: For christ's sake can't you reach out to *Pop!* For one lousy minute can't you mourn for poor Will? Will is dead and it's still Johnny, my Johnny. You are crushin' me with your love as sure as Will was caught and crushed by a timber.

Mrs. Farley: John . . .

Johnny: Leave me alone.

Mrs. Farley: You're all I got left.

Johnny: Don't say it.

Mrs. Farley: It's true.

Johnny: Get away.

Mrs. Farley: It's all right to cry.

Johnny:	Then why aren't *you* cryin'?
Mrs. Farley:	I'll tell you . . . every bit a my bein' is consumed with one thing, to keep some vestige a hope in my soul . . . bargainin' with the Lord to spare one a my sons.
Johnny:	Don't.
Mrs. Farley:	You think I don't weep? Why none a you here could conceive a my sorrow. Inside a my breast is a deep yawnin' hole and through it rushes a torrent a tears such as you've never seen! I have mourned Teddy and Robert and I mourn Will . . . but I will not mourn you Johnny! He's promised me you.
Johnny:	In exchange for them?
Cec:	She can't mean it boy. *He makes a gesture of support which Johnny brushes aside as he turns on his mother.*
Johnny:	God damn your church meetings and temperance!
Cec:	It's all right.
Johnny:	Nothin' is right! I'm goin'. I'm leavin'. I'm rentin' a room from Popovitch.
Mrs. Farley:	No.
Johnny:	And I got me employment at the Alberta Hotel.
Mrs. Farley:	The rumrunner.
Johnny:	Right. *He starts out.*
Mrs. Farley:	*Yells after him.* And what will you do with his whore?!

Johnny runs across the stage out of sight. We are left with fractured images of him fleeing. They glint as light fades.

Mrs. Farley:	John-ny!!

BLACKOUT

ACT TWO

Plaintive sound from the player piano. Rippling distorted image of Bill the Brit heralds his measured entrance on stage. He now wears a holstered revolver and his appearance is more solid and threatening. In repose he seems dangerous as opposed to silly. He stands at ease but watchful on the stage. He looks off and sees someone approaching. He smiles and removes his hat in greeting. It's Mrs. Farley. She bobs her head in greeting. He indicates she should look down the street.

She does so. Bill observes her, and steps away from her a bit. Mrs. Farley is torn between leaving and staying. She doesn't wish to be seen by Johnny whom she is watching, but she wishes to continue to observe him. He approaches. He sees her. He stops. She stiffens and sails past him like an iceberg in the North Atlantic. Johnny watches her go, catching sight of Bill. Johnny enters the Alberta Hotel.

The player piano melody brightens a bit as light builds on the Alberta Hotel. Leah stands by the piano. A strand of hair has come loose. She's running her thumb over the perforations in a piano cartridge. She stands in a stream of sunlight. Mr. Big sits, his lunch unfinished and forgotten in front of him. He watches Leah.

Mama is present, unobtrusive but busy as always.

Johnny looks at Mr. Big, at Leah; he stands in silent scrutiny.

Mr. Big: Leah? . . . Your hair.

She makes a motion to restore the strand to its place.

Mr. Big: No. Leave it . . . just as you were . . . the head tilted, the eyes . . .

She resumes her former position.

Mr. Big: How far between us . . . Johnny? *Mr. Big's eyes never leave Leah but he has obviously been aware of Johnny.*

Johnny: Eh?

Mr. Big: What would you ascertain the distance to be separatin' me—from her?

Johnny: I dunno.

Mr. Big: Hazard a guess.

Johnny:	Fifteen feet.
Mr. Big:	Fifteen feet it is, across the well-worn floor at the Alberta hotel?
Johnny:	'Bout fifteen.
Mr. Big:	Or is there stretchin' between us a great and gapin' abyss with a bottom a layered, feathery bones, thin and delicate as the scales of a pearl—and pressin' on t'other side at that—the Vaults a Hell?

Johnny gives a slow shrug.

Mr. Big:	Or are we so close there is nothin' between us but a hazy shimmer, insubstantial as a veil a dust motes driftin' in the sun . . . Eh Johnny?
Johnny:	I dunno.
Mr. Big:	You don't know . . . well then, try this. Why do I bestride my world like a colossus?
Johnny:	Diet?
Mr. Big:	Come on, do you know?

Johnny shrugs.

Mr. Big:	I've mastered the art a seein' the multiple realities a the universe, and more than that. I have embraced them, though they be almost always conflicting, but equally true . . . . Now, how far is it—fifteen feet, the abyss, or nothin' between us?
Johnny:	The car's ready.
Mr. Big:	As good an answer as any. *He finishes eating as he talks.* You know, if I could choose one image to carry me through all eternity, it would be that of Leah, as she stands there today, at this moment, elbow held just so, head tilted, a single strand of hair . . . what do you say, Johnny?
Johnny:	That's a long time.
Mr. Big:	Till Judgement Day?
Johnny:	Till then.

Mr. Big:	Ah yes. And when the good Lord called my name, I'd say, "Look, encompassed there, that's my life."
Johnny:	And what would He say?
Mr. Big:	Who?
Johnny:	God.
Mr. Big:	*Laughs.* . . . Well Mama, won't be long. *Kisses Mama's cheek.* Give Johnny some a that schnitzel. I'll just get my coat, Leah. *He exits.*

Mama exits with Mr. Big's dishes. Leah has continued to hold, relaxed and informally, the pose Mr. Big has described. Johnny stands staring at her. Eventually she turns to look at him.

Johnny:	. . . I don't suppose you got any idea a how stupid you look.
Leah:	Not your kind of image?
Johnny:	Didja ever meet Jack Cottrell?
Leah:	Should I?
Johnny:	He's a fellow from the Creek studied taxidermy by mail. You reminded me a one a his earlier efforts.
Leah:	Thank you.

Johnny turns to leave.

Leah:	Wait! Please . . . why . . . do you always sidle outa a room every time that I enter?
Johnny:	I don't.
Leah:	And if you stay, why are you always so rude?
Johnny:	I'm not.
Leah:	Or else pretend you can't see me . . . I'm not even there?
Johnny:	I don't do none a those things.
Leah:	Yes you do! And you been doin' them for ages!
Johnny:	Look, if you're gonna stand around strikin' affected poses and lookin' stuffed and actin' deaf, I just thought someone should tell you.

Mama is observing most discreetly. On the street, Bill is just a shadow.

Leah: Should be me's avoidin' you.

Johnny: Why's that?

Leah: 'Cause you said things to me that were lies, and I believed you. You said . . . you don't even like me!

Johnny: I do.

Leah: No you don't!

Johnny: Who said?

Leah: How people act is a lot more truthful than what anybody can say.

Johnny: I was tryin' to act like a friend!

Leah: When!

Johnny: When I told you you looked stuffed.

Pause. Then Leah suppresses a smile.

Leah: You wanna know somethin'?

Johnny: What?

Leah: *Whispers.* I felt stupid. *She smiles.*

Johnny: Well, you sure looked stupid—it was okay at first . . . it was when you kept standin' there it got stupid.

Leah: Do you know this is the most you ever said to me since that night? *Pause in which Leah sees Johnny's unease.* But we won't talk about that—you wanna know something else? You do, doncha?

Johnny: Sure.

Leah: From doin' . . . that . . . *She cranks and tilts her head in an exaggeration of the pose.* . . . I got a crick in my neck . . . right . . . here.

Johnny: Is it gone?

Leah: Mostly gone. Feel it. *She leans forward for him to feel it. He puts his hand out to feel it and stops.* The muscle's all . . . What is it? . . . What's wrong?

Johnny:	So why do you do it?
Leah:	I love him.

Johnny starts out.

Leah:	Now where are you goin'?!
Johnny:	Check on the car.
Leah:	You haven't had lunch!
Johnny:	Have it later.
Leah:	Come back here! What is the matter with you? At first I thought it was your brother—
Johnny:	Never you mind my brother!
Leah:	But it's six months now. . . . And then I thought it's because a your mother and you not speakin' and that gettin' you down—
Johnny:	I don't like people talkin' 'bout that!
Leah:	You might not like it, but we all do.
Johnny:	Well it's none a your business!
Leah:	Why did you say those things to me? You felt like you knowed me for a hundred years, that's what you said, and you liked me, and tried to make me say them too, and now you just. . . . Why did you do that? I'm not lettin' you go till you tell me!
Johnny:	. . . It . . . was a bet.
Leah:	A bet?
Johnny:	Yeah.
Leah:	With who?
Johnny:	Ahhh, Will, with Will.
Leah:	What for . . . to make fun a me?
Johnny:	Yeah.
Leah:	To make me look stupid.
Johnny:	I'm lyin'.

Leah:	Why?
Johnny:	It wasn't a bet, I just said that.
Leah:	What for?
Johnny:	I dunno. For fun.

Pause.

Leah:	I thought we were gonna be friends.
Johnny:	So what kinda friend do you want—a Mr. Big kinda friend?
Leah:	Whata you mean?
Johnny:	You know what I mean.
Leah:	No . . . Mr. Big is my friend, more than my friend—if it weren't for him and Mama, I wouldn't have anyone.
Johnny:	I'm not talkin' 'bout that.
Leah:	What are you talkin' about?
Johnny:	I'm talkin' 'bout you and him!
Leah:	You don't want me to love Mr. Big?
Johnny:	Jesus Christ you're stupid.
Leah:	Well you're cruel.
Johnny:	*I'm* cruel?
Leah:	I don't want you for a friend.
Johnny:	Pretty sad state of affairs when the "daughter" a the colossus a Blairmore's gotta look for a friend in the person of her father's employee!
Leah:	I *chose* you!
Johnny:	'Cause you don't have no others! Why's that I suppose?
Leah:	I have friends.
Johnny:	Name one.
Leah:	Dolly's my friend.

Johnny: And what's she but another hunka slag same as myself?

Leah: And me, what am I?

Johnny: You know what you are!

Leah: I'm his chosen daughter.

Johnny: Have you got no sense a what's proper, what's right?!

Leah: I'm his ch . . .

Johnny: Whore!

Pause. Fractured image of a car. Honk of horn offstage.

Johnny: Tell me it's just a story.

Mr. Big: *Offstage.* Leah!

Johnny: A mean story, ain't no truth in it.

Mr. Big: *Offstage.* Leah!

Sound of a car horn offstage.

Johnny: I wanted to talk to you a million times since that night. I meant every word I said. I mean it more now. *Mr. Big enters. Johnny whispers.* I love you.

Mr. Big: Leah?

Leah: Yes.

Mr. Big puts his arm around her in a warm, not an intimate, fashion.

Mr. Big: Here you are. Well, we'll be seein' you, Johnny.

Mr. Big and Leah exit. Johnny watches them leave.

Mama George: *Softly.* When he brought her home, she was just a tiny wee bit of a thing.

Johnny: Stealin' kids offa streets don't hardly seem right.

Mama George: Papa and I, we never had any.

Johnny: That don't make it right.

Mama George: She was runnin' away.

Johnny: So where was she runnin' from?

Mama George: Papa says her past, and into her future.

Johnny: What do you say?

Mama George: She told me—the William D. Purdy Home for Orphans. It was the sixth time she'd done it—and her only eleven. She'd been beat, her poor little backside and arms, they had bruises like overripe plums.

Johnny: Why are you tellin' me this?

Mama George: Because I want you to understand. . . .Why shouldn't she love him?

Johnny: There's love and there's love.

Mama George: Well, she'd have run from here if she hadn't been happy.

Johnny: Where would she run to?

Mama George: She'd run before, six times and only eleven.

Johnny: Maybe she was tired a runnin'!

Mama George: He picked her up and he brought her home and he gave her everything, a mama who loves her, a mama she loves, him who adores her—and you.

Johnny: I'm not a thing to be given to people.

Mama George: Maybe he don't realize that's what he's done.

Johnny: Then maybe I don't want her.

Mama George: You don't mean that.

Johnny: Well, a person can't be givin' people to people! He don't own her—nor me—and if her and me . . . it'd be our own business, have nothin' to do with him.

Mama George: That's right.

Johnny: But—I'd have to know, you see.

Mama George: Why?

Johnny: You say why, not what . . . you know what I'd have to know doncha?

As Mama moves to leave, Johnny stops her.

Johnny: You say she's like a daughter, more than a daughter, isn't that right? And those, you see, are the words I keep stumblin' on. Is a person takin' advantage of a person here, and which person is that!?

Mama George: Let me go.

Johnny: I gotta know, Mama.

Mama George: Where would you be if it weren't for him?

Johnny: In the mines! And you think I don't thank him for that? I find myself lovin' that man . . . and I owe him . . . I do owe him—he's . . . he's . . . like—yesterday when . . . when the Brit got onto our tail . . . Mr. Big was drivin' . . . you know what he did? The road lay ahead, and I thought, "Trust to the Whiskey Six, BC border or bust," and . . . and he swings the wheel one hundred and ten degree angle turn! We are off the road, and streamin' over those golden dips and mellow rises . . . and the Brit, I swear to God he broke an axle attemptin' the turn . . . and Mr. Big, he says, "We'll just snake our way into the 'Mericas, I know a man there who's into the marketin' of what slakes a powerful thirst. We'll do business with him." . . . It was . . . real sunny, no wind for a change . . . and we stopped on the top a one of them hills and we got outa the car and we stood there. . . . Far as you could see a rollin' sweep a foothills, and us two standin' there, with the car sittin' right on the top of one of them gentle rises, no trail leadin' to it or from it—and over it and us and all and around—the sky, like a big blue bowl. Him, with his foot on the runnin' board, and one hand in his pocket, and he says, "Johnny—we are standin' at the centre of the universe, Johnny, everything is in relation here"—and I believed him. . . . And he says, "We are the warp and woof in a divine tapestry, Johnny"—and I believed him. I don't know what the hell it means, but I believed him.

Mama George: You love Leah, that's all that matters.

Johnny: No—'cause inside a me, Mama, nestled 'gainst that

	gratitude is a grain a rot, and if I don't find out, that grain is gonna grow and spread.
Mama George:	Then you'll reap a harvest of tears.
Johnny:	I gotta have the acquaintance a the whole man!
Mama George:	Is that possible?
Johnny:	He says himself—a lie cannot endure. I don't wanna be commitin' myself to a lie.
Mama George:	He says there's many truths.
Johnny:	But him sayin' don't make it so. Lies can endure, and with no game playin', there's truth.
Mama George:	But whoever lived without playin' games?
Johnny:	I can stand knowin', it's not knowin' that kills.
Mama George:	If you love Leah, why does anything else matter but that? . . . I love him, and nothing else matters but that.
Johnny:	You've heard a my mum . . . inside a my mum, the milk a human kindness is curdled. She's like a thin mangy old cat that's gone wild. Nothin' left to nourish herself or her own. . . . But she would be rippin' out the belly and tearin' the throat, she would be killin' that tom that came on her kitten. . . . And there you are: warm and plump and lovin', givin', forgivin'. . . . What I'm wonderin' is—are you less than my mum?

Pause. Mama exits. Johnny stands alone, still. He looks out, his eye is caught by the vague shadow of Bill and Gompers. He watches them although he seems preoccupied as opposed to having some strong reaction at seeing them together.

Bill stirs in the shadows. Gompers approaches. Bill nods a greeting. The two of them draw together briefly. Gompers laughs, and leaves Bill. Bill's good cheer disappears as Gompers leaves him. Bill casually saunters off.

Gompers enters the hotel. Goes directly to look out and watch Bill's progress out of sight.

Johnny: . . . What did he want?

Gompers:	Nothin'.
Johnny:	What did he say?
Gompers:	Passin' time, that's all. *He moves to get a drink from the tap.*
Johnny:	. . . Watch him.
Gompers:	I don't need you tellin' me that.
Johnny:	Right.
Gompers:	*Drains his drink, gets himself another, looks at Johnny.* What're you starin' at?

Johnny looks away. Gompers sips his second drink.

Johnny:	. . . Did you know the Brit was waitin' for us yester-day?
Gompers:	I heard.
Johnny:	Seemed to know which route we was takin'.
Gompers:	You lost him, didn't you?
Johnny:	Ah-huh.
Gompers:	Well then, what the hell. He's always stakin' out this route or that. For once he got lucky.
Johnny:	Maybe.
Gompers:	He's keepin' an eye on the front too, thinks he'll catch us bringin' it out or in.
Johnny:	That's why it's stashed 'cross town.
Gompers:	He wants it real bad.
Johnny:	Ah-huh.
Gompers:	He's replacin' his vehicles with motorcycles.
Johnny:	So?
Gompers:	And they're puttin' machine guns on the front a them.
Johnny:	Where'd you hear that?
Gompers:	Around.

Johnny:	Who from?
Gompers:	Do you suppose a Whiskey Six can outrun fire from a Gatling gun?
Johnny:	Whata they want to bring guns into it for? They wouldn't open fire on an unarmed car that was just carryin' booze.
Gompers:	Lawbreakers is lawbreakers accordin' to the Brit. Murderers, rapists and rumrunners, all the same to the Brit. Principle of the thing he says.
Johnny:	What else did he say?
Gompers:	Nothin'.
Johnny:	You keep the hell away from him.
Gompers:	That's important information I got.
Johnny:	But what were you sayin' to him?
Gompers:	Nothin'!
Johnny:	Keep it that way. . . . Come on, we got work to do.
Gompers:	How did them that come last get to be first?
Johnny:	Drink up.
Gompers:	I don't take orders from you.
Johnny:	We got six kegs to load and deliver. Are you comin' or not?
Gompers:	*Drinks up.* . . . Gatlin' guns, Johnny.
Johnny:	If there's guns, they're for show. Let's go.
Gompers:	Don't it make you stop and think just a little?

The player piano ever so softly creeping in. One chair, the chair that Will sat in during the party in Act One, has light growing on it.

Johnny:	No. We'll cut across the foothills, helluva lot smoother ride than the road anyways.

Johnny and Gompers exit from the Alberta Hotel and head down the street.

Gompers:	You wanna know why I always win at poker? 'Cause I know . . .

Johnny: You lose at poker, Gompers. And just forget them motorcycles. Think a the jackasses ridin' them.

They disappear from sight.

The piano plays, growing in volume slightly, light building on the chair. Dolly enters. She listens to the piano. She takes a small photograph from her pocket, looks at it, places it flat on the table by the chair. She looks at it. She smiles. She extends her hand towards the chair, an invitation to dance. She dances with her imaginary partner. She is at first somewhat solemn and the dance slow, but it picks up in speed and merriment. It finishes quite merry and quick with Dolly responding, laughing, sharing the dance with a partner. The piano stops, not abruptly but at the end of the composition. Dolly releases her partner, extending a hand as he moves away from her. The light which has followed her dance returns to the chair. Dolly speaks quietly not trying to mimic Will's voice.

Dolly: . . . God but you're pretty. *She smiles.*

Cec enters followed by Old Sump. The light begins to fade slowly on the chair.

Old Sump: You and me, we know t'difference t'ere, Cec. Cec! I says we know t'difference.

Dolly: . . . I done it for you.

Cec raps vigorously on the bar.

Old Sump: T'ere's one drink and t'ere's two drinks and t'ere's t'ree. A man can have t'ree or four drinks and it don't mean a t'ing.

Mama enters; she will pour two glasses of liquor and refill Cec's flask for him.

Old Sump: Are you listenin', Cec? . . . And t'ere's not'in' wrong wit' a flask. I had me a real nice kinda shiny lookin' one, do you 'member it, Cec?

Dolly: Lemme hold your hand, Dolly.

The light on the chair is gone. Dolly's focus shifts from an inward one as she becomes aware of Cec and Old Sump.

Old Sump: But t' t'ing never went underground, do you hear what I'm sayin'?

He and Cec down their drinks. Mama refills them and exits.

Old Sump: I said t' t'ing never went underground, Cec.

Cec:	What's the time?
Old Sump:	First off, you needs your wits about you down t'ere, and number two, where would you be if t'ey caught you?
Cec:	What's the time?
Old Sump:	Out on your keester, so don't be carryin' t'at t'ing down wit' you.
Cec:	Ain't got no watch on you?
Old Sump:	Cec.
Cec:	Where's your watch?
Old Sump:	To hell wit' t'watch.
Cec:	What's the time Dolly?

Cec makes his way over to Dolly, followed by Old Sump.

Old Sump:	What t' hell's time to you, or you to time. We're talkin' important t'ings here.
Cec:	Dolly?
Old Sump:	She don't have t'time.
Cec:	Eh?
Old Sump:	Tell him.
Dolly:	I don't have the time, Cec.
Old Sump:	See?
Cec:	Don't anybody have a watch?
Old Sump:	No.
Cec:	Shit.
Old Sump:	No more takin' t' flask down wit' you, and no more a t' drinkin' till you drop—wit' t' exception a Friday and Saturday nights t'at is—and no more a t' 'avin' a short snort 'fore t' shift . . . Cec?
Cec:	I thought you was workin' this shift.
Old Sump:	Well, I am but I am sacrificin' my good sense to kee-pin' company wit' you.

Cec:	Oh.
Old Sump:	I don't want you drinkin' alone. *Cec nods.* And I made me a solemn promise wit' your boy, wit' Johnny. I made a promise to be t'ere to catch you when you fall down, t'see you home when I'm able, and t'watch you when we're working t'shift. . . . If I knowed then what I knowed now . . .
Cec:	What's that?
Old Sump:	Bein' t'ere is all right but . . . good god, Cec, seein' you home. Oh, t'at woman.
Cec:	Yup.
Old Sump:	She takes a strip right offa me front and down me back.
Cec:	Yup.
Old Sump:	What t' hell're you "yuppin'" for? You ain't even t'ere. You're out. While I suffer t'at woman's tongue, you lie where I lay you—right on t' floor. . . . Do you sleep on t'at floor, Cec? Or do she get you up t'bed?
Cec:	What's the time?
Old Sump:	You should be showin' her who wears t'pants.
Cec:	Is there someone don't know the answer to that burnin' question?
Old Sump:	Well t'en, you gotta reclaim t' pants.
Cec:	Who says I want 'em?
Old Sump:	It's not right for a woman t' be wearin' t' pants.
Cec:	I dunno.
Old Sump:	Eh?
Cec:	Some got a bent for it.
Old Sump:	But t'ey're not to be encouraged.
Cec:	I don't want the god damn things!
Old Sump:	You're not makin' sense.
Cec:	Got a heart like an axe-head in winter.

Old Sump:	It's t' liquor, Cec.
Cec:	Eh?
Old Sump:	Saturatin' the cells at t' brain.
Cec:	Oh.
Old Sump:	Soakin' it up. . . . Let's go.
Cec:	Now?
Old Sump:	T'at's right.
Cec:	We got a couple a minutes.
Old Sump:	Shift change now.
Cec:	In a minute.
Old Sump:	Now.
Cec:	What's the time?
Old Sump:	Come on, we're gonna be late.
Cec:	How do you know?
Old Sump:	I got an interior time-piece! Now come on.

Cec stands up and knocks over a chair.

Old Sump:	Jesus.
Cec:	I'm all right.
Old Sump:	You can't be showin' up like t'at.
Cec:	Los' my balance for a minute, that's all.
Old Sump:	Siddown.
Cec:	I'm all right.
Old Sump:	You're not all right.
Cec:	I'm fine.
Old Sump:	You're pissed.
Cec:	I just—
Old Sump:	You t'ink I don't know pissed when I see it? Now sid-down and stay t'ere! . . . Mama! . . . Mama!

Old Sump exits to find Mama. Cec looks at Dolly.

Old Sump: *Offstage.* Where's Johnny?

Mama George: *Offstage.* He and Gompers are 'cross town.

Old Sump: *Offstage.* Can you send someone for 'im?

Mama George: *Offstage.* If they haven't . . .

Old Sump: *Offstage.* I gotta git to t' colliery. I can't be clockin' in late. *Enters on the run, calling back to Mama George, who appears for a moment.* Tell 'im Sump's workin' and Cec ain't. Tell 'im 'e's 'ere! Now you sit t'ere, Cec, and you wait. *He's out of the hotel flying to work, yelling back . . .* See to 'im, Dolly!

Silence for a moment, then Cec reaches out and takes Dolly's hand. After a moment he releases it, and looks at his own hand.

Dolly: What's wrong?

Cec: I 'member . . . you're the one don't like the black. *He smiles. She takes his hand.* I used to tease him some, I did. . . . He was a real good boy. . . . Full a fun. Always laughin' he was. I 'member the time, him and me we was . . .

Sound of faint blast from the mine for a change of shift. Pause.

Dolly: Go on.

Cec: . . . He was just a good boy, that's all.

Ripple image of car.

Mr. Big: *Offstage, faint.* Leah?

Sound of door slam.

Mr. Big: *Offstage, a bit louder.* Leah!

Leah enters. She stops on seeing Dolly and Cec.

Leah: Oh . . . 'lo Dolly.

Mr. Big enters. Leah looks at him, goes over and sits with Dolly and Cec.

Leah: What're you two doin' here?

Dolly: I come over to visit.

Mr. Big:	Leah?
Leah:	I was out for a drive.
Mr. Big:	Leah.
Cec:	Somebody wants you.
Leah:	But I'm back now.
Dolly:	Oh.
Leah:	Aren't you workin', Mr. Farley?
Cec:	He wants you.
Leah:	Whatta you want?
Mr. Big:	I . . .
Leah:	What is it?
Mr. Big:	I thought . . .
Leah:	You go on by yourself.
Mr. Big:	Leah.
Leah:	Why don'tcha take Mama?
Mr. Big:	I want to take you.
Leah:	Why don'tcha take Dolly?—Do you wanna go with him, Dolly?
Dolly:	I dunno.
Leah:	You go with him, Dolly, it's fun.
Dolly:	Are you comin'?
Leah:	No.
Dolly:	Where is he goin'?
Leah:	He'll deliver a keg, then you'll stop for a while and . . . you'll visit the Butlers.
Cec:	What Butlers is that?
Leah:	You know the Butlers.
Cec:	No.

Leah:	Yes you do. . . . They got a fluffy white dog and a swing in the front and she always has cake and Mr. Butler and him sit on the porch and drink whiskey—isn't that right, Mr. Big?
Dolly:	I don't know the Butlers.
Cec:	'Cause there ain't any Butlers.
Leah:	I'd go but I been in that car for an age—my stomach's upset.
Mr. Big:	Is that it?
Leah:	Well what did you think! I said I felt sick!
Mr. Big:	That's what you said.
Leah:	And I do. So. Are you just gonna stand there?
Mr. Big:	No.
Leah:	So!? *Pause as Leah and Mr. Big stare at each other.* I . . . I'm . . . I'm sorry . . . I hurt you, I made you feel bad.
Mr. Big:	No.
Leah:	We . . . we . . . can go tomorrow.
Mr. Big:	That's what we'll do.
Leah:	. . . We . . . could go today—later today—if you want.
Mr. Big:	We'll make it tomorrow.
Leah:	You won't be mad that we don't go today?
Mr. Big:	Mad? *He moves to the bar to get a drink for Cec. Some of his former exuberance returns.* A definition of "madness," Mr. Farley!
Cec:	Eh?
Mr. Big:	*Dementia praecox.*
Dolly:	What's that?
Mr. Big:	Disordered reason. The question is—do I suffer from it—and if so, what could have caused it.
Leah:	I said I was sorry.

Mr. Big:	And I believed you. How could I be angry . . . *He goes to put his arm around her; there is the smallest apparently not deliberate move away from him on her part. He may be aware of it but he doesn't show it . . .* with you. *He incorporates her rejection—if such it is—into a move to Cec with his drink. As Johnny enters.* Now, Mr. Farley . . .
Johnny:	He's had enough.
Mr. Big:	Haven't you left yet?
Johnny:	We were late with the loadin'. . . . Come on, Pop.
Cec:	I was jus' fine, Johnny; it was Sump wouldn't wait.
Johnny:	Sure it was.
Cec:	I wanted to go.
Johnny:	Come on, I'm takin' you home.

Dolly touches Leah's arm to draw her attention to the photograph.

Mr. Big:	Johnny?
Johnny:	*Shouldering his dad up.* Yeah.
Mr. Big:	I've left a keg in my car out front.
Johnny:	What?
Mr. Big:	A touch of *dementia praecox.*
Cec:	Disordered reason.
Johnny:	Shaddup Pop. . . . What do you want me to do?
Mr. Big:	It'll have to be moved.
Cec:	Move it in here, sucker'll disappear like magic.
Johnny:	Where to?
Cec:	See? *Holds up his empty flask upside down.*
Mr. Big:	Pull the car 'round and . . .
Cec:	Nothin' left.
Johnny:	Shaddup Pop.
Cec:	Can't go home dry.

Mr. Big:	You best deliver him first.
Cec:	Sill kill me.
Mr. Big:	And see me when you get back.
Cec:	Don' wanna.
Johnny:	Right.
Cec:	Near the place.
Mr. Big:	Unless you want to use it to . . .
Johnny:	I'll walk him. *Gets Cec out the door with Cec rambling on as they disappear from sight.*
Cec:	Sill's gonna kill me Johnny oh god when se shees me that god damn Sump he wouldn't wait all his fault . . .
Dolly:	It looks just like him.
Leah:	Yes it does.

Mr. Big watches Leah and Dolly examine the photograph.

Dolly:	Isn't it strange they can do that?
Leah:	I suppose.
Dolly:	He had it taken for me.
Leah:	I know.
Dolly:	It wasn't studio-done.
Leah:	You told me before.
Dolly:	It was when that man with the camera and all came through. He took pictures a the colliery office, and then Mr. Wheatley, who's head of it all, had him and his wife and his family all in a group in fronta his house, and Will, when he heard, you know what he did?
Leah:	You told me, Dolly.
Dolly:	Well, he went right up to that man with the camera, and he said, "Hey there"—he never said sir—he said, "is that a val'able thing you got there?" And the fella

said, "You bet your sweet fanny ass it is," that's what he said, "and mind you don't touch it," and Will said, "Well, if it's val'able, I wouldn't be pointin' it at those ugly mugs there, 'cause surer than hell it'll break! You wanna capture a visage a heaven on a photographic plate—aim that thing this way." . . . He meant a picture of himself so's he could give it to me. And that's what happened. That's how come I got this picture a him.

Leah:	Dolly?
Dolly:	What.
Leah:	. . . It's a real nice picture.
Dolly:	It is, isn't it.
Leah:	. . . Dolly?
Dolly:	And I got it for all time 'cause a picture like this lasts forever. When I'm old, he's still gonna be young. . . . Do you think when you die, you stay the age that you die at?
Leah:	I wish you wouldn't keep talkin' like that.
Dolly:	Like what?
Leah:	All a that is over, Dolly.
Dolly:	I don't think so.
Leah:	It's past.
Dolly:	But it's still there.
Leah:	Where?!
Dolly:	It's not gone. Will isn't gone.
Leah:	He is, Dolly, and you got to face that!
Dolly:	No.
Leah:	It is past and over and done with!
Dolly:	No.
Leah:	You gotta forget about Will.
Dolly:	I don't want to.

Leah: You gotta start fresh.

Dolly: I couldn't.

Leah: Why not?

Dolly: Nobody can.

Leah: A course they can!

Dolly: What makes you think that?

Leah: They just can, that's all.

Dolly: But you're who you are and who you were and who you met and what you did and . . .

Leah: *Will . . . is . . . dead.*

Dolly: He's alive right inside a me, and caught in this picture is a little bit a him, and he is sittin' right over there where we used to sit, and in the mine where he used to work, and if you listen real close, which I know we can't but if we could, you could hear him, things he used to say and make everyone laugh, and you could hear us laughin' too!

Leah: Why can't you just leave him?

Dolly: That's what you wanta do, leave everything behind, pretend things never happened, but I don't wanta do that—and you can't do it either!

Leah grabs the photograph of Will from Dolly and tears it into little pieces which she drops on the floor. Dolly moves as if to bend down, to—what?— pick them up? Leah puts her foot over them.

Dolly looks at her a moment, then Leah turns and runs off. Dolly looks at the pieces of photo on the floor. She bends and gathers them up as lights fade on the hotel leaving Mr. Big, who has observed the scene, alone.

Cec:
Offstage singing.

Don't weep for me and mother,
Although I know 'tis sad.
But we try and get someone to cheer—

Light building on Mrs. Farley and Bill in the Farley home. They listen to Cec's approach; Mrs. Farley draws Bill to a place of partial concealment.

Cec:

Offstage, singing, closer.

And save my poor old dad.
I'm awful cold and hungry . . .

Cec and Johnny enter the house.

Cec: *Singing rather loudly.* She closed her eyes and . . . Shhhh! Shhhhh!! Shh Johnny not a sound! She'll be in here like a lion 'mong the Chris'ians, shh be quiet, you jus' leave me 'n ge' hell out. You go 'n don' worry 'bout . . .

Mrs. Farley steps into view.

Cec: Too late. Well! I just'n den he and we wereoohh 'n then ah so we come along there 'nd I 'n he and then it was jus' 'n thasa 'bou' how it was. *He sits.* So—don' be angry with 'im, be angry with me. Good night, Johnny.

Pause. Johnny turns to leave.

Mrs. Farley: Johnny.

Johnny turns back to his mother.

Mrs. Farley: I . . . I was . . . have you gotta get right back, Johnny? *Pause.* You wanna sit awhile? *Pause. Johnny sits.* I . . . I been missin' you . . .

Bill is present in the shadows. Johnny does not see him.

Johnny: Yeah.

Mrs. Farley: What?

Johnny: Me too.

Mrs. Farley: Here you are, right in town, and I haven't seen you since . . .

Johnny: You seen me.

Mrs. Farley: What?

Johnny: I said you seen me. You seen me lots a times.

Fractured slow image of constable taking shape outside the Farley's.

Mrs. Farley:	No, I . . . *She stops as Johnny stares at her in a silent rebuke. Pause.*

Johnny gets up to leave.

Mrs. Farley:	Johnny!
Johnny:	What.
Mrs. Farley:	You make it real hard for me! . . . Say somethin'.
Johnny:	I wish . . . I wish things was different, but they aren't . . . and . . . I don't see what I can do about that.
Mrs. Farley:	Things can change.
Johnny:	I don't see how.
Mrs. Farley:	I know they can. But you gotta have faith, and you gotta do somethin'.
Johnny:	Like what?
Mrs. Farley:	You gotta believe that by doin' somethin' you can change somethin'.
Johnny:	What're you talkin' about?

The figure of the constable, with careful observation, can be seen at his post outside the house.

Mrs. Farley:	*Smiles.* You're right I seen you. I went outa my way on the hope a gettin' a gawp at you. *She laughs.* And you seen me. I can say you did 'cause you said so. . . . I never set foot outside a this house my head wasn't full a possible places a glimpsin' you.
Johnny:	Not a word to me though.
Mrs. Farley:	I . . .
Johnny:	How come now?
Mrs. Farley:	*Takes Johnny's hand, pressing it between hers.* Because that's over and done with now. It's gonna be different now.

Pause. Johnny removes his hand, gets up, moves away, then turns back to his mother.

Johnny:	You gettin' outa temperance and bible-thumpin'?

Mrs. Farley:	I just . . .
Johnny:	That don't seem likely.
Mrs. Farley:	I was wrong.
Johnny:	'Bout what?
Mrs. Farley:	Come here and sit down.
Johnny:	What're you sayin' you're wrong about?
Mrs. Farley:	I got you an offer.
Johnny:	Eh?
Mrs. Farley:	Not the mines, Johnny. . . . Another job, a respectable job.
Johnny:	Doin' what?
Mrs. Farley:	You come just at the right time 'cause now we can talk and we can get things arranged and everythin'll be settled.
Johnny:	What was you wrong about?
Mrs. Farley:	There's people want to give you a chance. It's a real opportunity, Johnny. But people earn opportunities eh? Nothin' comes free. Do you understand what I mean?
Johnny:	Clear as a slough in summer.
Mrs. Farley:	Now don't be like that! I want you to listen and to . . .
Johnny:	And to what?
Mrs. Farley:	And to not be . . . to consider what I'm sayin' and not be. . . . Now what you want is a good job with a future, isn't that right? . . . Isn't that right?
Johnny:	That's right.
Mrs. Farley:	Soo? . . .
Johnny:	Look Mum . . .
Mrs. Farley:	You know Sergeant Windsor now don't you?
Johnny:	What about him?

Mrs. Farley: He's a good man, Sergeant Windsor.

Johnny: He'd piss in your pocket and swear it was rainin'.

Mrs. Farley: You said you would listen!

The constable shifts his position slightly.

Johnny: How'd the Brit come into this job thing?

Mrs. Farley: I gotta tell it in my own way so you'll—

Johnny: So I'll what?

Mrs. Farley: Understand!

Johnny: And what was you wrong about?

Mrs. Farley: Whatever I done was for you.

Johnny: I can do for myself. I . . . I gotta go now.

He turns to leave. Sergeant Windsor enters.

Bill: Johnny.

Johnny: What're you doin' here?

Mrs. Farley: He's come to warn you, Johnny, through me. And to give you a chance.

Bill: That's enough.

Mrs. Farley: He knows you're not like them others.

Bill: Mrs. Farley.

Mrs. Farley: Tell him.

Johnny: I'm late and I'm goin'.

Bill: I'd appreciate you hearin' me out.

Johnny exits from the house. The constable outside stops him. Johnny attempts to walk around him. The constable strikes him, knocking him down and giving him a boot as he lies on the ground. Then he grabs Johnny by the collar and flings him back into the house, and reassumes his position. Mrs. Farley, hearing the scuffle, makes a move to go to Johnny. Bill touches her arm. It is enough to stop her. Johnny is on the floor.

Bill: As I was sayin' . . . if you could spare me a moment . . . there's been a time in these parts where people have

	done as they please. Those times're changin'.
Johnny:	What the hell is this all about?
Bill:	There's some as think they're above the law, beyond the law. They're gonna learn different.
Johnny:	Christ!
Bill:	I'm talkin' respect and order.
Johnny:	Say it plain. *He wipes his mouth, looks at the blood on his hand, then at Bill.*
Bill:	Now I got a proposal to make. I'm makin' it to you 'cause you strike me as a smart boy, a good boy.

Johnny spits on the floor.

Mrs. Farley:	Listen.
Bill:	The whiskey . . .
Johnny:	Ain't got nothin' to do with whiskey! Mr. Big burns your ass and that's it in a nutshell! *Bill smiles.* You hate him 'cause he says that uniform and stupid accent don't make you one bit better than he is!
Bill:	We'll see if it does.
Johnny:	He's a man thinks for hisself and you can't stand that 'cause you let others think for you!
Bill:	A moral man don't need to think. *Laughs.*
Johnny:	You Don't Know Nothin'!
Mrs. Farley:	He's givin' you a chance to start somethin' new.
Johnny:	Get away from me.
Mrs. Farley:	He's offerin' you a job.
Bill:	In return for routes, delivery dates, information.
Johnny:	Do you know what he's askin' me to do?
Mrs. Farley:	He's askin' you to do what's right.
Johnny:	I'm leavin'.
Bill:	The man's engaged in a trade that killed your brother,

you support him, and you think *I'm* stupid?

Johnny: Dominion Colliery killed my brother 'cause the cost a replacin' rotten timber meant more to them than a man's life.

Bill: He was hungover from the booze. He should've seen it comin', he should've moved quick and fast and easy, and he would've—if it weren't for the booze. Rotten timber didn't kill William. The whiskey killed William.

Pause. Johnny wants to hit him but he doesn't. He turns and exits. The constable watches him go. He makes no move towards him. It is as if the previous encounter between him and Johnny had never happened. Bill turns to look at Cec slumped in the chair. He moves to him, looking down at him. He puts a hand under Cec's chin, tilting his face up.

Bill: . . . Hey . . . hey . . . wake up old man. *He gives Cec a light slap.* Wake up.

Cec makes a murmur of protest.

Bill: *Another light slap.* Come on. *Another slap.* Wake up.

Mrs. Farley stands silent, watching. She does not enjoy what she sees but she makes no protest.

Cec: Don'.

Bill: Wake up. *Another slap.*

Cec: Stop . . . don' . . . wha' . . . wha' the hell. . . .

Bill releases Cec's chin; Cec shakes his head. Bill steps away.

Cec: Oh. Ooohhh. *Puts a hand to his head.* Got the . . . got a terible head, does it to you you know. *He sees Bill. He looks around checking where he is. Back to Bill.* What a . . . what . . .

Bill: Mr. Farley.

Cec: Tha's right. Mister Brit. . . . Whatta you want?

Bill: I'm wonderin' if you could enlighten me as to the workin's a the taps at the Alberta Hotel?

Cec: You turn 'em to the . . . that way, 'cause it's opposite 'cause they're behind the bar, or the other way, and the beverage flows.

Bill steps closer to Cec, slaps his face with the back of his hand somewhat harder than before, still not a hard blow. Cec goes to get up. Bill shoves him back into the chair. Mrs. Farley turns her back and gazes out on the street towards the constable still at his post.

Bill: And the location a the warehouse where they're storin' the kegs?

Cec: . . . I . . .

Bill: In town or out?

Cec: I dunno.

Bill hits him a bit harder.

Bill: When he's out with the girl, is he makin' deliveries?

Cec: How should I know?

Bill: You're around.

Cec: He don't tell me those kinda things.

Bill hits him harder.

Cec: Whatta you . . .

Pause.

Bill: Now. *He moves. Cec reacts believing he's about to be hit. It's a small move but Bill sees it. He gives a dry smile. Pause.* What do you know?

Cec: Nothin'.

Bill begins methodically to beat Cec, no particular anger, no particular rush.

Cec: I don't know nothin'! . . . They don't . . . I . . .

Bill: Times.

Cec: Dunno.

Bill: Routes.

Cec: No.

Bill: Deliveries.

Cec is silent as Bill delivers two more blows and steps back. Cec falls to the floor. After a moment he speaks.

Cec: The . . . the only thing . . . I heered . . . is . . . he . . . he left a keg out front . . . in the car . . . out front . . .

Bill reaches into his jacket, pulls out a pint of liquor, tosses it to Cec.

Bill arranges his tunic and exits. Mrs. Farley turns to look at Cec who looks at her, then drinks from the pint. He gets up and leaves the room. Mrs. Farley follows him. Bill consults with the constable who checks his gun. The two move off.

Light slowly building on the Alberta Hotel. Mr. Big remains in the position from which he observed the Dolly and Leah scene.

A refracted image of glint on motorcycle and gun fades in and out.

Mr. Big: . . . Mama? . . . Mama! . . . Mama! *She enters.*

Mama George: What's wrong?

Mr. Big: . . . How old am I, Mama?

Mama George: How old?

Mr. Big: Don't you know?

Mama George: How old are you?

Mr. Big: Don't you remember?

Mama George: I remember everything.

Mr. Big: Do you?

Mama George: Of course. So do you.

Mr. Big: No.

Mama George: It's the important things you remember.

Mr. Big: It's hard to tell.

Mama George: Why's that?

Mr. Big: Does the fact they're remembered make them important? I get the feeling they're trivial things I remember. They don't add up to much . . . except for Leah.

Mama George: What a thing for you to be sayin'.

Mr. Big: Yet I do say it.

Mama George: Where is your vision a "intersectin' worlds cartwheelin' through space?" *Pause.* Can you no longer perceive people "glowin' and blazin' like crystal shards caught in a rainbow?" *Pause.* Is your great and glorious construction a the universe based on nothin' more than the frail embrace of a child?

Mr. Big: . . . Would it be . . . any less valid were that to be so?

Mama George: Children grow up.

Mr. Big: Do they? . . . I remember—a little boy . . . not so unlike Leah when I found her . . . but this male child, an unattractive child, an ugly child who found no Mr. Big . . . so he created one.

Mama George: He became one.

Mr. Big: Mr. Big.

Mama George: She's grown up.

Mr. Big: No.

Mama George: Do you remember when we met?

Mr. Big: I . . . I was erectin' canvas, two by fours, and papier-mâché worlds, barkin' on a midway—but just behind the eyes, that frightened little boy peeked out.

Mama George: I could see him.

Mr. Big: Can you see him still?

Pause.

Mama George: Do you remember the night we watched the shootin' stars, the night the sky was green with Northern Lights? . . . Do you remember? *She quotes Mr. Big from a former occasion.* "Had Lucifer not fallen from grace there'd be no such thing as choice!"

Mr. Big: "There is no Hell as men imagine it."

Mama George: "Hell is doing what other people tell you to!"

Mr. Big: *Semblance of his former self.* "Men are most like animals and least like gods when they relinquish choice! Heaven is freely choosing with respect for the choice of others."

Mama George: *Calls out, as if from the crowd.* "What's that mean?"

Mr. Big: "It means the one thing that keeps us from achievin' Holy Grace is government!"

Mama George: Go on!

Mr. Big: "For governments remove choice. It's only when individuals choose and suffer the consequences of their actions that humanity can progress!"

Mama George: Live by those words! . . . I believed them. . . . Do you remember the night you brought Leah home?

Mr. Big: For you.

Mama George: I could never give you that most valuable thing.

Mr. Big: That didn't matter.

Mama George: It mattered to me—and to you.

Mr. Big: We had Leah.

Mama George: But that wasn't the same.

Mr. Big: You do love Leah?

Mama George: It's you I love most of all. *Pause.* Do you think I don't know why I find you sitting alone? . . . Did you think I never knew? Did you think, with all the things we shared, I wouldn't know? . . . Did you think she wouldn't tell me?

Mr. Big: Tell you what?

Mama George: You picked her off the street, you gave her everything, and in return she . . .

Mr. Big: She what?

Mama George: Paid.

Mr. Big: It was not like that!

Mama George: I know how it was.

Mr. Big: She never told you that!

Mama George: She was afraid.

Mr. Big: It was not like that!

Mama George: She was tired of runnin'!

Mr. Big: She did not say that!

Mama George: I know what she said!

Mr. Big: She did not seduce me to assure . . .

Mama George: How does a child seduce?

Mr. Big: Nor did I seduce or force her!

Mama George: With what devices could a child resist?

Mr. Big: She never said those things to you!

Mama George: And it was me she came to. . . . Do you know what I did? . . . I reassured her.

Mr. Big: She didn't need it.

Mama George: Oh, but she did. See how I love you.

Mr. Big: You've done none a this outta love.

Mama George: I have.

Mr. Big: Then it's a despicable thing.

Mama George: Despicable things are done in its name—could you argue with that?

Mr. Big: And grand things as well!

Mama George: She's leavin' you, Mr. Big.

Mr. Big: Where would she go?

Mama George: You need me now.

Mr. Big: Who would she go to?

Mama George: Who'd have her now? Who would she have?

Mr. Big: I see you plain.

Mama George: She didn't go with you today.

Mr. Big: You want to tarnish, to destroy, to vandalize.

Mama George: She won't tomorrow either.

Mr. Big: You know nothing!

Mama George: I know who she loves. Do you?

Mr. Big begins to laugh.

Mr. Big: Yes! I know who she loves! She loves me!

Mama George: No.

Mr. Big: It's me who she loves!

Mama George: You've gone blind starin' at stars. . . . It's Johnny she loves.

Mr. Big: Johnny? . . .

Pause.

Mama George: We are old, Mr. Big.

Mr. Big: Don't.

Mama George: We're old.

Mr. Big: No more . . . I . . . beg you . . . leave me alone . . . go.

Mama George exits.

He shuts his eyes. After a moment he gets up, goes behind the bar to get a glass. He stops. He brings out the gun which is beneath the bar. He looks at it. He cocks it, places it on the bar. He gets a glass and pours himself a drink. Johnny enters as Mr. Big's back is towards him so that Mr. Big is not aware of his entrance. Johnny moves to the bar. When Mr. Big turns around Johnny is there. A pause. Mr. Big gives Johnny his own drink and pours himself another. He notices the bruise on Johnny's face. He tilts Johnny's face up to look at it, reaches under the bar, brings out a cloth, dips it in the liquor, puts it to Johnny's face. Johnny holds the cloth against his face.

Johnny: *Low.* Bastard . . . sayin' things . . . I shoulda . . . I—bastard! *He hits the bar with his fist.* The Brit, he's sayin' things, makin' offers, who the hell does he think he is! He's sayin' things! To me! I won't have that dirty son of a whore . . .

He goes to take a drink. He stops. Looks at it. Pause. He puts it down. He looks at Mr. Big.

Johnny:	I want you to tell me . . . what was it that killed William?
Mr. Big:	*Searching, not his usual self.* . . . A . . . coming together . . . of random . . . incident . . . timber spongy from some rot within, pressure from above, then, from below, Earth sighed, a tiny tremor, not even one you'd notice . . .
Johnny:	Why?
Mr. Big:	Perhaps she's angry at the violation, the intrusion.
Johnny:	Whyn't he move, jump clear, he must've, *must've* felt it comin', shiftin'.
Mr. Big:	Perhaps.
Johnny:	Whyn't he move!?
Mr. Big:	He chose not to.

Pause.

Johnny:	. . . He had a head that mornin' . . . from the drink.
Mr. Big:	I expect he did.
Johnny:	And?
Mr. Big:	And what?

Johnny picks up the glass of booze and throws it. It breaks. Johnny stands there. After a moment he looks at Mr. Big.

Leah enters drawn by the sound of the breaking glass. She sees the two men. She stops. They look at her. She looks at them, then she stoops to clear up the glass. Johnny rushes over.

Johnny:	No . . . don't . . . I'll do it. It's all right, I'll do it.

The two of them pick up the glass. Mr. Big watches them without expression. Once they reach for the same piece, and look at each other, then back to the picking up of glass. When they're finished, Leah goes to get up and leave. Johnny grabs her hand and draws her up as he gets up. They become aware of Mr. Big's gaze. A pause with Johnny maintaining his grip on Leah's hand. She does not protest.

Mr. Big:	What is it?

Johnny: *Releases his breath which he did not realize he was holding.* I wanna ask you somethin'.

Mr. Big: Yes.

After a moment Johnny looks down.

Mr. Big: . . . I'm waiting.

Johnny: I—

Leah: *Low.* Don't.

Mr. Big: What is it?

Johnny: It's somethin' important.

Leah: *Low.* No.

Johnny: Maybe Leah shouldn't be here.

Mr. Big: Does this matter of import touch upon Leah?

He will not look directly at her through this section. He is garnering what appears to be the very last of his strength. Although there is no loss of control, it is taking everything to maintain his façade.

Johnny: Yes it does.

Mr. Big: Then it's imperative she's present.

Johnny: I don't think . . .

Mr. Big: Leah stays.

Johnny looks at Leah and she looks at him. It seems she acquiesces to Mr. Big's statement.

Johnny: If that's what she wants.

Mr. Big: And in her rightful position.

Johnny: What?

Mr. Big: By my side, where she's been since eleven.

Leah looks at Johnny, he releases her hand, she joins Mr. Big. Johnny looks at the broken glass he holds in his hand; he places it on the bar.

He sees the gun.

Johnny: It's a serious question.

Pause. Mr. Big is still, silent. His largesse of style and manner are gone. He looks directly at Leah for the first time.

Mr. Big: A serious question. *Mr. Big looks at Johnny, then he looks at neither but seems caught in an inward vision. . . .* Touchin' upon Leah . . . did I ever tell you . . . how I found Leah?

Johnny: I heard.

Mr. Big: *To Leah.* You told him, did you?

Leah: No.

Mr. Big: *Low.* Incandescence.

Johnny: What?

Mr. Big: Radiance.

Johnny: What's wrong?

Mr. Big: Stars . . . flarin' up . . . a brilliance consumin' all in its orb, then shrinkin' to a black pinhole in space . . . 'bout the size of a fist in the void . . . 'bout the size a my heart, but black, charry black, and cold . . . .You wanted to ask me. . . . The first time I saw Leah . . . I thought I'd slipped through a wrinkle in time and was seein' myself. . . . It was rainin', and she was walkin' a purposeful walk, and her eye was fixed on a destination so distant no mortal eye could discern it, and both of her arms were wrapped 'round herself, embracin' herself, maintainin' herself . . . and I sat in my car and I wept for her . . . and for all of us here.

Johnny makes a move as if to speak. Outside the hotel there is the glint of sun on metal, gun, motorcycle, appears, disappears. Perhaps it's the glitter of the odd star in the cosmos.

Mr. Big: Let me . . . continue. Your question must wait, for I too have something of import to say that touches on Leah.

Leah: Mr. Big?

Mr. Big: I must, Leah. I'm hearin' it said that my . . . fantastical comprehension of a cosmic design does not spring from revelation or wisdom, intuition or

insight. . . . It is, rather, mere invention—and lies—
which serve . . .

Johnny places his hand near the gun.

Mr. Big: . . . to legitimize . . . an on-going affair . . . with a
child.

*Johnny places his hand over the grip of the gun but he does not fully grasp
it or pick it up.*

Mr. Big: . . . If—if all mankind could read the skies as I can,
do you know what they'd do?

Johnny: What?

Mr. Big: They'd never lift their eyes from off the path in front
of them! They fear dimension. They live in cracks
between the baseboard and the wall in one corner of
a mansion whose beauty and proportion is as bound-
less as the heavenly firmament! Is it strange that their
thoughts turn dark and ugly? Look at her! She's the
product of my vision, not the inspiration of it! Could
falsehood and contrivance bring forth such perfec-
tion? I ask you. Look at her . . . of course I love her.
Who would not love her? . . . She is proof that my
grasp of all worlds, real or imagined, is sound—and
that soundness is proof that she's sound. I swear to
you Johnny, Leah is without flaw or injury. She is
founded on truth. *He appears spent.* And my love . . .
for her . . . which I do not deny . . . is as . . . my
love . . . for you . . . whom she loves . . .

He does not look at Leah.

Johnny: Leah?

*Glitter and glint from refracted images outside hotel. Gompers runs down
the street.*

Gompers: Johnny? Johnny!

Johnny: *Whose attention is on Leah.* What do you want?

Mr. Big is so still, so quiet that Gompers seems not to know he's there.

Gompers: Where the hell've you been?

Johnny:	Here. I been here. *He glances at Gompers.* Are you loaded?
Gompers:	Hell yes, I been waitin' for you; but didja take a look on the street?
Johnny:	*Attention on Leah.* Yeah?
Gompers:	On the street!
Johnny:	What?
Gompers:	The Brit's got her blocked off at the west end.

Johnny moves to look into the street.

Gompers:	What the hell's he up to?
Johnny:	I dunno.

Leah and Mr. Big look at each other.

Gompers:	What're we gonna do!
Johnny:	Gimme a minute.
Gompers:	What're we gonna do!

Widow Popovitch scurries down the street towards the hotel.

Johnny:	Where'd you leave the car?
Gompers:	Right where we loaded.
Widow:	Vere's Mama? I haf—do you know vat is happening out dere?
Johnny:	Take the alley east, cut across the double that ain't fenced and go for the hills.
Widow:	Mama!
Gompers:	Jesus Johnny, what if—
Widow:	Mama dey haf guns pointed down da street.
Johnny:	Go!
Widow:	Dey're coming d'other vay too.
Johnny:	*Yells after Gompers.* You let the Brit stop you I'll kill you!
Widow:	Look at dem Johnny.

Johnny: Jesus Christ there's a keg out front.

Widow: Dey haf da guns at one end . . .

Johnny: Are cars blockin' the street?

Widow: No cars, jost da guns on dose motorcycles.

Johnny: I can bust through that easy. Where's the keys?

Mama joins The Widow looking out on the street. Leah tries to keep Johnny from leaving.

Johnny: There's a keg in the car out front.

Leah shakes her head trying to hold him from going.

Johnny: Where's the keys? *He finds the keys. He pushes her aside.* I bust through them motorcycles, we're clear!

Leah: Johnny!

Johnny: I'll ditch the keg in Bossy's Creek, and I'll be right back. I'll be right back. Meet me at the corner lot. The corner lot, Leah!

He runs out the door, ducking and dodging, slowly making his way to the car without being seen. Mama and The Widow follow him out. Their voices are heard offstage.

Widow: Careful, Johnny.

Mama George: He's got to move that car.

Sound of car door slam. Image of the Whiskey Six flashing. Leah turns to listen. The engine revs up and the car pulls out. Amongst the offstage voices we can hear . . .

Mama George: Look!

Widow: Look! He's headin' for them!

Sound of shots.

Widow: They're shootin'!

Mama George: He's gonna . . .

Sound of crash as the car hits the motocycles.

Mama George: He's through!

Widow: Vight trew dem!

Sound of car receding in the distance.

Mama George: He's gone!

Widow: Broke trew.

The car fades away. Silence. Leah looks at Mr. Big.

Leah: Did . . . Did you think you could just tell a story and everything would be right? *Pause.* If he ever finds out . . . what will I do? . . . And if he believes you . . . how can I live like that?

Mr. Big: Pretend.

Leah: I'm tired of pretending. . . . Why didn't you leave me, Mr. Big? Why didn't you leave me that day in the rain? . . . But—you can still make it right. Yes you can. *She picks up the gun.* Here. Take it. . . . Hold it, Mr. Big.

He takes the gun.

Leah: Now—make it right.

Mr. Big: I can't.

Leah: Pretend. . . . Look. . . . I'm turning . . . I'm runnin'. *She turns and starts to run towards the door.* I'm runnin' to him! *She is almost at the door.* Now!

Mr. Big fires at Leah hitting her in the back. She collapses knocking over a chair. Lights fade. Plaintive note from the piano reminiscent of Act One opening. Will, Dolly, Cec, Old Sump, Mama, the Widow, Gompers seen in shifting light with the piano music growing, the figures swaying. Leah is seen amidst them as they begin to dance as at the beginning. Mr. Big joins them. The odd change of partner. Fluid. Not overly sad. Not sad at all. Bill the Brit watches. Johnny enters, moves past them, through them, obviously not of them. He picks up the chair, restoring it to its former position.

Dolly: *Voice-over.* And round.

Will: *Voice-over.* And whirl.

Cec: *Voice-over.* 'Cause to keep goin'.

Widow: *Voice-over.* Favourite.

Mama George: *Voice-over.* Love.

Mr. Big:	*Voice-over.* Visage a heaven.
Dolly:	*Voice-over.* Just so.
Will:	*Voice-over.* You're pretty.
Mama George:	*Voice-over.* He believes it.
Dolly:	*Voice-over.* Lasts forever.
Mr. Big:	*Voice-over.* Collidin' conjectures.
Cec:	*Voice-over.* Good times him and me.
Old Sump:	*Voice-over.* T'at's what we called it.
Leah:	*Voice-over.* Was it?
Mr. Big:	*Voice-over.* Invincible, Leah.

The voice-overs become murmurs, the wind on the foothills; the figures' movement becomes more static, light dimmer.

Johnny has taken off his jacket, slung it over his shoulder. He looks quite a bit older. He speaks to the audience.

Johnny: I was caught in his kaleidoscope worlds cartwheelin' through space. I believed in his crystal-shard people radiatin' light like a rainbow. She was livin' proof a transcendence.

The gossamer depiction of the Crowsnest Pass seen at the beginning slowly obscures Blairmore.

Johnny: Mr. Big once asked me—what do you suppose an oyster thinks of a pearl? . . . What does an oyster think of a pearl? I didn't know. He didn't tell me.

He takes a few steps whistling. Stops.

Johnny: It may all have been lies, but that still doesn't mean it weren't true.

Whistle of the train. He looks. The headlight of the train grows. It appears he plans on catching it. The sound of the train increasing. Light of train grows as train approaches. Johnny starts to exit to catch it.

BLACKOUT

Bibliography

PUBLISHED STAGE PLAYS

Pollock, Sharon. "Blood Relations." *Canadian Theatre Review*, 29 (Winter 1981): 46-97.
_____ "Blood Relations." *Plays By Women, Vol. 3*, ed. Michelene Wandor. London; New York: Methuen, 1982: 91-122.
_____ *Blood Relations and Other Plays*, eds. Diane Bessai and Don Kerr. Edmonton: NeWest Press, 1981, NeWest Press, 2002.
_____ *Doc*. Toronto: Playwrights Canada, 1986, c1984, Broadview Press, 2002.
_____ "Doc." *Modern Canadian Plays*, ed. Jerry Wasserman. Third edition. Vancouver: Talonbooks, 1994: 129-167.
_____ *Fair Liberty's Call*. Toronto: Coach House Press, 1995, Broadview Press, 2002.
_____ "Getting it Straight." *Heroines: Three Plays*, ed. Joyce Doolittle. Red Deer: Red Deer College Press, 1992.
_____ "'It's All Make-Believe, Isn't It?'—Marilyn Monroe." *Instant Applause: 26 Very Short Complete Plays*. Winnipeg: Blizzard, 1994.
_____ *The Komagata Maru Incident*. Toronto: Playwrights Co-op, 1978.
_____ "The Komagata Maru Incident." *Six Canadian Plays*, ed. Tony Hamill. Toronto: Playwrights Canada Press, 1992.
_____ "Prairie Dragons." *Playhouse: Six Fantasy Plays For Children*, ed. Joyce Doolittle. Red Deer: Red Deer College Press, 1989.
_____ *Saucy Jack*. Winnipeg: Blizzard, 1994.
_____ *Walsh*. Vancouver: Talonbooks, 1973.
_____ "Walsh." *Modern Canadian Plays*, ed. Jerry Wasserman. 3rd ed. Vancouver: Talonbooks, 1993: 237-271.
_____ "Whiskey Six Cadenza." *NeWest Plays By Women*, eds. Diane Bessai and Don Kerr. Edmonton: NeWest Press, 1987: 137-247.

UNPUBLISHED STAGE PLAYS

Pollock, Sharon. *And Out Goes You?* Vancouver: Vancouver Playhouse, 1975.
_____ *Angel's Trumpet*. Calgary: Theatre Junction, 2001.
_____ *Chautaqua Spelt E-N-E-R-G-Y*. Calgary: Alberta Theatre Projects, 1979.
_____ *A Compulsory Option*. Vancouver: New Play Centre, 1972.
_____ *End Dream*. Calgary: Theatre Junction, 2000.
_____ *The Great Drag Race or Smoked, Choked and Croaked*. MS., Commissioned by the Christmas Seal Society of British Columbia, 1974.
_____ *The Happy Prince*. Adaptation of the Oscar Wilde Story. Vancouver: Playhouse Theatre School, 1974.
_____ *Hon/Harold*. MS., 1972.
_____ *Lesson in Swizzlery*. New Westminster: Caravan, 1974.
_____ *Mail vs. Female*. Calgary: Lunchbox Theatre, 1979.
_____ *Mother Love*. MS., 1972.
_____ *Moving Pictures*. Calgary: Theatre Junction, 1999.
_____ *My Name is Lisbeth*. Vancouver: Douglas College, 1976; rewritten as *Blood Relations*.

_____ *New Canadians*. Vancouver: Playhouse Holiday, 1973.

_____ *The Rose and the Nightingale*. Adaptation of the Oscar Wilde Story. Vancouver: Playhouse Theatre School, 1974.

_____ *Star Child*. Adaptation of the Oscar Wilde Story. Vancouver: Playhouse Theatre School, 1974.

_____ *Superstition Throu' the Ages*. Vancouver: Playhouse Holiday, 1973.

_____ *Tracings: The Fraser Story*. Edmonton: Theatre Network, 1977.

_____ *Untitled Libretto*. MS., Commissioned by Banff Centre of the Arts, 1978-1980.

_____ *Wedjesay?* Vancouver: Playhouse Holiday, 1974.

_____ *The Wreck on the National Line Car*. Calgary: Alberta Theatre Projects, 1978.

RADIO AND TELEVISION WRITING

Pollock, Sharon. "The Making of Warriors." *Airborne: Radio Plays by Women*, ed. Ann Jansen. Winnipeg: Blizzard, 1991.

_____ *31 for 2*. TS. CBC Radio, 1971.

_____ *The B Triple P Plan*. TS. CBC Radio, 1972.

_____ *Country Joy*. Six 30-minute scripts. TS. CBC Television, 1978.

_____ . *Generation*. TS. CBC Radio, 1979.

_____ *In Memory Of*. TS. CBC Radio, 1975.

_____ *Intensive Care*. TS. CBC Radio, June 1983.

_____ . *The Komagata Maru Story*. TS. CBC Radio, 1976.

_____ *The Larsens*. TS. CBC Television, 1974.

_____ *Mary Beth Goes to Calgary*. TS. CBC Radio, 1980.

_____ *Mrs. Yale and Jennifer*. Eight Episodes. TS. CBC Radio, 1980.

_____ *The Person's Case*. TS. Access Television, 1979; first appeared under the working title, *Free Our Sisters, Free Ourselves*.

_____ *Portait of a Pig*. TS. CBC Television, 1974.

_____ *Ransom*. TS. CBC Television, 1976.

_____ *Split Seconds in the Death Of*. TS. CBC Radio, 1971.

_____ *Sweet Land of Liberty*. TS. CBC Radio, 1981.

_____ *Waiting*. TS. CBC Radio, 1973.

_____ *We to the Gods*. TS. CBC Radio, 1972

CRITICAL ARTICLES AND INTERVIEWS

Agnew, Theresa. *Let Her But Breathe: Changing Representations of Women in Plays By Prairie Women Playwrights*, MA Thesis. Edmonton: University of Alberta, 1994.

Balcon, D. "A Question of Copyright: The Sharon Pollock Case." *Cinema Canada*, 102 (December 1983): 26-27.

Bessai, Diane. "Introduction." *Blood Relations and Other Plays*. Edmonton: NeWest Press, 1981: 7-9.

_____ "Sharon Pollock's Women: A Study in Dramatic Process." *A Mazing Space: Writing Canadian Women Writing*, eds. Shirley Neuman and Smaro Kamboureli. Edmonton: Longspoon/NeWest Press, 1986: 126-136.

_____ "Women Dramatists: Sharon Pollock and Judith Thompson." *Post-Colonial English Drama: Commonwealth Drama Since 1960*, ed. Bruce King. London: Macmillan, 1992: 97-117.

Belliveau, George. "Daddy on Trial: Sharon Pollock's New Brunswick Plays," *Theatre Research in Canada* (forthcoming in 2002).

Clement, Susan, and Esther Beth Sullivan. "The Split Subject of *Blood Relations*."
 Upstaging Big Daddy: Directing Theatre as if Gender and Race Matter, eds. Ellen
 Donkin and Susan Clement. Ann Arbor: University of Michigan Press, 1993:
 53-66.

Conolly, L.W., ed. *Canadian Drama and the Critics*. Vancouver: Talonbooks, 1987: 134-
 135, 259-276.

Dufort, Lynn. "Sharon Pollock Talks About Her New Work." *Foothills*, 2.2 (1986): 3-5.

Dunn, Margo. "Sharon Pollock: In the Centre Ring." *Makara*, 1.5 (August-September
 1976): 2-6.

Gilbert, Reid. "'My Mother Wants Me To Play Romeo Before It's Too Late': Framing
 Gender On Stage." *Theatre Research in Canada/Recherches Théâtrales au Canada*,
 14.2 (1993): 123-143.

_____ "Sharon Pollock." *Profiles in Canadian Literature 6*, ed. Jeffrey M. Heath.
 Toronto: Dundurn, 1986: 113-120.

Gilbert, S.R. "Sharon Pollock." *Contemporary Dramatists*, ed. James Vinson. 3rd ed.
 London: Macmillan, 1982: 642-645.

Grace, Sherrill. "Sharon Pollock's Portraits of the Artist," *Theatre Research in Canada*.
 (forthcoming in 2002)

Hayes, Christopher. "Miss Pollock Downs Her Axe. She Settles Out of Court: The
 Borden Film Goes On." *Alberta Report*, 10 (June 20, 1983): 45.

_____ "Miss Pollock Gives CFCN 40 Whacks: The Court Freezes the TV   Adaptation
 of Her Lizzie Borden Play." *Alberta Report*, 10 (May 16, 1983): 38.

Hofsess, John. "Families." *Homemaker's Magazine*, 15 (March 1980): 41-60.

_____ "Sharon Pollock Off-Broadway: Success as a Subtle Form of Failure." *Books in
 Canada*, 12 (April 1983): 3-4.

Hohtanz, Marie. "Passionate Playwright." *Calgary Herald Sunday Magazine* 29
 November 1987: 6-10.

Hustak, Alan. "A Very Dramatic Exit: Playwright Pollock Quits Theatre Calgary."
 Alberta Report, 11 (September 10, 1984): 40-41.

Ingram, Anne. "Right Theatre at the Right Time: Sharon Pollock Takes New
 Brunswick by Storm." *Performing Arts*, 24 (July 1988): 12-13.

Jansen, Ann. "Change the Story: Narrative Strategies in Two Radio Plays."
 Contemporary Issues in Canadian Drama, ed. Per Brask. Winnipeg: Blizzard,
 1995: 86-102.

Kerr, Rosalind. "Borderline Crossings in Sharon Pollock's Out-law Genres." *Theatre
 Research in Canada*, 17.2 (1996): 200-215.

Knelman, Martin. "Daddy Dearest: Sharon Pollock's *Doc*." *Saturday Night*, 99 (October
 1984): 73-74.

Knowles, Richard Paul. "Replaying History: Canadian Historiographic Metadrama."
 Dalhousie Review, 67 (1987): 228-243.

Loiselle, Andre. "Paradigms of 1980's Quebecois and Canadian Drama: Normand
 Chaurette's *Provincetown Playhouse, juillet 1919, j'avais 19 ans* and Sharon
 Pollock's *Blood Relations*." *Quebec Studies*, 14 (Spring/Summer 1992): 93-104.

Loucks, Randee. *Sharon Pollock: 1973-1985. Playwright of Conscience and Consequence*,
 Unpublished MA Thesis. Calgary: University of Calgary, 1985.

McKinley, Marilyn. "Sharon Pollock's Bloody Relations: A TV Adaptation of Her Hit
 Play Enrages the Calgary Writer." *Alberta Report*, 10 (February 28, 1983): 36.

Messenger, Ann P. "More Utile than Dulce." *Canadian Literature*, 65 (Summer 1976):
 90-95.

Metcalfe, Robin. "Interview with Sharon Pollock." *Books in Canada*, 16 (March 1987): 39-40.

Miner, Madonna. "'Lizzie Borden Took an Ax': Enacting *Blood Relations*." *Literature in Performance*, 6 (April 1986): 10-21.

Much, Rita, ed. "Reflections of a Female Artistic Director." *Women on the Canadian Stage*. Winnipeg: Blizzard, 1992: 109-114.

_____ "Theatre by Default: Sharon Pollock's Garry Theatre." *Canadian Theatre Review*, 82 (Spring 1995): 19-22.

Mullaly, Edward, J. "The Return of the Native." *Canadian Theatre Review*, 63 (Summer 1990): 20-24.

Nothof, Anne. "Crossing Borders: Sharon Pollock's Revisitation of Canadian Frontiers." *Modern Drama*, 38 (Winter 1995): 475-487.

_____ "Gendered Landscapes: Synergism of Place and Person in Canadian Prairie Drama." *Great Plains Quarterly*, 18.2 (Spring 1998): 127-138.

_____ "Staging the Intersections of Time in Sharon Pollock's *Doc, Moving Pictures*, and *End Dream. Theatre Research in Canada* (forthcoming in 2002).

Nothof, Anne, ed. *Sharon Pollock: Essays on Her Works*. Toronto: Guernica, 2000.

Nunn, Robert C. "Sharon Pollock's Plays: A Review Article." *Theatre History in Canada*, 5.1 (Spring 1984): 72-83.

Page, Malcolm. "Sharon Pollock: Committed Playwright." *Canadian Drama*, 5.2 (Fall 1979): 104-111.

Perkyns, Richard. "Generations: An Introduction." *Major Plays of the Canadian Theatre, 1934-1984*. Toronto: Irwin, 1984: 605-608.

Plant, Richard. "Precious Blood." *Books in Canada*, 11 (April 1982): 8-12.

Pollock, Sharon. *Canadian Literature*. Toronto: CMEC; Calgary: Access Network, c1984; videorecording.

_____ "Dead or Alive: Feeling the Pulse of Canadian Theatre." *Theatrum*, 23 (April/ May 1991): 12-13.

Rempel, Byron. "Not a Diplomat, Pollock Returns Dismayed at Canadian Theatre." *Alberta Report*, 16 (November 6, 1989): 56-57.

Rudakoff, Judith, and Rita Much, eds. *Fair Play*. Toronto: Simon & Pierre, 1990: 208-220.

Russell, David. *The Direction of Whiskey Six*, Unpublished MFA Thesis. Edmonton: University of Alberta, 1987.

Saddlemyer, Ann. "Circus Feminus: 100 Plays by English-Canadian Women." *Room of One's Own*, VIII.2 (July 1983): 78-91.

_____ "Crime in Literature: Canadian Drama." *Rough Justice: Essays on Crime in Literature*, ed. Martin L. Friedland. Toronto: University of Toronto Press, 1991: 214-230.

_____ "Two Canadian Women Playwrights." *Cross-Cultural Studies: American, Canadian and European Literatures 1945-1985*. Ljubljana: Edvard Kardelj University, 1988: 251-256.

Salter, Denis W. "Biocritical Essay. (Im)possible Worlds: The Plays of Sharon Pollock." *First Accession*, eds. Apollonia Steele, and Jean Tener. Calgary: University of Calgary Press, 1989: ix-xxxv.

St. Pierre, Paul Mathew. "Sharon Pollock." *Canadian Writers Since 1960*. 2nd ser. *DLB* 60: 300-306.

Stone-Blackburn, Susan. "Feminism and Metadrama: Role Playing in *Blood Relations*." *Canadian Drama*, 15.2 (1989): 169-178.

Unknown. "Sharon Pollock: *Doc*." *Contemporary Literary Criticism: Yearbook 1987*, 50, ed. Sharon K. Hall. Detroit: Gale Research, 1988: 222-227.

Walker, Craig Stewart. "Sharon Pollock: Besieged Memory," *The Buried Astrolabe:Canadian Dramatic Imagination and Western Tradition*. Montreal & Kingston: McGill-Queen's University Press, 2001.

Wallace, Robert, and Cynthia Zimmerman, eds. *The Work: Conversations with English Canadian Playwrights*. Toronto: Coach House Press, 1982: 115-126.

Wylie, Herb. "'Painting the Background': Metadrama and the Fabric of History in Sharon Pollock's *Blood Relations*." *Essays in Theatre*, 15.2 (1996): 191-205.

Zichy, Francis. "Justifying the Ways of Lizzie Borden to Men: The Play Within the Play in *Blood Relations*." *Theatre Annual*, 42 (1987): 61-81.

Zimmerman, Cynthia. "Sharon Pollock: The Making of Warriors." *Playwriting Women: Female Voices in English Canada*. Toronto: Simon & Pierre, 1994: 60-98.

_____ "Towards a Better, Fairer World: An Interview with Sharon Pollock." *Canadian Theatre Review*, 69 (Winter 1991): 34-38.

_____ "Transfiguring the Maternal," *Theatre Research in Canada* (forthcoming 2002).

Ziraldo, Christiana. *Replaying History: A Study of Sharon Pollock's* Walsh, The Komagata Maru Incident, *and* Blood Relations, MA Thesis. Guelph: University of Guelph, 1996.

SELECTED REVIEWS

Allen, Bob. "Laughs Aimed at Politicians in a New Play." *Vancouver Province* 21 March: 35.

Allen, Bob. "Stratford Discovers the West." *Vancouver Province* 5 April 1974: 3.

Anonymous. "Dramatic Feuding: Theatre Calgary's *Walsh* Garners Controversy." *Alberta Report*, 15 (February 15, 1988): 41.

Anonymous. "*The Komagata Maru Incident*: You Can Look For A Message Made Palatable." *Vancouver Sun* 16 January 1976: 31.

Anonymous. "Playwright Pollock's a Hit in San Diego." *Alberta Report*, 6 (November 23, 1979): 46.

Anonymous. "Sharon Pollock: National Arts Centre." *The Globe and Mail* 12 May 1983: 25.

Ashley, Audrey M. "Stratford Director, Cast and Playwright's Delight." *Ottawa Citizen* 25 July 1974: 50.

Baldridge, Harold. "Calgary." *Canadian Theatre Review*, 2 (Spring 1974): 118-120.

Bale, Doug. "Longshot Steals Show at Stratford Festival." *London Free Press* 25 July 1974.

Brennan, Brian. "*Komagata Maru Incident* Heavily Loaded with Propaganda." *Calgary Herald* 13 January 1979: A8.

_____ "Playwright's Account of Lizzie Borden Effective Drama." *Calgary Herald* 14 March 1980: C9.

_____ "Plays Bogs Down in Enigmatic Historical Difficulties." *Calgary Herald* 12 January 1988: E2.

_____ "Pollock Offers Best Work Yet." *Calgary Herald* 8 April 1984: F2.

_____ "*Whiskey Six* is Pollock's Best Play Yet." *Calgary Herald* 11 February 1983: F1.

Brunner, Astrid. "Getting it Straight." *Arts Atlantic*, 9 (Spring-Summer 1989): 59.

Conlogue, Ray. "A Theatrical Gem Reflects the Last, Best West." *The Globe and Mail* 7 March 1983: 15.

Deakin, Basil. "TAG's *Walsh*: Should Be Stuff of Good Theatre." *Halifax Chronicle*

       Herald 14 June 1984: 42.

Dibbelt, Dan. "Walsh." *Windspeaker*, 5 (January 29, 1988): 14.

Doolittle, Joyce. "Walsh." *NeWest Review*, 13 (April 1988): 13.

Downton, Dawn Rae. "Blood Relations." *Arts Atlantic*, 9 (Winter 1989): 62-63.

Fraser, Matthew. "*Doc* May Be Tough Pill for New Brunswick." *The Globe and Mail* 7
       March 1986: A12.

Freeman, Brian. "In Review: *The Komagata Maru Incident*." *Scene Changes*, V.9
       (December 1977): 20-21.

Freedman, Adele. "NAC Brings Little to Wild West Yarn." *The Globe and Mail* 12 May
       1983: 25.

Garebian, Keith. "In Review: *One Tiger to a Hill*." *Scene Changes*, VIII.6 (September/
       October 1980): 37-38.

Godfrey, Stephen. "Debate Soars Above Earthbound Historical Drama." *The Globe and
       Mail* 29 January 1988: A18.

Hale, Amanda. "Family Flashback." *Broadside*, 6 (November 1984): 11.

Hustak, Alan. "Sharon Pollock's Triumph: A Hit for Theatre Calgary's New Boss."
       Alberta Report, 11 (April 30, 1984): 54-55.

Johnson, Bryan. "Sikh's Play, *Komagata Maru*, Bitter and Austere, But True." *The Globe
       and Mail* 24 October 1977: 15.

Loukes, Randee. "*Whiskey Six*: Observations of a First Performance." *ACTH Newsletter*,
       7 (Fall 1983): 17-18.

Milliken, Paul. "In Review: *Generations*." *Scene Changes*, IX.4 (June 1981): 39-40.

Peterson, Maureen. "Centaur's *Blood Relations* Everything A Play Should Be." *Montreal
       Gazette* 9 January 1982: 34.

Portman, Jamie. "Calgary I." *Canadian Theatre Review*, 1 (Winter 1974): 118-120.

———— "Calgary II." *Canadian Theatre Review*, 2 (Spring 1974): 121-123.

———— "Sharon Pollock Demonstrates Immense Gifts With Latest Play." *Calgary
       Herald* 20 March 1980: D1.

———— "*Walsh* Signals Red-Letter Event for TOL." *Calgary Herald* 9 November 1973.

Rich, Frank. "Theatre: *Tiger to a Hill* Canadian Prison Drama." *New York Times* 14
       November 1980: C3.

Webster, J. "Another Stage Triumph for Sharon (Pollock)." *Atlantic Advocate*, 64
       (August 1974): 50.

Whittaker, Herbert. "Canadian West at Stratford." *The Globe and Mail* 22 July 1974: 14.

———— "*Walsh* Beautiful, Tedious Too." *The Globe and Mail* 13 November 1973: 16.

———— "*Walsh* Serves Up Sad History Straight." *The Globe and Mail* 25 July 1974: 13.